CW01034015

Rich

Happy reading, and
maybe you'll return
to Laos one day ...

Christophe Whitehouse

# Lone Buffalo
## Conquering adversity in Laos, the land the West forgot

Born in London in 1959, **C.J.C. Whitehouse** is a writer/researcher with a wide range of interests that include choral music, hill walking and playing bridge. Prior to writing *Lone Buffalo*, he worked in protein redesign at Oxford University, where he completed a D.Phil., published several papers and helped to develop a technology that is now in the early stages of commercialisation. He met Manophet, whose life this book describes, during his first visit to Laos in 2001, and resolved there and then to tell his story in writing. But by the time he finally got round to tackling the project a decade later his inspirational subject had passed away. It took several years to track down and interview his family, friends and the key figures from his past, who were by now scattered across three continents. *Lone Buffalo* is the resulting narrative – partially fictionalised: the tale of a local hero determined not to be beaten by his circumstances.

Manophet Mouidouangdy 1969-2010
(Photo: Mak Yiing Chau [www.clovemcreative.com])

# Lone Buffalo
### Conquering adversity in Laos, the land the West forgot

C.J.C. Whitehouse

Arena Books

The right of C.J.C. Whitehouse to be identified as author of this book
has been asserted in accordance with the Copyright, Designs and
Patents Act 1988.

First published in 2016 by Arena Books

Arena Books
6 Southgate Green
Bury St. Edmunds
IP33 2BL

www.arenabooks.co.uk
Distributed in America by Ingram International, One Ingram Blvd., PO Box
3006, La Vergne, TN 37086-1985, USA.

C.J.C. Whitehouse
  **Lone Buffalo** *Conquering adversity in Laos, the land the West forgot*


British Library cataloguing in Publication Data. A catalogue record for this
Book is available from the British Library.


ISBN-13   978-1-909421-65-3

BIC classifications:- BGH, BTP, HBJF, 1FML.

Printed and bound by Lightning Source UK

Cover design
by Jason Anscomb

Typeset in
Times New Roman

In memory of Manophet Mouidouangdy

1969 – 2010

# AUTHOR'S NOTE

The early chapters of this book are, of necessity, heavily fictionalised – though the events that I describe did, insofar as I can ascertain, occur. The later chapters, by contrast, draw on transcripts and stored electronic records, some of which I have reproduced almost verbatim. However, it may be a mistake to suppose that the later material is more reliable. Truth is fluid in parts of Southeast Asia, particularly in societies that write nothing down and rely on the spoken word. Stories can grow or bend in the telling. Memories have a way of playing tricks. I have come to view the discrepancies that became apparent during the course of my research as integral to the story, and have elected not to try and conceal them.

Certain names have been altered, in accordance with the wishes of those concerned.


# ACKNOWLEDGEMENTS

I am indebted to all those who allowed me to interview them, particularly Manophet's family, who received me so warmly and gave me permission to weave this story around his life. I would also like to thank everybody who read the book prior to publication and provided feedback, and those who were kind enough to supply photographs.

The excerpt from Fred Branfman's *Voices from the Plain of Jars* is reprinted by permission of The University of Wisconsin Press, © 2013 by the Board of Regents of the University of Wisconsin System.

# ONE

His earliest memory was of a dome of light. How old he had been when the image became imprinted on his mind, he could not tell. Nor could he say what it was or where it might have originated. All he could rely on was the curving outline of the brilliant glow against the shadow. It was not geometrically perfect. A thin segment had been sliced away at the bottom, flattening the underside, and the base was always at an angle, sloping gently upwards from left to right. Sometimes the vision would appear when he was drifting off to sleep, reconnecting him with the forgotten world to which it belonged, teasing him with fleeting details: melancholy shapes quivering silently in the murk, cool air that never seemed to move, a sense of being possessed by the surrounding darkness. The splash of a water droplet striking a rock could conjure up the same unearthly atmosphere; so too the smell of smouldering tinder. Was it real, or had it only ever been a dream? Manophet knew his family would say he was making it up if he told them about it. They never believed anything he said. But he had thought of a way to turn the situation to his advantage. He would keep it a secret from *all* of them! The idea filled him with exhilaration. He would have something that was his and nobody else's, a little nugget of contraband with which to run away to one of his hiding places and console himself when they made fun of him or told him he was in the way.

He hated getting up in the morning. The sun emitted a fearsome heat as soon as it climbed over the horizon, baking the parched dust that carpeted the ground, stinging his feet when he walked and hurting his eyes if he did not screw them up. Most days, his belly groaned for want of food. Insects bit him if he went about without a sack to cover up his torso. Often he suffered from one of the illnesses that flared up periodically. There was never anything to do. It was too hot to run around, and nobody could afford to make time for him. 'What will we eat if we spend all day playing with you?' his older brothers and sisters would scold. 'We have to go out and look for food.' And his mother had another new baby at her breast. Having one younger brother was bad enough. Now there were two clamouring for her attention: nine people living on top of one other in the tiny allocation of space – ten when his father was present. Whenever he asked for anything to be explained, the rest of them delighted in telling him he was too young to understand. Jun was the worst. How come *she* knew so much when she was only two years older than he was? How he longed to be seven, like her. But at least she would share her knowledge with him occasionally. Thanks to her, he knew now that rain came from clouds, that caterpillars turned into butterflies, and that their lives would improve out of all recognition when they could finally return home.

Perhaps, when he reached the age of seven, he would be able to understand why his family had tried to give him away. Several months had passed since that bewildering episode, but it continued to cast a menacing shadow. He would never forget the storm of panic that had broken over him as he grasped the notion that he had been brought to his uncle's house not for a visit but to be left there. Why was he not wanted any longer? What had he done wrong? His small world had been dashed into a thousand pieces. For the first few hours, he had lain on the ground howling. He was not used to being indoors, and he felt suffocated by the stagnant heavy air. The wooden floor magnified every tiny sound. Sinister scraping noises from other parts of the house curdled his blood. Alarming crashes jolted the breath from his body. But at length a plan of action began to form in his mind. He pretended to fall asleep. Then, when he was satisfied that his uncle and aunt had decided he no longer needed watching and had turned their minds to other things, he slipped outside as quietly as he could and started walking. Remembering that he needed to head downhill, he followed the dirt road until it levelled out. But now he was lost. Should he go left or right? For what seemed like hours, he wandered back and forth without happening on any territory that looked familiar. Eventually, at the far end of a long winding track, he spotted a hillock that he recognised. His reappearance threw the family into mayhem. He was examined, scolded, pointed at, dabbed with herbal ointment where his feet had blistered. His mother started crying and said he was the naughtiest boy she had ever known, but Manophet knew she was not really cross. 'Your uncle wants to adopt you,' she explained when everything had calmed down. 'He is such a kind man, and he and auntie Nang have no children of their own.' Manophet looked up at her tired, prematurely lined face. 'But I don't want to be adopted,' he said. 'I want to stay here and live with you.'

Their lives carried on as though nothing had happened. Boun came back dejected from the market evening after evening, apologising for the meagre haul of threadbare green leaves at the bottom of her basket. Sing, who had already turned twenty, continued to exhaust himself hauling heavy stones away from a piece of land that he was clearing. Lar kept them all awake half the night with his crying. But the memory of what had happened would not leave Manophet in peace. You could not just give a person away. A fistful of rice or a carved bamboo maybe, but not a person – and certainly not a member of your own family. And why him? Why not Thong or Kone? It must have been a punishment for not always doing what he was told. Somebody or other was forever upbraiding him for disobeying their instructions. He was never allowed to do what *he* wanted. It was so unfair! To make things worse, they had tried to trick him into believing it would have been better for him if the adoption had gone through. His uncle had a proper house of his own, it was true, and several chickens and a big barrel where he could store water that was safe to drink, but what compensation were a few vainglorious luxuries for being severed from your family? Bossy and exasperating though they could be, he had missed them terribly during the few hours that he had been away and was desolated to think they might not have felt the same way.

His mother was determined to instil positive karma into her children, their challenging circumstances notwithstanding, and there was no shortage of rules to observe. He found it a struggle to survive for more than a few hours at a time without falling foul of one or other of them. "Right Speech" was the discipline he was most often deemed to have infringed – not speaking truthfully, but "Right View" was almost as much of a nemesis. It was so *dull*, resisting the exotic fantasies that laid siege to his imagination whenever he was left to his own devices and trying instead to see the world as it really was. Satisfying the requirements of the "Right Action" principle should have been more straightforward as it came naturally to him to be kind to other people and to help them. Unfortunately, his offers of assistance seldom seemed to go down well with those on the receiving end, who would always manage to contrive a reason for not wanting him under their feet. The only merit for which he received praise was not grumbling about the conditions in which they lived – though it had never been clear to him why this should be considered such an achievement. Nobody else in the family grumbled – indeed, the others would sometimes claim that their lots had improved. And yet their protestations always had a hollow ring. He began to grasp that the life to which he had been born was not as it should have been. It was not normal, it seemed, to have so little to eat, to feel unwell so often, to live in a big camp instead of a home. Nobody really wanted to be here – that was the unspoken truth. 'When are we going back to our house?' he would ask. 'When the war is over,' they would always reply.

It was the war that was responsible for their father's periodic absences – this much he understood. Days at a time could go by without them setting eyes on him. Then, without warning, he would reappear and spend a week in the camp recovering from his exertions, or sometimes longer. There was always a stir when his lean authoritative figure crossed back into their precinct. He was even more of a stickler for discipline than his wife, and all his children, from the eldest to the youngest, made a point of being on their best behaviour. There were so many questions that they wanted to ask, but he was not allowed to talk about the situation outside the camp. Instead, he would quiz them individually about their conduct. 'And you, young man,' he would say to Manophet, 'have you been kind to your brothers and sisters since the last time I was here? Have you been helpful to your mother? You must look after her, you know. She cannot do everything on her own. You must make sure she does not get too tired when I am away.' And Manophet, struck with awe by the rugged boots on his father's feet, the masculine smell that emanated from his faded shirt and the luxuriant moustache that sprouted above his mouth, would gaze up nervously at the commanding presence and nod timidly back.

It was not just Lar who kept them awake at night. At least once a month, one or other of his elder siblings would have a nightmare and lurch up violently from the mat on which they were sleeping, wracked by sobs or screaming. The family did not go in for histrionics, and these outpourings of emotion jarred horribly against the calm that otherwise prevailed. When Manophet had nightmares, he could shrug them off as soon as he awoke. Why were his brothers and sisters different? Even Sing, the eldest, who slept next to him, had once woken up and started shouting out frenzied warnings about burning rain. Whenever such an episode took place, one of the others would immediately rise and hurry across to offer words of comfort. 'It was just a nightmare,' their soothing voices would cajole. 'An evil spirit came wandering through the camp and entered your dream.' But Manophet knew there must be more to it. They were always resorting to imagery as a way of keeping the truth from him. It was as though a line had been drawn through the family, dividing it into two parts. On one side were his parents and his older brothers and sisters, on the other the three juvenile children, who were considered too young to be entrusted with grown-up knowledge. But the line was in the wrong place. He had been born in the family's homeland, like his older brothers and sisters. It was only Thong and Lar who had been born here in the camp. Why was he excluded from the senior group?

His mother was usually too busy cooking or cleaning or sewing or looking after Lar to spend more than a few minutes at a time with him, and his father had given him instructions not to bother her with questions when she had so much to do. But obedience was usually the loser in the battle with curiosity where Manophet was concerned, and he chivvied away at her whenever she gave him half a chance. Why was there a war? Who was fighting? When would it end?

'It is difficult to explain,' she said. '*Falang* have controlled this region for a long time, even though there is no reason why it should belong to them. Now they are being challenged.'

12

'What are *falang*?' he asked.

'*Falang* are men with white skins from far away who believe we are incapable of managing our own affairs and need them to tell us what to do.'

'Is my father fighting against them? Is that why they knocked our house down?'

'It is the other way round,' she said. 'It is because they destroyed our house that your father became a soldier for the other side. It was not just our house. They knocked down every building in our town. That is why we had to leave. There was nowhere left for us to live.'

'Is it dangerous for my father, being a soldier?'

She shook her head. 'It was dangerous where we used to live,' she said, 'but there is no fighting down here at the moment. It is only in other parts of the country. When your father goes away from the camp, it is not to fight. He is trying and find out what preparations the enemy is making in case there is fighting later on.'

'Will the enemy try and attack the camp?'

'Manophet, I have told you a dozen times you should pay more attention when you are near the pot,' she exclaimed. 'You will get scalded if you stand right beside it like that. Run along and see if you can stop Thong making that silly racket.'

Sometimes, if he thought for long enough about the dome of light, it would swell up and consume the surrounding darkness, leaving only a dazzle of grand confusing shapes. Away on the blurred horizon, rich unfamiliar flecks of colour seemed to gleam. Closer to, glossy cloudlike formations clustered along lazily converging diagonals. What were these massive pillars that soared into the sky above, and these tunnels of tangled green? They did not correspond to any facet of the drab landscape around the camp. The ground here was nothing like the floor of the rocky cauldron where the shadows danced. It had a springy feel, and the air fizzed with a heady mixture of sharp resins. Pools of shimmering dappled light spilled out from under serrated overhangs. Was this a snake, this green and yellow creature? Manophet had never seen a snake, but it answered the descriptions he had been given. And that impudent gaudy-looking bird – could that be a parrot? If only he could glimpse a little more of the picture. It had an air of paradise to it, this fabulous realm, a magical beauty. And yet he could tell from the thud-thudding of his heart that every moment spent within these borders was fraught with danger. Suddenly it all came hurtling back. Something terrifying was chasing him. He needed to run away, but it was impossible. He was trussed up in a sack. His limbs would not move. And now the sky was trembling, and a terrible violent shaking was starting to break the beautiful image apart.

During the summer months, the temperature could rise above forty degrees for days at a time. Rain became a distant memory. The sun would blaze down, sucking every drop of moisture from the land, reducing what little vegetation survived to scrubby brown clumps. They were free to wash in the Mekong, but it was a long walk away, and they were so dusty by the time they arrived back at the camp that it was scarcely worth the effort. Manophet had allowed his thirst to get the better of him the first time he had been allowed into the water unsupervised, and had gulped down a few turbid mouthfuls. Over the next few weeks, he suffered recurrent stomach cramps and bouts of diarrhoea. Only when some medicine was purchased at prohibitive cost did the illness abate. 'Perhaps that will teach you to do as you are told occasionally,' his mother had remarked as he lay convalescing beside the still where she produced the rice wine that had paid for the medicine.

The ground seemed too hard even to lie on now. All but the rubberiest plants had died. But at last a bank of clouds began to form on the horizon. Rumbles could be heard from the skies, and a few drops of drizzle fell. For a week or two there was jubilation. People raced out into the open whenever a shower passed overhead, laughing as the raindrops pelted down on them, cleansing their grubby clothes and bodies. A week or two more, and there was frantic activity, a frenzy of hoeing and furrowing and planting. Another fortnight, and the skies opened in earnest, transforming the land at a stroke. In place of the dust through which they were wont to shuffle, a carpet of red mud oozed underfoot, sucking though the gaps between their toes, splattering their legs when they walked. Puddles formed, expanded and joined themselves into impromptu canal systems. Water slurped up through the ground, saturating their sleeping mats, leaving them perpetually damp. A few families scavenged corrugated tin roofs and rigged them up on shaky bamboo poles, but the deafening rattle of the heavy rain left most of the refugees feeling they were better off getting wet.

Jun sidled up to him one day. At first he ignored her. Nobody ever stopped what they were doing when *he* came to be companionable. 'What are you up to?' she asked.

'Nothing,' he retorted, closing his fist around the sharp stone that he was holding. What was wrong with carving notches in a coconut shell that nobody else wanted?

She squinted at the battered object. 'Is it a clock?'

'A clock? Of course not.'

'Well, what are those marks round the edge?'

'It's a secret,' he said defiantly, putting it behind his back where she could no longer see it. 'What's a clock?'

'It tells you what the time is. Uncle has one.'

'You've been crying,' Manophet challenged.

'No I haven't.'

'Anyhow, I *hate* Uncle.'

Jun let out an incriminating sniff. 'I can keep a secret,' she announced huffily. 'I know lots of secrets.'

'Tell me one then. Tell me a secret.'

'Why should I?'

'*Please* tell me a secret,' he implored. 'If you tell me a secret, I won't tell the others you've been crying.'

She weighed her position. 'You were in my dream,' she said. 'Last night.'

'What happened?'

Suddenly the vitality drained out of her. The corners of her mouth drooped, and she looked down at the ground. 'I don't want to talk about it.'

'I had a dream about an *aeroplane*,' he countered triumphantly.

But now Jun's eyes began to overflow with tears. Slumping down beside him, she wept noisily into the ground. Manophet felt cheated. He wanted to tell her about the aeroplane, which was vivid once more in his mind. He could remember huge wheels coming out of its belly. But Jun was too upset to listen. 'I didn't mean it when I said I wanted to kill you,' she sobbed. 'I'm so sorry.' All her self-control had gone.

Manophet wanted to run and fetch his mother, but Jun was holding his arm too tightly.

'You were so heavy,' she said. 'I couldn't carry you any further. And you kept crying and crying when you needed to be quiet.'

From that day forward, he was closer to her than his other brothers and sisters. They fell out periodically, as children do, but always made up. She understood his frustration at not being trusted with the information to which the older family members were privy, and divulged little snippets on condition that they stayed between her and him. He learned that his family had lived on the outskirts of a provincial state capital named Muang Khoun, and that he had been born in a hole in the ground in the rainy season in 1969 because every last house had been destroyed. Through talking to Jun, he began to grasp why this was not enough to place him on the right side of the family dividing line. It was not where he had been born that mattered. It was that he was too young to have any memories of his life prior to the family's admission to the camp. His sister, with her two and a half year advantage, had grown up in a different realm. There was nothing the family could do to insulate her from her past.

Manophet was fascinated by the great Mekong River. The land through which it flowed seemed not to slope at all, yet the water always knew which way it was supposed to go. When he waded in up to the tops of his thighs, he could feel the current tugging at his legs, threatening to knock him off balance and sweep him downstream. He would carry sticks or big leaves in from the shore and drop them on the surface so that he could watch them float off into the distance. Now and then, a longboat would buzz past, leaving a foamy trail in its wake. He would wave and wave, in the hope that the boatman would wave back, but most of them seemed oblivious to his presence. If you could reach the far bank, you would find yourself in another country, according to his mother – a land with its own king, full of people who spoke a different language. Manophet watched the figures on the distant shore as they went about their business, but they appeared so tiny across the wide channel that it was impossible to tell whether they had any peculiarities. One day, when he was old enough, he would build a boat and sail across to take a proper look. And after that he would let the boat carry him all the way to the vast ocean into which the river fed. How badly he wanted to be the first member of his family to see the sea, to do something, *anything* that one of them had not already done before.

The arid land on which they had been settled was available only because the locals deemed it too marginal to farm. It bruised their heels when they tried to break up the soil, devoured their sweat, and gave pitiful crop yields in return. The precious rice grains that they had brought with them were not adapted to lowland conditions and disappeared without trace into its brutal embrace. They made no headway trying to keep chickens. Unable to eke out an existence, the birds languished, laid no eggs and eventually grew so scrawny that slaughtering them was barely worthwhile. The surrounding terrain offered limited opportunities for supplementing their diets. There were few wild animals to hunt. Fish were fiercely competed for by every hungry family group with the means to catch them. Any edible plants growing wild had long since been torn up and consumed. Manophet had been malnourished since birth. He was used to being skin and bones. But the portions in his bowl seemed to grow smaller by the day. Once or twice, consignments of rice in bulging sacks were brought in to the camp by elephant, enough to form a pyramid that was even taller than Jun when they were unloaded and piled on top of one another. These were tokens of recompense from the *falang* who had knocked their houses down, apparently. But within a matter of weeks the rice had all been consumed, and the only legacy was the wrangling over how the empty sacks should be shared round.

His father called him across one day as he was playing. 'Sit down, please,' he said. 'I have something to say to you.' Manophet squatted nervously in front of him. His mother was seated close by on a low mound. 'Things have become very difficult for our family,' his father said in a low voice. 'We have lost our home and all our possessions. We have no water buffalo left, no pigs. We have nowhere to fish. Things have reached the point where we no longer have enough food to keep ourselves from starving. I'm afraid we have no alternative now but to take drastic measures. I know this will be difficult for you to understand, but there is only one solution, and that is for your uncle and aunt to adopt you. I have been over to see them, and they are prepared to forgive you for behaving so foolishly the last time you went to their house. You must accept my word that this is the best thing that could possibly happen to you. Your uncle and aunt do not have the same worries that we have. They are in better circumstances, and they will be able to give you a happier life.'

Manophet's stomach had caved in on itself. Nothing in the world terrified him more than the idea of returning to his uncle's house. A scream of defiance welled up from the depths of his being, but it stuck in his throat, refusing to release. The only sound that he could produce was a low jerky moaning. His small body started shaking. His shoulders slumped. It was as though his organs were turning to jelly. He teetered forwards onto his knees, then keeled over completely, landing on his face.

'Now don't be silly,' his mother said in a trembling voice, picking him up and brushing the dust out of his hair. 'It will be so much better than what you are used to. They will be able to feed you properly, and you will have clothes of your own. Even shoes! I'm sure they will buy you a pair of shoes if you want. And you will be able to stay cool indoors when it is too hot instead of getting sunstroke, and dry when it rains.'

'You must be a good boy and not cause any trouble for your new Father and Mother,' his father said sternly. 'They have been very kind, offering to do this for you. And do not for one second imagine you can run away as you did before, because I shall simply take you straight back.'

There was worse in store. His uncle and aunt had built a fence around the house, and the latch on the gate was out of reach. It was impossible for him to leave. His aunt did her best to mollify him and make him feel at home, but Manophet was beside himself with rage at the betrayal he had suffered. He did not wear the shoes that were procured for him, and took no interest in the toys that were bought, not even the football, which he secretly longed to kick about. He loathed the carbuncle on his uncle's bulbous nose, and detested the way his aunt's hair always smelled of cooking oil. He felt wronged, abandoned, misunderstood, desperately alone. He could tell that his uncle was offended by the lack of gratitude with which his generosity was being met, and refused to call him Father as a way of compounding his discomfort. The one aspect of his new existence with which he could not find fault was the food that his aunt served up. He made a pretence of disliking it, but hunkering down to sleep each night with a full belly was seductively pleasurable. He began to put on weight. Minor ailments that had afflicted him for as long as he could remember receded or vanished. He was able to run faster. But his aunt and uncle made the mistake of pointing out these advances to him. The more they made of the improvement to his lot, the stronger his distaste for his own wellbeing became. How could he enjoy living like a prince when Jun and his other brothers and sisters were going hungry night after night?

The days dragged interminably by. He had nobody to talk to. His only solace was his imagination. He dreamed that an elephant would come charging out of the jungle and trample down his aunt and uncle's fence. He would give it all their bananas as a reward, and it would pick him up with its trunk and carry him to Muang Khoun, where their house had been, so that he could drive out the *falang* with a big stick. *That* would teach them! Then he had a more practical idea: he would save up a little of his food each day so that the rest of his family could have it. His aunt and uncle would not miss it. They always had plenty in the house. From then on, he left two mouthfuls of food unconsumed on his plate at the end of each meal, and later counted out two hundred grains of rice from the sack by way of compensation when his aunt and uncle were not looking. These he hid in a hollow bamboo. Little by little, the bamboo grew fuller. But one day his aunt caught him raiding the rice sack. His uncle was furious. What sort of behaviour was this, stealing rice when their backs were turned? Manophet faced them truculently. He was *not* stealing. But he could not afford to tell the whole truth or they would find the bamboo and take away the rice that he had saved, so he remained silent. His recalcitrance was taken as an admission of guilt, and he was made to stand in a corner in disgrace. The punishment did not have the desired effect. The longer he faced the wall, the fiercer his sense of injustice grew, and the stronger his determination to avenge the wrongs that he had been done became. By the end of the week, he had worked out how he could loop a long curved stick around the high bolt on the gate in the fence and tease it open.

He crept out during the night, carrying his rice carefully in its bamboo casing, now with a big banana leaf wrapped over the opening so that it did not spill. This time, he knew which dirt track to follow. Within a couple of hours he was back at the camp. He was not expecting a warm reception. His father was a man of his word, and there was little doubt in Manophet's mind that he would be turned around and marched smartly back the moment he showed his face. But at least his family would have the rice. As luck would have it, however, his father was off on a mission, and his mother was laid up with a fever, so neither of them was in a position to make the journey. His mother wept when he explained to her about the rice and, although no promises were made, he was allowed to stay for two days, then another two, and so it continued. Jun was thrilled to have him back. 'I was afraid I was never going to see you again,' she admitted. 'We were talking about you the way we talk about –' She had grown even thinner in the interim, and there were sores on her body left by infected insect bites.

'Why is it always *me* that has to go?'

She shrugged her shoulders.

'I don't see why we can't take it in turns. That way, we could all have some of their food.'

He went to tell Mr Phaothan he was back in the camp. Mr Phaothan was a cheerful fellow who would always take the trouble to say good morning to him, and could sometimes be prevailed on to tell stories about his grandmother, who had once met the king. But Mr Phaothan was nowhere to be found. 'Gone away,' said the man sitting on the log where he usually sat. 'Not here any more,' confirmed a quietly spoken girl who Manophet had seen with him in the past and was presumably part of his family. Later that day, he received the same explanation for the disappearance of three of Mrs Xi's children. Perhaps he was not alone in having been sent off to be adopted by relatives. He hid behind a sleeping mat that had been hung out to air and watched Mrs Xi as she went about her chores. She moved listlessly, as though indifferent to whether or not she completed them. Every so often she stopped to attend to the young child at her feet, testing the knots in the *baci* strings around its wrists. Gradually the display of half-hearted activity petered out, until she stood motionless, staring idly down at the dust, her arms slack at her sides. A neighbour who had been keeping a surreptitious eye on the proceedings came across and placed an arm around her.

He knew it could only be a matter of time before his father returned. With a sinking heart, he watched him stride in past the straggle of mangy dogs that hung around the camp entrance. He could run away and hide, but that would only make his parents more irritable when they found him. Tears pricked the backs of his eyes. It had been such a happy few days. But events now took an unexpected course. His father ordered all his children to make themselves scarce, and then spent several hours deep in consultation with his wife. At length he emerged, summoned Sing, and spent a few minutes talking privately to him. After that, he called for Boun, then Neung. By the time it came to Manophet's turn, the sun was low in the sky.

'My son,' he said softly, 'I am so sorry you have had to grow up in such difficult times. It has not been easy for you. How I wish you could have enjoyed a more normal childhood. This terrible war has been going on since long before you were born and, although we are very close to victory now, the final stage is the most dangerous one. Our soldiers have made great advances in recent weeks. They are only a few miles away, and I must leave again tomorrow to join up with them.' He reached out his arms and gathered Manophet up in a tight embrace. 'I am afraid this may be the last time we will see one another. You are a good boy at heart. I have always known that. And I know you are very fond of your mother. I want you to promise me that, if I do not survive, you will look after her to the very utmost of your ability until the day that she dies.'

For once, his father was wrong. Resistance melted away as the army for which he was fighting pushed south, and scarcely a drop of blood was spilt as they took control of the capital. The last few *falang* fled hastily back to wherever they belonged, and the war was at an end. The country had finally won its independence. Five years after entering the camp, the refugees were free to return home.

# TWO

It took a week to reach Muang Khoun. Families who still had money arranged rides on carts or joined bicycles together to transport their possessions, but most of the refugees travelled on foot, the older ones taking turns to carry the smaller children. Manophet, now almost six, walked the full distance unaided, keen that nobody should have any excuse to think about sending him back to his uncle's house. It was slow going during the early stages. There were checkpoints to negotiate along the road out of Vientiane, and they had to manage without his father's know-how as he had military duties to fulfil elsewhere in the capital. Edgy soldiers scrutinised their faces and delved into the shapeless sacks of belongings that they carried with them before allowing them to pass. Manophet eyed their shiny rifles, longing to know how heavy they were and how the wood was joined to the metal, but he knew he must not touch them. They stopped frequently to sound out the locals in the hope of ascertaining which roads were passable, which regions unsafe, and where they stood the best chance of finding food along the way. Not so long ago, he would have found such formalities tedious, but he had begun to appreciate that listening in on conversations not intended for his ears could be a rewarding exercise, and he tried to follow the exchanges. The older members of the group were worried about how closely they could afford to approach the enemy's last stronghold, Long Chieng. Apparently this was where the defeated soldiers' villages were located. But how could a town or a village be hostile? Surely it was against foreigners (or *falang*, as they were generally known) that his father had been fighting. It was all very baffling.

They walked from first light until mid-morning and then again from mid-afternoon to dusk to avoid the worst of the noon heat. Manophet's feet hurt, but he was determined not to complain. Kone and Neung chattered away about places they would see again and childhood memories, not caring that their older siblings showed no appetite for joining in. The mountains in the distance changed colour with the movement of the sun – now black, now purple – but never seemed to get any closer. Manophet thought about the soldiers' guns. Had they used them to kill other soldiers? He had never given much thought to the business of killing and how it was carried out. Now it began to trouble him. What happened when you died? Was it quick, or did you writhe around on the ground until the pain became too much? Was your body eaten up by flies and crows the way an animal's body was? The sinister shadow of his country's recent troubles began to steal across him. Perhaps this explained the nightmares from which the rest of his family suffered, and why they kept him in the dark about so much to avoid upsetting him. It could even be the reason why his father had grown tearful on his last day in the camp. Although he was a soldier, he had no gun of his own with which to defend himself. He must have been afraid that he might be killed in the final battle. Suddenly it was all too much. Tears began to run down Manophet's face. Luckily there was an aeroplane rumbling overhead, and nobody noticed.

Jun was not far ahead. He ran to catch her up. 'Are the enemy soldiers at Long Chieng *falang*?' he asked.
She shook her head. 'Hmong mostly.'
'Hmong? What are Hmong? Are they the same as *falang*?'
'The Hmong are a tribe,' she said.
'Are there other tribes?'
She nodded.
'How many?'
'Loads – Phouane, Khmu, Iumien. We share the land. It belongs to all of us.'
'Are *we* a tribe?'
'No, not really. There are too many of us. Tribes are smaller. They live in separate villages and have their own languages. And they wear different clothes. You can tell which tribe a person belongs to from what they're wearing.'

On the fourth day, the road finally began to climb. In place of the familiar shrivelled thorn trees and brown clumpy weeds, delicate green bushes sprang up by the wayside. Tall grasses waved in the faint breeze, and the chirruping of cicadas filled the air. Ahead, a couple of startled wild pigs shot off into the undergrowth as the party rounded a bend. Manophet was astonished by the abundance of wildlife that surrounded him. Here was a tiny gold beetle making its way around a mud rut while, overhead, birds exchanged serenades as they fluttered from tree to tree. He was not used to nature. It saturated his senses, filled his ears with heady music. They stopped beside a tumbling stream where, to his surprise, the family lay down one by one to drink. Was this not the same alluring water that flowed down to the great Mekong and turned your stomach to liquid if you allowed it pass your lips? But it was not the time to argue, and he took his turn like the rest. How sweet it tasted. No wonder so many creatures made their homes here. The higher they climbed, the easier it became to endure the heat. The air grew clearer. Jagged limestone outcrops began to dominate the horizon, then vertiginous mountain ridges that reached up to touch the clouds. Deciduous trees gave way to thick forest evergreens that crowded in on the road, blocking out the view for minutes at a time, shrouding the party in a thick pulsating silence.

They stopped to confer. Was there enough time to cross the next karst ridge and descend into the valley before dusk? They needed to find a village in which to spend the night, but could the tribes who lived in the region be relied on to make them welcome? Some cousins who were travelling with them remembered there being a Yao settlement a couple of miles further on, but that had been eight years ago. Even in peacetime, tribes were liable to abandon villages if the surrounding land ceased to be productive and move away to other parts. There was no knowing what had taken place here during the war. The villagers might not even be aware it had ended. Nervous eyes surveyed the silent conifers. Would it be safer to sleep in the open? What if they were ambushed? Somewhere in these mountains, desperate enemy soldiers were hiding. Although they would probably not hurt civilians, they would have no qualms about plundering their food and possessions if an opportunity arose. The debate was cut short by a sudden shriek. Manophet turned to see Kone bolting off into the forest, closely followed by two of their cousins. For a moment there was panic. Sing and Boun leapt to their feet and grabbed their sacks from the ground. His mother scooped up Lar as though to follow. Another moment, and the leading trio had stopped in their tracks and were turning back. Sheepishly, they began retracing their steps. Jun, still breathing hard, released

Manophet's arm, which she had been gripping tightly. In the distance, the rumble of a plane could be heard.

They passed through another checkpoint at a road junction and turned east towards Vietnam. A few miles further on, they crossed into Xieng Khouang, the family's home province. Here, there were gentle hills, intersected by meandering rivers. The sunshine, which had long since ceased to be its usual fiery self, felt pleasantly warm on Manophet's back as he walked, and the dust-free air was a joy to breathe. But ugly scars disfigured the panorama. Fire had consumed long stretches of forest. Skeletal white-grey trunks spiked up through carpets of ash, branch stubs angling out like amputated limbs. Once-green farmlands lay barren and ochre-stained. From one derelict expanse, a rusting hoe projected forlornly towards the sky, unaccountably still upright. Here and there, the remains of wrecked houses could be seen, tangles of charred timbers strewn across disused fields, uprooted fencing flattened by years of inattention and left to rot in shallow ditches. The devastation grew more extensive the further they travelled. No birds flew in the skies above. No creatures showed themselves. The land was dead. Ahead, on a distant hillside, Manophet noticed a strange sandy pockmark. When the road finally wound past it many minutes later, it turned out to be a crater deeper than the height of a fully-grown man, and at least three times as wide.

The road to Muang Khoun was in woeful condition. Sections had been gouged out or blasted away, making it impassable to carts, and in places they had to clamber over boulders or skirt around deep shafts. Manophet found it increasingly difficult to contain his excitement as the moment of arrival drew closer, but the older members of the group insisted on stopping to inspect every plant they found growing by the wayside, every piece of timber or metal, and the final few miles took an eternity to traverse. Even rocks were picked up, turned over and passed around for comment. They spent an age beside a small gully, cautiously tasting the brackish water. But at last, as the road crested a hillock and swung round to the left, a sudden urgency took hold of the party. A few hundred yards further on, they could no longer hold themselves back, and broke spontaneously into a run, their aches and pains temporarily forgotten. After five gruelling years in exile it was finally time to reclaim their inheritance. Manophet gazed at their home with dismay. It bore no resemblance to the picture in his head. He had known the house would be in ruins, but where were the beautiful fruit trees about which they had talked, the river off which the sun sparkled, the blue dragonflies, the grassy bank down which you could roll if you held your arms tightly by your sides? The place was just a jumble of wreckage, like all the others they had passed along the way. They stood in a ragged huddle, nobody wanting to disturb the past. At length his mother advanced, gingerly shifting lengths of charred timber to create a path. A muffled gasp slipped from her throat as a small stack of rotten planks collapsed, revealing the skeleton of a cat.

At first, the enormity of the task confronting them appeared overwhelming. The land had been lush and fertile before the war, but the enemy had dropped poisonous chemicals on it from their aeroplanes, causing the fruit trees and other vegetation to die. From there, the toxins had leached into the rivers, wiping out all the fish. How long would nature take to heal the environment? Here and there, weeds were starting to take hold, but would rice be capable of flourishing in their place, and would it be safe to eat? Without rice, feeding the family would be even more challenging than in the camp. Almost all the forests in the vicinity had been razed to the ground. Gone were the wild animals that they were used to hunting, the birds, the forest plants. As for rebuilding the house, there were more difficulties than they had foreseen. A bomb had landed no more than a few yards from the site on which it had stood, leaving a deep crater. A new plot would have to be cleared and levelled. But they needed advice about where they should locate it before they could start, and on the more technical aspects of construction such as how to splice roof beams. Normally there would have been neighbours to ask, but the community of which they had been part no longer existed. The centre of Muang Khoun was considered too dangerous to resettle, and so far only a handful of other families had returned to the area. Besides, where was the wood to come from? Most of the old timber was spoiled and no longer fit for purpose.

Trying to explain away the past with ambiguous half-truths was futile now that Manophet could see the legacy for himself, and his elder siblings were more forthcoming when he asked questions about the war. As the days went by, he began to build up a picture of what had taken place. Aeroplanes had started dropping bombs five years before he had been born. Peasants had watched in bewilderment as the terrifying machines had burst out of the sky and blown their painstakingly maintained rice fields to pieces. Smallholdings that had been tended by successive generations of the same family for decades or even centuries had been wiped out in the blink of an eye, leaving the owners' livelihoods hanging by a thread. What had they done to deserve such treatment? There were suggestions that the *falang* flying the aeroplanes had mistakenly dropped their bombs on the wrong side of the border with North Vietnam, not knowing exactly where they were. But back they had come, more and more of them as the years went by, annihilating harmless livestock, setting fire to woodlands, destroying houses. The dazed inhabitants had dug holes in the ground in which to shelter from the huge blasts and the shock waves that followed. Any human movement on the ground during daylight hours brought aircraft swarming down like hornets, and the townsfolk had stayed indoors, out of sight, stealing down to their damaged rice fields at the dead of night to try and patch them up. But the *falang* had kept returning, targeting every structure visible from the sky, until the last building in Muang Khoun had been wiped out, the last rice field destroyed, leaving the townsfolk with no choice but to abandon their homeland and take refuge in the forest.

The family had been on the run for several weeks at the time of Manophet's birth, inching laboriously towards Vietnam, where the patriotic forces were stronger, staying motionless under trees whenever aircraft passed overhead, going to any length to avoid attracting the attention of patrolling Hmong soldiers. Manophet's father was off fighting with the patriots, and they did not know whether he was alive or dead. Food had been almost impossible to find. They had scavenged as best they could, living mostly off leaves and berries. Manophet had been a perpetual liability, wailing for sustenance at times when they desperately needed him to be silent, and limiting the group's mobility. Other families had given their newborn babies opium to hush their crying, but Manophet's mother had been determined to resist this practice. It had been during one of the tensest episodes in this game of cat and mouse that Jun had lost her temper and declared that she wanted to kill her little brother. The bombing raids had become so frequent and intense that they had been forced to take refuge in a limestone cave, along with a number of other families. Here they had remained for several months, venturing out by night to search for food. Jun remembered water dripping through the roof and forming a dank pool on the rocky floor from which they had occasionally been forced to drink even though they knew it might be contaminated.

Manophet knew what aeroplanes looked like, and he could imagine bombs dropping out of their bellies, but he found it difficult to grasp what happened when a bomb struck the ground. What *was* an explosion? Neung said it was like a terrible thunderstorm, but that left him no closer to understanding how a bomb could turn into a crater. Living in a cave, on the other hand, he found easy to visualise. They had passed one on the road from Vientiane and stopped to look inside. Fancy making your home in one of *those*! You would live in the dark – like a bat, or a mouse in a hole. The roof would be so low in places that you would only be able to move about by slithering on your tummy like a snake. Or perhaps, if you were good at digging, like a mole, you would tunnel through to other caves so that you could meet other people without the enemy knowing where you were. And now he was gripped by a tantalising thought: what would you see if you looked out from the back of a cave towards the entrance? Surely an image similar in outline to the flattened dome of light that periodically enraptured him in dreams. And the sound of rain droplets splashing down that often seemed to accompany his earliest memory – could that not be the sound of water dripping through a cave roof? He had been there. There *was*, after all, a thread connecting him to his family's odyssey.

For several weeks, they avoided the centre of Muang Khoun. Unexploded bombs were reckoned to lie half-concealed at every turn. Nor was Manophet's mother in any hurry to lay eyes on the ruins to which the town in which she had grown up had been reduced. However, intrepid settlers from surrounding areas made the journey and returned with the opinion that visitors were in no danger unless they stepped off the beaten track. Eventually the family summoned up the courage to walk the two miles. Not a building had survived. The remains of the hospital – two corner-pieces and a wall punched through by gaping window voids – perched groggily at the top of a short flight of steps strewn with masonry. Manophet tried to stop himself thinking about what might lie beneath the moss and creepers that had already begun to swallow up the remnants of the civilisation that had flourished here. In the eerie silence, they picked their way carefully along a path that led to Wat Phia, one of the oldest structures in the town. A vast cross-legged Buddha had somehow survived the bombing and now towered above the ruins, framed between tottering pillars against a backdrop of distant hills. Years of wind and rain had weathered away the gold leaf that had once adorned it, exposing the mottled stone from which it was hewn. A piece from one arm was missing, but the naked figure was otherwise intact, even the line of short stone hairs carved into its head. It was as though the nation's suffering had been distilled into the expression on the Buddha's face: a crooked mouth frozen in an abortive smile, the resigned half-closed eyes seemingly too heavy to shed tears.

He was still confused about what the Hmong and the *falang* had to do with each other.

'The white men did not want to bring soldiers of their own to fight in the forest, so they asked the Hmong to fight on their side,' one of his cousins explained. 'The Hmong thought they would be safer fighting with the *falang* than against them because their aeroplanes gave them a big advantage, so they said yes.'

'But why did the *falang* attack us?' he asked. 'What did we do wrong?'

'*Falang* are like buffalo,' his cousin replied. 'They have natural impulses that they can't control. Every so often a herd panics and goes on the rampage. When that happens, they don't notice what's under their feet.'

His father was less equivocal on the subject when he visited. 'The Hmong were guilty of carrying out atrocious acts during the war,' he said. 'The new government has promised to hunt down the ringleaders and bring them to justice.'

'Will they be sent to a re-education camp?' Manophet asked.

'How do you know about re-education camps?' his father retorted testily. 'You are never to mention that subject again. Do you understand?'

'Those are for the Lao who took sides with the king against the new government,' Sing explained later when his father was out of earshot.

Now Manophet was even more confused. He had caught the words "re-education camp" in a conversation to which he was not supposed to have been listening the previous day, but he had no idea what went on there. Had his own people, the Lao, fought on both sides during the war? Surely they should have realised that was not a sensible thing to do. And what on earth had the king been thinking, fighting *against* the patriots?

Work on the house came to an abrupt halt one morning when a sharp crack rang out from across the valley, followed by a faint cry. A plume of smoke billowed up on the hillside from which the noises had come. It was land farmed by a family that had returned to the plain at about the same time as Manophet's. Thong started crying, unnerved by the violence of the report which, even at this distance, left a ringing in the ears. After exchanging hurried glances, Sing and his cousin dropped their tools and started running. Manophet watched as his two relatives, now small across the slope, approached the spot where the smoke had risen. Other figures were converging from different parts of the hillside to gather round a figure lying on the ground. Sing was tight-lipped when he returned on his own half an hour later, and Manophet had to piece the story together from scraps of conversation that he contrived to overhear during the days that followed. The woman lying on the ground had been breaking up the soil in a field ahead of the rice planting season. Her hoe had struck some buried ordnance left over from the war, causing it to explode. She had lost a leg and also had abdominal injuries. Their missing cousin had set off immediately in the direction of Khang Khan with the aim of finding a doctor, though more in hope than expectation. Apparently this was not an isolated incident. Three or four tragedies of a similar kind had taken place in the surrounding area during the preceding few weeks.

From time to time, while listening in on older members of his family conversing amongst themselves, he would catch the name Bua. The first time he heard it, he assumed they were talking about Boun, but then Boun herself spoke the name, and went on to imply that Bua was male rather than female. Jun was part of the group within which this exchange took place, so she was evidently in on the secret. Manophet felt the old resentment surge inside him. Why should she be privy to this information and not him? However well he tried to behave, the family's sinister conspiracy against him kept rumbling on in the background. He confronted her one day when they were alone together, demanding answers. Who was Bua? Why did they always whisper when they talked about him? A look of dismay entered Jun's face. He knew exactly the emotion that was tearing through her: it was the one that had overcome him when his aunt had caught him raiding the rice sack during his stay at his uncle's house. Her arms sagged by her sides. 'I can't tell you,' she said forlornly. 'I promised not to.'

Later in the week, his mother called him in. It was rare for her to summon him formally, and he feared for his fate – even though he could not recall having put anybody's nose out of joint during the past few days. Uncle Athakhanh might be safely out of reach in Vientiane, but his parents had several other brothers and sisters living nearby on whom they were capable of foisting him at a moment's notice if they felt so disposed. However, her business was not of a recriminatory nature. 'I have something important to tell you,' she said. 'It is something about our family that we haven't mentioned to you before because it upsets us whenever we think about it. It will make you very sad, I'm afraid, but I think the time has come when you should hear the truth.'

He stood awkwardly in front of her, uncertain what to expect.

'A long time ago, you had another brother,' she said. 'His name was Bua. He was our third child. He was born after Boun and before Neung.' She took his hand. 'He was wounded during the war. It was around the time you were born, when we were living in the forest. There were bombs falling everywhere. We had to run away from them as fast as we could. But some shrapnel hit him in the back while we were trying to find somewhere to hide. He was seriously hurt. His injury was so bad that he couldn't walk any more. We didn't know what to do. It was too dangerous for us to stay out in the open, with all the bombs falling.' There were tears in her eyes. 'In the end, your father and uncle carried him to a little cave and made him as comfortable as they could. That way, at least he would be safe for a while.' She put a hand to her mouth, unable to continue.

Her distress was scaring him. How could there have been another child in the family? There was nothing, *nothing* to suggest that a person was missing. He did not want to hear the end of the story. He tried to back away, but she would not release him.

'They left him there,' she said at length.

'On his *own*?' he blurted out.

He had never seen her look so guilty. 'There was nothing else they could do.'

28

'How old was he?'

'Twelve,' she said. 'Your father told me where the cave was before he went off again to fight, and I went back with a doctor once it was too dark for the bombers to keep flying. We searched for a long time. There were two or three caves that seemed to match the description your father had given, but there was no sign of him.'

'He disappeared?'

'We don't know what happened to him,' she said. 'We couldn't be sure we had found the right cave.'

'Perhaps he managed to walk out by himself.'

'He could not have walked anywhere,' she said. 'We are certain about that.'

'Well, perhaps he just got better then.'

His mother shook her head. 'Your father cut his ear lobe before he left him.'

Manophet turned the curious disclosure over in his mind, wondering what it meant. 'Why did he do that?' he asked eventually.

'To see if there was any blood flow. It is a way of telling whether somebody close to death will survive. If some blood flows out, the person will live.'

Manophet fingered his own ear lobe as he tried to digest the idea.

'There was no blood flow,' his mother said quietly.

Food remained scarce. Before the war, crops of all descriptions had flourished on the high plain where they lived. They had kept chickens, ducks, pigs, water buffalo. Now, like every other family, they were starting again from scratch. Livestock could only be sourced at prohibitive cost, and it was no longer safe to allow them to roam at will as they were too easily lost to poisoned grazing or buried bombs. The river yielded up a fish or two from time to time, but stocks were pitifully low. Neung showed Manophet how to catch swallows. First of all, you had to find a long straight stick. After that, you needed to tie three or four short sticks tightly to one end using creepers so that they stuck out at right-angles. The crown was then coated with a gluey black pitch, and the contraption was raised to the vertical in an open field, planted firmly in the ground and left to stand. If your luck was in, a swallow would fly down to perch and become stuck in the pitch. It was a wearisome business. Swallows hardly ever fell for the deception unless another swallow had already blundered into the trap and started chirping, giving the impression it was safe to land. And, on the rare occasions they were successful, the reward scarcely justified the effort involved. There was precious little meat to be had off a swallow, and they took forever to pluck.

Boun would sometimes tell him stories about the old days, as the family habitually referred to the times before the bombing. 'We used to visit the Wat all the time,' she said, 'sometimes to give alms to the monks when they came by with their bowls in the morning, sometimes to make a special offering for one of our ancestors. Sing was going to become a novice monk, but then the temple was destroyed and it wasn't possible. Not that he was all that disappointed. He hadn't been looking forward to having his head shaved.' She gave a mischievous chuckle. 'The monks were very wise, especially the oldest ones. People travelled from all over the province to take lessons from them. If you needed something translated from a foreign language, for instance, or you wanted to learn some history, you would go to the Wat. But the best thing about Muang Khoun was the market. Villagers from different tribes would travel to the town from all over Xieng Khouang on market days to trade with each other. They would bring every kind of merchandise you can possibly imagine – food, clothes, silver jewellery, peculiar animals in baskets, cooking pots, musical instruments, carved wooden boxes – all kinds of curiosities. The streets used to throng with people dressed in their own special costumes. It was always so colourful and lively.'

'Were some of the people who came Hmong?' Manophet asked.

'Hmong, Khmu, Phouane – lots of Phouane.'

'Did you hate the Hmong?'

She shook her head. 'There was never any bad feeling in those days. We had more than enough food and water and sunshine to go round. We lived peacefully side by side, sharing the rivers and the forests and the beautiful mountains. None of us wanted there to be fighting. But the Pathet Lao started going round individual villages asking the villagers to fight on their side in the war. And so then representatives from the king's side tried to get the villagers to be on *their* side. It wasn't easy to know what to do. If a village said it wanted to stay neutral, *both* sides suspected it of being hostile, so that was no good. Lots of villages just pretended to back one side or the other. If they were instructed to attack a neighbouring village, they would send messengers ahead with a warning so the people who lived there had time to make themselves scarce before they arrived.

He longed to impress his family, but they remained unmoved by his finest accomplishments. When he managed to knock a huge pine cone down from a tree by throwing a stone they shrugged their shoulders. And when he snared his first swallow without any help from Neung there was universal scepticism. Was he sure he had not found it lying on the ground already dead? 'You tell too many fibs,' his mother scolded when he flew into a rage. 'How are we to know when to believe you?' "In the way" was an aspersion that flew regularly in his direction. If he tried to help Sing and

Neung with the construction of the house, or when they were moving earth or heaving boulders, they would instantly find fault with some aspect of his initiative. He should not be standing so near the building site. Something heavy might fall on him. Under no circumstances was he to move the wheelbarrow. He was not to pick up the heavy hammer in case he dropped it on his toe. It was almost as bad if he sat in when Kone and Jun took cooking or needlework lessons from his mother and older sister. Heavy hints were dropped that it was not appropriate for a boy to be acquainting himself with women's work. 'Why don't you go and mind Thong?' somebody would suggest. '*That* would be helpful.' Manophet had nothing against his younger brother, who was an amiable soul who always did what he was told and never seemed to upset anybody. But minding a three year-old for hours at a time was as boring an assignment as it was possible to imagine. How was *he* to learn anything useful if he was expected to spend all day doing that?

A rare opportunity to shine came his way when his mother promised to lend their cousins a cooking pot. 'Somebody will need to carry it there,' Manophet pointed out. As usual, there were those who doubted his ability to perform such a task. It was a good hour's walk. Would he not get tired? Was he sure he could remember the way? But for once he was trusted and, after some stern reminders about the dangers of straying off the path, he was despatched with his cargo. At last he had been given some responsibility. How important he felt! He strode along briskly, greeting everybody he met with a cheery *sabaidee*. The path weaved its way over the hill and descended into a burned-out section of forest on the other side, where tree corpses swayed and creaked as though they were about to crash down on top of him. But these soon gave way to verdant soaring evergreens that had somehow survived the war years. Tiny flowers adorned the path now, and the pine needles gave off a crisp resinous smell. He walked more slowly. There was no need to hurry through such a beautiful place. Suddenly he heard a muffled shooshing a few yards ahead. Was a wild beast lurking in wait for him? A moment later, a girl of about his age emerged from an opening between the trees to the left. She was dressed in an elaborately embroidered costume and had a wicker basket containing a stack of large banana leaves strapped to her back. Manophet trotted up to say hello, relieved to discover she was not a tiger. Her response, insofar as he could judge, was friendly, but there was a complication: he could not understand a word she was saying. For a second or two, they stood staring at one another, unsure what to do. Then, at exactly the same time, they started laughing. Would two cats have been unable to comprehend one another if they had met on the path, or two goats? Of course not. But it was not such a difficult obstacle to overcome. Once they had mastered each other's names, it did not take them long to begin exchanging words.

He thought often of My during the days that followed. It bothered him that he did not know which tribe she belonged to. If she was Hmong, he should not have made friends with her. Her family might have fought against his father in the war and committed atrocities – whatever those were. But she did not *seem* a horrible person. With her searching eyes and wide crooked smile, she looked unlike anybody he had met before. The scarf that she wore across her head, the ear-rings, the complicated slip-knots with which she attached her basket to her wrists – none of these were things a Lao girl would wear or use. He did not mention her to his family. They had no patience with patterns of life that deviated from those that they regarded as normal. But Manophet had bigger dreams. He was determined not to spend his days doing exactly as his ancestors had done. He would travel far and wide, meet exotic strangers, learn to speak their languages, discover what *they* thought. More than anything, he wanted to fly in an aeroplane, like the *falang*. He could not imagine anything more exciting than being able to look down at the earth from high up, passing through clouds, speeding from place to place at hundreds of miles per hour. His mother was amused when he announced his ambition. 'But you have already flown in an aeroplane,' she said, laughing when his mouth fell open. 'How do you suppose we got to the camp in Vientiane? The *falang* had so many aeroplanes by 1970 that they decided they might as well use them to clear us all off the plain so it would be easier to bomb.' Manophet crept away, trying to conceal his disappointment. Like every other important event in his life, the airlift had taken place when he had been too young to be aware of what was going on. He had been born too late.

# THREE

Stage by stage, the family clawed its way back from the brink of destitution. The house was completed. Rice fields were painstakingly scoured for signs of unexploded bombs, patched up and brought back into service. New fruit trees were planted. One by one, chickens were acquired and – after much soul-searching and at fearsome expense – a pig. Everyday affairs were overseen by Manophet's father, who was permitted to spend more and more of his time at home as the months went by. The government could not afford to pay its soldiers, and there was no need for them all to continue serving full-time now the war had been won. The family faced a continual uphill struggle to make ends meet, but they consoled themselves with the knowledge that conditions were worse in other parts of the country. Prior to their expulsion, the unprincipled *falang* had been pumping large sums of money into the economy to ensure that the Royalist government continued to do as it was told. Now that this cash river had dried up, there was widespread financial hardship as the country was not used to having to manage without it. Sing had left the household after winning a Soviet-funded place at university in Moscow, and Boun had married and moved away to Phon Hong. But another new baby boy had arrived, Phanh, leaving the house almost as crowded as before. Manophet, now ten years old, rose at dawn each morning to walk to the ramshackle schoolhouse on the other side of the hill, a three mile journey that took him an hour and a quarter to complete.

He enjoyed lessons. At the beginning, he had found them difficult to understand, being one of the youngest pupils in a large class containing children of a wide range of ages. But, now that he was used to the teachers and their routines, he looked forward to soaking up the odd mixture of information that they were able to supply. Geography was his favourite subject. He loved the big map of Laos that hung on the classroom wall. Each of the country's seventeen provinces – all of which he could identify by their shapes, and whose names he knew by heart – was shown in a different colour. The thick-lined international borders particularly intrigued him. Beyond these lay a galaxy of mysterious foreign powers – to the south, Cambodia; to the west, Burma and Thailand. The border with Burma was drawn in blue to show that it ran along the Mekong, as did long stretches of the border with Thailand. It was a long way to the great river from Xieng Khouang, but his childhood dream of letting it carry him away had lost none of its allure. How badly he wanted to set foot in a foreign country. Vietnam to the east was the closest. It would surely take no longer than two or three days to walk there. And, across the short frontier to the north, the outline of vast China mushroomed like an enormous leafy tree. Populations were another topic that intrigued him. Why were there fifteen times as many people in Vietnam as in Laos – more than fifty million – when Laos took up almost as much space on the map? According to his teacher, it was because Laos was mountainous and had no coastline, but this did not sound much of a reason to Manophet. China was ten times as densely populated as Laos even though half of it was covered in mountains. His own parents had done what they could to redress the imbalance by bringing ten children into the world, but they could hardly be expected to rectify the entire problem on their own.

History he also found absorbing. It left him inspired and dejected by turns. What a stirring achievement winning independence had been. One by one, the proud *falang* occupiers had been sent on their way – the Thais, the French, the Japanese, the Americans – until at last the people of Laos could stand proudly on their own feet and call themselves the Lao People's Democratic Republic. It had taken terrible sacrifices. Many lives had been lost, and the country was woefully disadvantaged as a result of the battering it had taken. But conditions would improve over time as long as they all continued to work hard together in the fields, and provided the *falang* did not decide to start another war – that was the line taken by the Party official who came to lecture at the school from time to time. And yet what hope was there that the interfering *falang* would leave them alone for long enough to put their lives back together, given the regularity with which invasion had followed invasion over the centuries? The government had closed all the country's borders to prevent any more foreigners slinking in, but a few border guards would be no match for a hostile power equipped with aeroplanes and bombs and sophisticated guns. 'We are too small and too poor for other nations to take us seriously,' Manophet's grandfather sighed when he solicited his opinion. 'The one good thing is that, if a *falang* army tried to invade now, it would be in for a tough ride. Its soldiers would not be able to move around the country without blowing themselves up on the bombs that were dropped the last time they were here.'

At first, Laos had tried not to take sides in the war, their history teacher explained, not wishing to fall out with either of the formidable combatants involved, and the Americans and the North Vietnamese had both agreed to respect its neutrality by signing a treaty. But neither party had honoured the undertakings enshrined in it. The Vietnamese had carried on moving troops across the border, to the point where tens of thousands of its soldiers were amassed on the Plain of Jars, as the area around Muang Khoun was known. America, for its part, had set up a secret military base at Long Chieng, a facility that developed rapidly into the second busiest airport in the world. Not taking sides had soon ceased to be an option for anybody living along the fault line. In the north of the country, the Pathet Lao had worked hard behind the scenes to win the hearts and minds of the villagers, encouraging them to support the North Vietnamese and press for independence. Further south, in Vientiane, the Royalist government, now fatally dependent on American aid, had clung cravenly to power. Civil war had become inevitable when the Americans attempted to exclude the Pathet Lao from government by falsifying the general election result. This, together with their penchant for bombing anything that moved, hardened opinions against them and eroded the resolve of those in favour of remaining neutral. The upshot was that independence, when it finally arrived, had not been the tumultuous unifying event that Manophet had once liked to suppose. The *falang* might be gone, but there were still plenty of other scores to be settled.

There was a frisson of anticipation when their cousins succeeded in borrowing a cart for a day. It was big enough to transport the whole family to Phonsavan, which had assumed the role of state capital following the destruction of Muang Khoun. Not so long ago, Phonsavan had consisted of little more than a glorified road junction, but it was said that there were now dozens of new roads and buildings. They loaded up an assortment of items that they hoped to sell in the marketplace – plants from the forest, a couple of squirrels, a porcupine, all the scrap metal that they had salvaged over the years including a heavy bomb casing, which they had been told should fetch a good price if they bargained cannily, skirts and tapestries embroidered by Manophet's mother with some help from Kone, rice wine, a wooden Buddha carved by one of their cousins. Phonsavan lay almost twenty miles away, and they set out at first light. Although the road was in better condition than when they had traversed it at the end of their long journey from Vientiane almost five years ago, it remained richly endowed with potholes, and at times they could have walked as fast as it was safe for the cart to travel. Manophet kept his eyes on the horizon, hoping to catch sight of one of the great megalithic urns from which the Plain of Jars took its name, about which he had learned at school. An ancient civilisation was thought to have hewn them from rock many centuries earlier. Thousands of these vast relics were strewn across the region, and it was to either side of this stretch of road that they were said to be most heavily concentrated.

They had counted on having to spend most of the day in the marketplace, but their wares were snapped up more swiftly than they had anticipated. After trading a few of the kip that they had earned for some food, they wandered around the town, taking in the atmosphere. Not since leaving Vientiane had Manophet seen buildings fabricated from concrete rather than wood. Many were still under construction, enmeshed in twirly-twig scaffolding. Jun, who had recently hatched ideas about becoming a doctor, gazed longingly at the beginnings of the Lao-Mongolian Friendship Hospital, a huge structure in the making, though at this point little more than a forest of metal rods poking up through a maze of concrete squares. Manophet noticed that his mother was becoming increasingly subdued. 'Is something wrong?' he asked her eventually. She smiled and put an arm around him. 'Muang Khoun used to be a lovely town,' she said. 'In some people's eyes, it was even more beautiful than Luang Prabang. There were stupas and temples, monasteries, peaceful courtyards where you could sit in the shade beneath tall trees when it was too hot. But it took many centuries to build. Phonsavan is being thrown together as fast as possible, and with the cheapest materials they can find, so that Xieng Khouang can have a proper capital again. Unfortunately, nobody has thought about how it will look when it is finished. I'm afraid it is going to be very ugly.'

Manophet thought back to the temple that they had just visited. He had been rather taken by its ornate decoration and racily painted exterior, but the cheapness of the effects now began to dawn on him. The golden statues in the inner sanctum had none of the charisma of the great stone Buddha that towered above the ruins of Muang Khoun. He had lost count of the number of times he had been to contemplate that lonely battered figure. Its weather-beaten face still had the power to stop him in his tracks. His mother was right: there was nothing spiritual about Phonsavan. And yet he could not help liking the town. Its liveliness infected him with energy and optimism. What were those boys doing, for instance? He ran across to the open grassy space to get a better look. About twenty teenagers were kicking a ball backwards and forwards, closely observed by a few youngsters dotted along the periphery, hoping to be allowed to join in. Using only their feet, the boys wearing shirts appeared to be striving to force the ball between a pair of upright sticks driven roughly into the ground at one end of the field, while the bare-chested boys were aiming towards a matching pair of sticks at the other. What a magnificent idea for a game. He longed to continue watching, but the rest of the family was already heading away to inspect a lavishly appointed house perched above a rice paddy. The remainder of the day passed in a blur as he dreamed of holding a soccer match back at home in Muang Khoun. There was a square of dirt behind the house that might serve as a playing area if it could be extended by a few yards. Goalposts would be simple enough to improvise, but what about a football? Perhaps he could stuff a rattan ball with crushed banana leaves or damp rags to make it heavier.

Luckily, My had turned out to be Khmu and not Hmong, and Manophet had been allowed to remain friends with her. It took five hours to walk to her village and back, so they saw one another only a few times a year. Manophet was usually the one who did the walking. He loved immersing himself in the culture of her tribe, observing their curious rituals, having to speak Khmu instead of Lao. None of the children in the village understood Lao, which meant there was no point in them attending the school, where it was the only language spoken. But My was as keen to master Manophet's native tongue as he was to conquer hers. She was always hungry for new words and good at absorbing them – though explaining to her how to arrange them in the correct order was more a challenge. If they grew bored of that pastime, she would take him to visit her pig, or they would scramble up the slope on the other side of the village fence and see if they could see what the shaman was up to through the hole in the wall in his house. The shaman was an alarming man with only one eyebrow, revered by the villagers on account of his ability to gauge the moods of the forest spirit and the water spirit. Most of the children in the village believed he could make himself invisible, but neither Manophet nor My was inclined to buy into this story without first seeing the evidence with their own eyes. Which was not to say that My regarded him as a charlatan, or doubted his other spiritual powers. On the contrary, his ability to divine which spirit was responsible for any illness or misfortune that struck the village filled her with as much awe as the rest of her tribe, and his relationships with the spirits of her ancestors were too sacred for her even to consider talking about to an outsider such as Manophet.

Manophet badgered one of his school teachers for more information about the country's ethnic makeup. How many tribes were there? How many different languages? The teacher shrugged his shoulders, and said nobody really knew. Wave upon wave of migration had taken place from China, a process spanning several centuries, with the result that any number of different hill-tribes now lived in northern Laos, and at least as many again in Burma, Thailand and Vietnam. Many lived such remote existences that the only reliable means of characterising them would be to track them down and find out whether they resembled any of the groups that had already had their identities documented. It was something that made the government's life very awkward, he lamented, because many of the minority tribes did not identify with Laos at all. Some probably did not even know they were Lao citizens. Manophet felt sorry for the government, which he knew, from listening to his father's conversations with friends and neighbours, had all manner of troubles on its plate – not least the continuing refusal of the Hmong to surrender their weapons. It had shown such fortitude in winning independence for the nation, and was surely now entitled to expect the villagers on whose behalves it had struggled to give it their unconditional support. And yet a third of the population probably had no notion of what independence was, let alone what the word patriotic meant. How could such a fragmented population be persuaded to pull together for the common good?

To everybody's surprise, Manophet had established himself as the most proficient fisherman in the family. Sitting patiently by himself when there was nothing to do had never been one of his strong points, and it was a mystery to the rest of them why he became so much better at it when there was a fishing rod in his hands. But there was little that gave him as much pleasure as catching a fish big enough for every member of the family to receive a mouthful or two at dinner. Now his parents could be proud of him: that was *his* fish they were eating. Thong came with him one Saturday morning to try his luck with a rod. He had tagged along once or twice before, without ever catching anything, but his mother wanted him out of the house so she could clean, and he had nothing else to do. The sun beamed down through the shimmer of haze, reflecting fierily off the glassy water, and there was hardly a breath of wind. Their chances of success in these conditions were not high. Manophet concentrated all his energy on the smooth surface of the river, trying to divine where the deeper currents ran. What would entice a fish into the open on a day like this? It was not long before Thong grew restless. He started conversations, forgetting that this might scare the fish away, and then kicked a stone into the river. Manophet tried to suppress his irritation. It was not really his brother's fault that he was bored. He was not old enough to enjoy activities of this kind. 'You can go off and play if you don't want to fish any more,' he whispered condescendingly. 'Just don't make a noise and don't play near the river.'

For a time there was peace. Birdsong drifted across from a covey of trees clustered around an abandoned farmstead further down the valley. Then Manophet saw the water stir. Beneath the surface, a dark shape swerved suddenly out of the shadow, bringing up a little puff of mud before vanishing once more into its hiding place. Carefully, he adjusted his position, making sure he did not disturb the rod. His heart was pounding softly. He took in a long slow breath to steady himself.

'I found a bombie,' Thong announced.

Manophet battled to contain his exasperation. Remarkably, the fish seemed not to heed the disturbance. Keeping his eyes on the stretch of water where it had shown itself, he gestured to Thong to keep quiet. For a moment, it appeared the crisis had been averted, but then Thong chimed in with another salvo. 'I'll just throw it away then, shall I?' he said huffily. 'In case it explodes.'

Manophet was already leaping to his feet. Too late, he had realised this was not something Thong would have said in jest. He turned to see his brother's arm raised high above his head, his podgy fist clutched precariously around a cluster bomb. The sun caught the shiny metal casing as he launched the device into the air. '*No!*' Manophet screamed. But by now it was already looping on its way in an absurd slow-motion arc. Presumably Thong's intention had been to throw it as far as possible from where they were fishing, but it was a plan he did not have the skill to execute. Instead of flying towards the relative safety of the neighbouring field, the bombie hurtled directly towards a dead tree standing no more than a few feet in front of him.

The earth stood still. The moment seemed to last an eternity. Then there was a brilliant eruption of light accompanied by a brutal deafening report. Manophet clapped his hands to his ears and reeled backwards, instinctively shutting his eyes. Catching his heel on a tussock of grass, he overbalanced and tumbled to the ground in a confusion of useless jellified arms and legs. A tremendous ringing filled his temples, above which he could hear nothing. Opening his eyes again, he saw smoke spouting up from the tree. For an instant, he thought it was on fire. What had happened to Thong? He staggered back to his feet. There he was on the ground. Not moving. Cold fingers closed around Manophet's heart. He could see blood. Finally a high eerie wail telling of indescribable pain began to be audible above the din in his ears. Manophet hesitated. Was it safe to go any nearer? Inch by inch, he crept across the ground that separated them. His brother was a horrible sight. There was a gaping wound in his stomach. Bits of his insides were spilling out, and there was gore everywhere. Thong had his hands around the hole, trying to close it up. Manophet did not know what to do. He could not think of any words to quieten or comfort the howling figure on the ground. His brother was dying. He did not want to abandon him, and yet he knew he must go and fetch help.

He was exhausted after sprinting all the way to the house, and had to gasp for breath before trying to speak. Leaping to his feet, his father barked out a command that immediately brought Neung haring across the fields, and grabbed some poles and a length of cloth from behind the house. Wasting no time, he set off towards the river, leaving his two sons to keep up as best they could. By the time they reached Thong, he had lost consciousness. His breathing was shallow and irregular. Grey with worry, Manophet's father went about his business precisely, coaxing the displaced organs and tissues back into position, gently bandaging up the wound. Manophet tried to watch, but the sight was too gruesome, and he threw up over his own feet. Groans came intermittently from Thong as his father worked. Neung tied the material they had brought to the poles to create a makeshift stretcher, and they eased it underneath the motionless form. With Neung at the front and his father taking the rear, they set a course across the hill towards the house of a distant relative who had been a nurse in one of the cave hospitals during the war. 'Go home,' his father told Manophet when he tried to follow. 'You are not needed any more.' Quivering with emotion, he watched them recede into the distance. After a few minutes he slumped down beside the path. He was certain Thong could not survive. You could not just push a person's intestines back inside them after they had been blown out and expect them to live. Human beings did not work like that. The little brother who had slept by his side at night ever since he could remember, the brother that he had teased and helped, shared jokes with and bullied had been plucked away and replaced by an unthinkable empty space.

Manophet's world had changed forever. Until this moment, the war had been something that had danced around him. He had seen it reflected in ravaged landscapes and faces frozen in blank expressions. He had heard its echoes, struggled to find the sun amongst its long shadows. Now that the taste of death had finally entered his mouth, its bitterness appalled him. It was not out of vindictiveness that the older members of his family refused to talk to him about what they had been through. Their memories were locked away for a reason. The methodical efficiency with which his father had worked as he tried to save his son struck Manophet with particular force. He had known exactly what to do. Casualties were nothing new to him. He had dealt with suffering and death as a matter of routine while serving as a soldier. But it went further than that. This was not even the first time he had knelt beside a dying son. Ten years ago, he had cradled Bua's lolling head in his arms. It was beyond Manophet to fathom the torment that his father had endured during his lifetime. The only certainty was that he would never be able to never match up to him as a man. Hot tears ran down his face as he remembered the contempt with which his father had dismissed him from the scene as he and Neung had borne Thong away. He was in no doubt that he would be blamed for the disaster, and this time there could be no question that it was blame he deserved. Thong had done his best to attract his attention, but Manophet had been so obsessed with catching fish that he had closed his ears to what his little brother had been trying to tell him.

Two days went by. Then came news that nobody had really expected. Thong was out of danger. It would take a few weeks, but the nurse saw no reason to believe he would not make a full recovery. A storm of relief broke over Manophet, releasing his tortured soul from its agony with the same exhilarating violence as monsoon rains sweeping across parched ground at the end of the dry season. It was an outcome for which he had not dared to hope, and one that left him filled with an overwhelming sense of obligation to his ancestral spirits, or whoever else was responsible for the miracle. But what could he do to repay his debt? He wrestled for many hours with the problem, until at last the perfect solution occurred to him: he would resolve to be a good person for the remainder of his days. Nobody could make adequate reparation for having a life restored to them, but by solemnly undertaking to spend his whole life trying, he would surely be doing as much as he reasonably could.

He made a start by visiting his brother every week on his own initiative while he was convalescing and, for a time, the pledge that he had made to himself seemed straightforward enough to keep. But as the months went by he began to realise that telling good from bad could be more complicated than telling black from white. And it was not always easy to determine exactly how good he needed to be. Was it enough to be kind and respectful and eschew the forms of behaviour disapproved of by his parents, or did it require something more? He had a strong instinct that a good person needed to *make* good things happen, rather than just keep out of trouble.

Not wanting to broach the subject of unexploded ordnance with his father, Manophet turned to one of his school teachers for background information, a man who had served alongside him as a Pathet Lao soldier in the war and had friends in the Vietnamese intelligence services. It transpired that the most lethal aspect of cluster bombs – or bombies, as they were known locally – was that they were designed not to activate until after they had been released by an aircraft. If they were dropped below a certain altitude, they would hit the ground before they had had time to arm themselves, and would fail to detonate. The *falang* had sprinkled them across the province like confetti, and in all likelihood tens of thousands of unexploded devices were still lying around. One theory was that the pilots had got wind that most of the casualties that they were inflicting were civilian and had resorted to dropping bombs from lower altitudes on humanitarian grounds, failing to appreciate that this would prolong the suffering of those affected by many decades. Another was that they had been given orders to render the Plain of Jars uninhabitable with the aim of clearing the North Vietnamese off it for good. Bombies could lie harmlessly beneath the ground for years as long as they were not disturbed, his teacher explained, but they were liable to explode if struck by a farmer's hoe or subjected to any other sudden impact. Fire could also rouse them from slumber, making the slash-and-burn agricultural practices favoured by many of the minority tribes especially hazardous. Under every clod of earth a potential threat lurked. Nor was the Plain of Jars the only region of the country to have been affected. Payload upon payload had been jettisoned in sparsely inhabited areas by aircraft returning to their bases in Thailand after aborted missions over Vietnam, this being deemed safer for the pilots than landing with full bomb loads aboard.

Thong had been lucky. More than half the victims of bombie accidents failed to survive, and those who did pull through were typically left without limbs or eyes, or had organs full of shrapnel that they could not afford to have removed. The *falang* had also dropped other types of ordnance. His teacher had a scar on his hand where a fleck of phosphorus had landed and burned away the flesh over a period of days. He was reticent when it came to sharing personal stories of this kind, but Manophet managed to wheedle one or two out of him. One of his assignments had been to carry rice to families who had taken refuge from the bombing offensive in caves.

Supplies had been hard to come by, and days used to go by when there was nothing to deliver. He remembered returning to a cave after such a hiatus to find only two of the five families still alive. The rest had been so hungry that they had crept out into the forest to forage for food, returning with a few leaves. Fearful of lighting a fire, the smoke from which could have caught the attention of any bombers patrolling the area, they had eaten these raw. Within minutes, they had started to foam at the mouth. By morning, all fourteen were dead.

These days, when Manophet thought about caves, he thought most often of the great caves at Vieng Xay where the Pathet Lao had been headquartered during the war, a labyrinthine limestone warren in which there had existed a bakery, a hospital, even a theatre, all safely out of reach of the *falang* bombardment. What an exciting place that must have been. Thousands of Lao had lived and worked there, marshalling secret intelligence, masterminding military strategy and communications. How he longed to be able to see that scarcely imaginable complex for himself, to set foot inside the offices that had been used by the leaders of the revolution and look at the big maps and charts that were said to hang on the cave walls to this day. His dream was still to travel across the ocean in an aeroplane to a far-off land, but he was old enough now to recognise that he was liable to be disappointed if he did not scale back his ambitions. *Any* opportunity to leave the bomb-strewn outskirts of Muang Khoun behind for a few days and visit somewhere glamorous would be worth seizing. Perhaps Vieng Xay was a more realistic goal. If he was lucky, he might even be able to catch sight of the king at Camp Number One. Of course, it was not certain that the king was still alive. There were rumours that he had died of malaria. And there was no guarantee that Camp Number One would be as open as the camp near Vientiane in which Manophet had grown up: it might not be possible to stand at the perimeter fence and gaze in at the people living there.

It intrigued him that his father refused to hear any mention of Camp Number One. Even his teacher clammed up if the subject of re-education camps arose. What were they concealing? Manophet's feelings towards his father were powerful and complicated. He had never really forgiven him for trying to farm him out to his uncle for adoption, but he was fiercely proud of the role he had played in helping to liberate the country, and as intimidated as ever by the air of authority that he exuded. There was never any ambivalence or indecision to his father's pronouncements. His children were to stand up straight and speak clearly when they talked. They were to be kind and generous to others. They should respect elder members of society. The amount of rice the family would plant to meet the requirements of the cooperative was specified to the handful. The Party official who came to collect the tithe was to be given a single cup of tea and then sent on his way. Manophet was torn between conflicting impulses: to be a good person and accept what he was told; or to keep on asking questions after his father declared a topic closed and risk being shown up as a foolish boy. He allowed the question of why his father was troubled by what was going on at Camp Number One to rest. But his inquisitiveness got the better of him shortly after Thong was brought home. If Thong had survived his accident against all the odds, was it not possible that Bua too had survived all those years ago on the battlefield? Surely there was a chance that he was still alive if nobody had been able to find his body. He had the sense to put the idea to his mother rather than his father, but it was still a bad mistake. Disappointment he had reckoned with, even disapproval and censure, but it had never occurred to him that the suggestion might make her so angry. He crept away feeling small and ridiculous, having been instructed never to mention the topic again.

# FOUR

Ten years had passed since the family's return to the Plain of Jars, and Manophet had turned sixteen. Though still short for his age, he was growing into a handsome young man with a captivating smile. The family continued to find itself on the wrong end of his pranks from time to time, but his serious side was more often in the ascendant. He found it impossible to put the hazards amongst which they lived out of mind for any length of time. The grassless bomb crater beside the site of the old house was as much of an eyesore as ever, and rising population levels across the province ensured that bombie accidents remained depressingly common. His country's situation impinged on every aspect of his daily life, and it was inevitable that he should reflect periodically on his lot in the hope of making sense of it. Could all their travails be blamed on the war and its legacy, or was it more complicated? How bad *was* the economy? Was it true that Laotians were significantly worse off than their Vietnamese counterparts and even the Cambodians? The letters written by his brother Sing from the USSR provided a modicum of context, but most of his information came from copies of a newspaper published in Vientiane that one of his teachers would sometimes bring in to the school and leave for the pupils to peruse. When Manophet's turn to read came, he would start by leafing quickly through the pages in case there were any soccer scores or – better still – match reports. Once that ritual had been performed, however, he would settle down and work his way through the weightier material.

The nation's misfortunes and adversities were documented with feverish zeal by the columnists. No wonder his parents had kept so much from him while he had been growing up. On every side, Laos was hemmed in by malign forces. The Thais were trying to annexe defenceless border villages, aided and abetted by the Chinese. The Americans were undermining the government's cooperative schemes by subversively encouraging merchants to disregard the fixed prices set by the authorities. Sinister unnamed westerners were creating discord and unrest by promoting alien social practices too vile for a respectable newspaper to describe. Hmong bandits loyal to Vang Pao, who had led the anti-patriotic forces during the war before fleeing to America with his tail between his legs when they were routed, were continuing to launch sporadic attacks against the nation's long-suffering army. How was a tiny country like Laos to defend itself against such a panoply of onslaughts when its hard-pressed people were already at full stretch trying to feed themselves? As a general rule, the paper ended its articles on an optimistic note: the enemy's dastardly schemes had been shown up for what they were before any harm could be done; the bandits had been heroically routed. But heartening conclusions of this kind did little to deflect from the journalists' sense of outrage that morality should count for so little in the reckonings of the dark forces arrayed against their small nation. Time and again, *falang* with hare-brained ideological agendas had trampled Laos underfoot, and there was a palpable apprehension in the writing of some of the contributors that history might be on the verge of repeating itself.

As time went by, however, Manophet began to sense that readers were not expected to take every article at face value, and he began to read more carefully between the lines. It was impossible not to feel bitter towards the Americans, but it could hardly be reasonable to blame them for sabotaging the government's cooperative schemes when they were not even allowed to set foot in the country. Indeed, the general public would have no inkling of what Americans at large thought, were it not for the glee with which classroom teachers and newspaper editors dragged their political and economic ideas into the open so that they could declare them flawed or denounce them as subversive propaganda. He decided that the dark forces to which the newspaper's editors were fond of referring were deliberately blown out of proportion with the eminently sensible aim of keeping readers on their guard. It would be all too easy for villagers to grow complacent about the threat posed by the outside world, given how little ever happened in their parochial lives. The most dramatic event to have taken place in Xieng Khouang during the past five years had been the failure of the rains in 1984 and the resulting drought. Manophet could appreciate why a quiet life might appeal to men and women who had lived through the dark days of the war but, for his own part, he found the uneventful Muang Khoun lifestyle insufferably boring. Newspapers offered him a precious opportunity to alleviate the monotony for a few hours – dismal though the process of slogging through articles about disappointing rice harvests or imperialist aggressors ravaging innocent peasants in far-off lands could often be.

In truth, a good many of the news stories were dull. Why anybody should want to know that a delegation of Lao Party officials had met a delegation of Vietnamese Party officials to tell each other what excellent fellows they were, it was beyond him to understand. But he could often find a thought-provoking idea or two on the correspondence pages. Was it permissible to move into houses belonging to villagers who had fled the country, one reader wanted to know? The paper advised him that all homes abandoned by their owners became the property of the State. It was the question rather than the starchy answer that interested Manophet. It seemed inconceivable that the houses in question had been standing empty since the war. They must have been vacated recently. And yet why should villagers be fleeing the country *now*? Were foreign living standards so much higher that it was worth giving up a *house* to take advantage of them? In a subsequent story, it was announced that hundreds of Hmong fugitives had returned to Laos from Thailand, having discovered that life on the other side of the border was intolerable. How had they managed to leave Laos in the first place, Manophet wondered? There were rumours that it was possible to escape across the Mekong by night if you had a boat, but the Thai border guards were known to have orders to shoot on sight, so it would be an immensely risky proposition. He was also puzzled that the authorities had greeted the returning tribesfolk so warmly, welcoming them home with gifts of mosquito nets. Since when had the Hmong become popular with the Party?

Another exchange that intrigued him related to the local wildlife:

Correspondent: *I sometimes have a chance to go from Vientiane to Ban Keun, a distance of quite a few kilometres. While on the bus, we do not see so much as a single animal crossing our path. They have all been completely wiped out. This is because the authorities in each village and in the rural areas all have guns to kill them. It is even worse when those in the army who have guns use them to shoot the animals. All along the way, we cannot avoid seeing wood being cut and the forest being destroyed. The forest is all gone everywhere, especially where it used to be at the flat part of Phou Pha Mountain. What measures should be taken in this matter?*

# LONE BUFFALO

Response: *Have you forgotten the devastation of our country, in particular the damage done to nature, mountains, cliffs, forests, various animals, rivers and streams, rice fields etc. because of the imperialists and their running dogs? The nation's history records that the American imperialists brought over three million tons of bombs to destroy Laos. That was one ton of bombs for every Laotian. From the north of the country to the south the land is bare and empty, with only bomb craters as a hated memorial for the Lao people. Wherever there were dense forests, they sprayed chemicals to kill the trees until all the forests were ruined.*

*We do not know where you were then. If you did not come to look at it or help to resist those who brought ruin to us then, why are you complaining now? The poison made even the field crickets come out of the ground and die, not to mention birds, mice, and other wildlife – how could they tolerate the poisoning? This is the cause of the extinction of nature in our country. It will take at least another twenty-five years for the land that was bombed by the imperialists to revive. We cannot deny there is some careless slaughter by our people and some cadres nowadays. However, we believe there is very little because it is more the case that there are no animals left to be hunted, as you can see. Indeed, the policies of our Party and government clearly indicate that forests and wildlife should not be damaged.*

*If you ever travel abroad by aeroplane, you should look down. The spectacle of "dense forest" is almost non-existent. All the mountains as well, even the remote ones, were burned and annihilated and became barren. This is the deplorable legacy that the imperialists' war of aggression has bequeathed to the people of Laos. The fact that nature in our country should have been so devastated leaves us brimming with resentment.*

While the Editor could be patronising, it was rare to see him lose his temper with a correspondent like this. Apparently the accusations had struck a nerve. The writer had been audacious in suggesting that soldiers were involved. It was a miracle the letter had been published at all. Possibly he imagined the soldiers were acting on their own initiative, and wanted to blow the whistle on them, when in reality they had only been following orders, cutting down timber so that the government could sell it off to raise funds. But, if the soldiers' activities were above board, why was the Editor so hot under the collar? Were they supposed to have been carrying out their mission in secret? It was not at all clear how far the government's spectrum of covert activities extended, and the Party seemed to be in no hurry to clarify the position, if the evidence of a previous article was to be believed. Even though Manophet had read the short paragraph several times, he was still unsure what it meant:

*As you know, the Party has been out in the open since 1980, and members are no longer as secretive as they were before. But you should not assume that all the work that we do will be in the open, with no secrets. If we operated like that, we would be taking an extreme rightist position which, just like an extreme leftist position, could be harmful.*

He was caught off guard when his father sat him down one day and told him he thought he ought to become a monk for a trial period. 'I was a novice once,' his father said, leaning forward in his chair so that his powerful eyes could be close to his son's. 'Almost every Lao boy would spend some time in the temple. It was normal in the old days. You might take to that way of life and decide to be ordained. Monks are learned and well-respected members of the community. But, if not, you can come back after a few weeks and carry on with your education. That is up to you.'

'Neung never became a novice,' Manophet pointed out.

'That is because the State and the Sangha were still at loggerheads when he was your age,' his father said. 'Do you know what I mean by the Sangha? The Sangha is the name by which the Buddhist community is known. I may as well tell you what went on since you will hear it all from the monks in due course if you decide to go. In other communist countries, religious activities are frowned on because it is believed that they can interfere with economic progress. But almost all those countries are Christian. Laos is unusual in being both communist *and* Buddhist, and Buddhism and communism have some important principles in common. After all, the Buddha himself gave up his royal status and possessions so that he could follow the path to enlightenment. Monks became widely respected during the time that Laos was under French rule. There were no schools in those days so, unless you belonged to the elite, you had to go to a monastery if you wanted an education. But, if somebody who had studied at a monastery tried applying for a government job, they would always be turned down on the grounds that their education had had a religious bias, making them unsuitable for the position. All the worthwhile jobs were given to the elite. The result was that many ordinary Lao became disenchanted with the Royalist government, and at the same time favourably disposed towards the Sangha. And so, when war broke out, it made sense for the Pathet Lao to forge an alliance with the Sangha and encourage the monks to go out and preach its vision of greater equality in the villages. Well, you can probably guess what happened. Buddhism and communism are not one and the same, and parts of the message that the monks started spreading were inconsistent with the Party's ideals. There wasn't much the Party could do to correct the discrepancies during the war, but after independence it tried to iron out what it saw as the errors in the monks' beliefs –'

Manophet smiled to himself, knowing this was as close as his father would come to admitting they had been sent for re-education.

'However, the Sangha refused to compromise the Buddha's teachings, and relations between the two organisations broke down. For several years, the government tried to discourage Lao boys from becoming novices. It even set up vocational schools to lure them away from the monasteries. But the Sangha needed the Party just as the Party needed the Sangha. A stand-off did not help either of them. In the end, the Sangha agreed to place more emphasis on its role as custodian of traditional Lao values and culture. That chimed better with what the State was trying to achieve, and relations between the two institutions have now started to normalise.'

Although Manophet had never devoted much serious thought to Buddhism, it would have been impossible, growing up near Muang Khoun, to have avoided wondering what the great Buddha brooding over the ruins of the town signified. Immense and venerable, it could hardly have looked more out of place in the crater-pocked landscape amidst which it stood. And yet, in mirroring the dilapidated condition of ordinary people, it declared its commonality with them. There were no monks left in Muang Khoun these days, but his parents still held the Buddha site sacred, and would make offerings there from time to time. 'Bua came in to my dream last night,' his mother would say. 'Perhaps he is hungry. I had better take some food up to the temple.' The status of Bua's soul was not well understood by the family. It was thought possible – assuming his body had not been given the proper funeral rites – that his spirit might still be lingering close to the home of the family's ancestors, and there was nothing to be lost by catering for this contingency. If, on the other hand, all was well and he had succeeded in making the transition to his next incarnation, it could do no harm to show that he had not been forgotten, even after all these years. For a day or two, Manophet was unsure how to respond to his father's proposal. Spirituality and religion were all well and good for certain kinds of people, but were they for *him*? Then, of a sudden, he became certain this was the right course to take. At least it would be different. Who could tell where such an adventure might lead?

The family held a *baci* ceremony in his honour the evening before he departed. His mother and sisters worked feverishly all day preparing the food and the *pha kwan* – elaborate arrangements of banana leaves and blossoms in wooden baskets. He offered to help, embarrassed that they should be going to so much trouble, but this merely precipitated an outburst of indignant chirruping, followed by stern exhortations not to enter the house until they were ready. A distant relative who had once been a monk arrived shortly before sunset to officiate at the ceremony, and at last Manophet was allowed indoors. He had never seen so many eggs! No wonder they had been in such short supply during the past fortnight. His sisters must have been sneaking them out of the chicken coop first thing in the morning and stashing them away. White candles crowned the magnificent display, white being the colour of peace, good fortune and honesty. The elderly relative, now seated on the opposite side of the *pha kwan*, lifted his voice and invoked the *kwan* – the soul's vital forces, summoning any that might be roaming back to their places as the guardians of Manophet's wholeness of spirit. Unfurling the white cotton thread that extended from the pinnacle of the *pha kwan*, he tied it around Manophet's outstretched wrists, symbolically binding the *kwan* in their rightful place. The *baci* string was not to be untied for at least three days, the elder advised him gravely, and under no circumstances was he to cut it off. Manophet was unsure how seriously he was supposed to take the ceremony, a tradition that stretched back many centuries. But he was deeply touched by the expense to which the family had gone on his behalf, and it seemed politic to err on the side of respectfulness.

He had not lived apart from his family for any length of time since being left at his uncle's house, and he found it difficult to adjust to living in the monastery, which lay far away, on the outskirts of Vientiane. The monastic way of life brought an unsettling sense of isolation, particularly the extended periods of time when there were no set tasks. It was not so much the rigours of going without food from lunchtime onwards that made the long afternoons a challenge as the fact that he had so little to keep him occupied. He would much have preferred to be gaining merit by doing selfless deeds. What a good feeling that must engender – giving of yourself for the benefit of somebody in greater need without expecting anything in return. But novice monks seemed to furnish others with more opportunities to gain merit than they obtained themselves. According to Buddhist teaching, it was a novice's parents who enhanced their spiritual wellbeing by allowing him to enter the temple rather than the novice himself. And, while the townsfolk were believed to do their souls no end of good by dragging themselves out of bed at five o'clock in the morning and bringing offerings of sticky rice to the temple, they had the advantage over the recipients of their largesse. Wrapped only in thin orange robes, barefoot and shaven-headed, the novices would try not to shiver involuntarily as they held out their bowls, and could often manage to think no further than how much longer the ceremony would drag on. Manophet would sometimes glance at the almsgivers as they handed over their donations to see whether they betrayed any signs of ascending to a higher spiritual plain, but as a rule they lowered their faces when they knelt, concealing their expressions.

He struck up a friendship with a novice from Muang Kham named Keola. Like Manophet, Keola had no memories of the war and was reliant on his family for stories. The house in which they had been living had caught fire when a bomb had landed in a neighbour's rice field. In the ensuing panic, his mother had run out of the nearest door, taking him and two of his sisters, and been swept up in a stream of villagers fleeing east towards Vietnam. His father, meanwhile, accompanied by Keola's two remaining siblings, had bolted through the other door and become attached to a band of villagers fleeing south. For more than five years, the two sides of the family had lived separate existences, neither knowing whether the other had survived the bombing. But at the end of the war both parties had made their way back to Muang Khan, and there had been a joyous reunion that Keola could still remember.

Keola had been lucky. An aunt and uncle of his had wanted them all to take shelter from the increasingly frequent bombing raids in a cave several miles away, but Keola's mother, fearing that her son was too ill to travel, had refused to make the journey.

'In the end, they decided to go to Tham Piu without us,' he said. 'If I had not been sick at that time, the four of us would have died there beside them. Sometimes I wonder if there is a reason why I am still here. Perhaps I am supposed to become somebody important, or do something special.'

It was a sentiment Manophet recognised and could sympathise with. 'My parents always change the subject if the war comes up,' he said. 'I can understand why it is difficult for them, but concealing the truth doesn't make it go away. Our generation has to come to terms with what happened too. It is no good just shutting us out.'

They let up from sweeping the temple floor to allow an elderly monk who had emerged from the main sala to pass, bowing their heads when he paused to nod approvingly at their efforts before continuing on his way.

'Do they know how many people died at Tham Piu?'

'Three hundred and seventy-four. There were no survivors.'

With the exception of this aunt and uncle, Keola's immediate family had come through the war unscathed, but there had been a sting in the tail. His brother had married a girl with whom he had fallen in love whilst sojourning in one of the refugee camps around Vientiane, and in due course she had given birth to a daughter. Her father, who had served as a General in the Royalist army, had fled to America as soon as the war had ended, fearing he would not survive incarceration in a re-education camp. Three years later, he had sent instructions that the rest of his family should join him, including his daughter and her child, as he feared their lives were still in danger. Keola's brother had not seen his bride or their daughter since that day.

'Why could he not go with them?' Manophet asked.

'The government would not give him a passport.'

Manophet leant his broom against the temple wall so that he could rearrange his robe. Sing had not had any difficulty with his passport application, but perhaps he had been a special case. 'How does he keep in touch with her?' he asked. 'Can you post letters to America from Laos?'

'He has never tried to contact her.'

'But that is terrible.'

'He felt betrayed. She knew he would not be allowed to leave Laos, and yet she chose to move to America without him.'

'I suppose – if her life was in danger –'

'As far as I know, she never tried to contact him either. He will probably be on his own for the rest of his life.'

Manophet mulled the story over. 'I don't think it quite adds up,' he ventured after a couple of days had gone by. 'The General's family would never have been sent for re-education such a long time after the war had ended.'

Keola shrugged his shoulders. 'They might have heard rumours that they were on a black list and not known whether they were true. My brother says the Party prefers it if there are rumours going around because that keeps everybody guessing. He thinks it may even start some of them itself.'

'But isn't it more likely the General was deceived by American propaganda about how bad things were in Laos?' Manophet persisted.

'It could just have been a cover story,' Keola conceded. 'My brother's mother-in-law never liked my brother. She thought her daughter was too good for him. Maybe they just wanted an excuse to get him out the way.'

Manophet put an arm around his friend's shoulders, touched by his frankness and aware that the humiliation rubbed off on the whole family. 'I don't suppose it can really be so much better living in America than living here.'

'They all have televisions in their houses, and machines that wash your clothes and cook your food, Keola replied gloomily. 'People work in buildings thirty storeys high. They say you can fly hundreds of miles to visit relatives in a different part of the country whenever you feel like.'

'Well, they are hopeless at soccer,' Manophet countered. 'They failed to qualify for the World Cup finals even though the rules were changed to allow twenty-four teams through when there are usually only sixteen.'

Keola gave a rueful smile. 'My brother is happy that he doesn't live there. He says he would feel sick if he was surrounded by people who could spend so much money destroying a tiny country thousands of miles away and then just forget about it.'

'Perhaps it is because they are not Buddhists,' Manophet suggested. 'If they were Buddhists, they would know that the pursuit of money never leads to happiness.'

'But are we happier than them, do you think?' Keola asked.

'It would be nice to have *some* money,' Manophet admitted. 'Enough to buy a soccer ball, for instance. Enough to give a few kip away to other people occasionally.'

He looked forward to the structured periods of the day. Some of the other novices grumbled about having to spend so long chanting in the morning, but Manophet had immediately picked up the knack of losing himself in the ebb and flow of the Pali verses. Away would go his worldly preoccupations, to be replaced by a sense of tranquillity not unlike the one that settled over him when he went fishing. The challenge of being a good person always seemed easier to rise to after starting the day with a long rhythmic *Araham*. Another satisfying ritual was the daily procession through the town. He loved filing out into the cool light of the rising sun knowing that he was participating in a centuries-old tradition. Such an air of solemnity the older monks managed to conjure up as they crossed out of the sacred temple precinct and into the humdrum everyday world beyond. Only when the procession finally came to a halt to receive alms did he start to become conscious of the cold. Religious instruction classes featured too prominently on the curriculum for his liking, but the monks also taught subjects never mentioned by his school teachers at home. History lessons focussed on ancient times rather than the injustices suffered by the country during its recent past. He heard the legend of Khun Cheung and the race of giants said to have hewn the two thousand year-old stone urns that littered the Plain of Jars, and learned the story of king Fa Ngun, who had ruled over a Lao principality known as the Kingdom of a Million Elephants during the fourteenth century.

Had the Lao words for Million and Elephant not rhymed, historians might have been less generous in estimating the number of elephants under Fa Ngun's jurisdiction, Manophet reflected. But there was no doubting that there had been a great many, since laws had been enacted to prohibit injuring, killing or stealing a neighbour's elephant, with strict penalties for those who broke them. On the face of it, it had been no more exceptional to possess an elephant than to keep chickens or a pig. It was as though these great beasts had come to be regarded as indispensible accessories, allowing ordinary Lao to travel effortlessly through the jungle from village to village, hunt tigers without fear of being clawed to death, or haul trees from the forest if they needed wood. By the seventeenth century, Laos had become the greatest civilisation in all of Southeast Asia, controlling extensive swathes of territory that had since become part of Thailand in addition to its existing lands. But then the kingdom had fragmented. Marauding *falang* had poured in from all sides to plunder its treasures and strip it of its dignity, and it had not been strong enough to resist them. The Siamese had destroyed Vientiane. The Vietnamese had annexed Xieng Khouang. One day, perhaps, the country would rise from the ashes and reclaim its rightful inheritance. His mind filled with stupendous dreams. Muang Khoun would be rebuilt in its former glory. The great Buddha would be covered once more with a magnificent layer of gleaming gold and occupy a new temple surrounded by a thousand stupas. 'You are better at dreaming than meditating,' Keola pointed out, and Manophet knew his friend was right. It was becoming clearer by the day that he was not cut out to be a monk.

His favourite teacher was the oldest monk in the temple, a diminutive thick-spectacled octogenarian who had studied with the old Sangharaja, and who made no attempt to remain within the bounds of political acceptability laid down by the Party when he was teaching. Marxism was never mentioned in his lessons, and he seldom seemed more at home than when digressing onto a tabooed subject such as the Sangharaja's escape across the Mekong to Thailand a few years earlier on a raft constructed from inflatable tubes. He would reminisce about a period before the Second World War that he referred to as the golden age, during which Laos had been at peace with itself despite being under French rule. This was a time, he told them, when Buddhism had been the country's moral and cultural heartbeat, and materialism had been seen as the common enemy against which the people must unite. Nor was he afraid to shine light on the murkier aspects of his own doctrinal position. 'One thing you should understand,' he told the novices, 'is that spirit worship is not a practice that was ever advocated by the Buddha. It is peculiar to Buddhism here in Laos. When you hold a *baci* ceremony, you are following an ancient Lao tradition designed to bring good luck by invoking the spirits or *kwan* that watch over the soul, one that may even pre-date the arrival of Buddhism in Laos – in spite of the fact that the ceremony is usually conducted by a monk. There are many different tribes in our country, as you know, and few if any of them subscribe to Buddhism. However, the great majority practice spirit worship in one form or another, and that is what binds us all together.'

Manophet stayed behind after one of his classes had ended in the hope of learning more about the likely state of Bua's spirit. 'What happens if somebody is never given a proper burial?' he asked.

The old monk placed his fingertips together as he contemplated the question, his eyes half closed behind the bulging lenses of his spectacles. 'It is not given to us to understand how souls migrate from one life to the next,' he said at length. 'We believe that, when a soul is released from a body, it spends a period of time wandering because the path that it needs to follow is not immediately made clear. Our funeral rites are intended to surround a departed soul with love and reassurance as it begins this process. We prohibit women who are expecting children from attending funeral ceremonies in case the presence of an unborn baby confuses the spirit about its intended destination. But the truth of the matter is that we do not really know how effective these practices are. Very occasionally, certain unexplained phenomena suggest that a departed spirit has continued to wander for too long because it cannot find the path that it needs to take, but these events are rare. If your brother's spirit has not troubled you during the years since he departed, I think you may rest assured that it has found its new dwelling place.'

He felt a little nostalgic on the morning of his final procession. He was looking forward to seeing his family again, but he would miss the monks. It was easier to be a good person when you were living among role models, and he had enjoyed learning from them. For the last time, he took his place with the other novices in the silent crocodile as it followed the familiar route into the town, their orange robes brilliant against the grey sky. Bleary-eyed townsfolk were kneeling at their stations as usual, ready with their offerings. But today a group of soldiers had come to watch the ceremony. There were seven of them dressed in the distinctive uniform of the Russian army, rifles slung over their shoulders, conversing loudly in their mother tongue. The almsgivers threw disapproving glances in their direction to indicate that they should be quiet now that the monks had arrived, but to no avail. At length, one of them rose from his knees to remonstrate, but the soldier pushed him roughly to the ground. 'Why are you feeding these scroungers?' he shouted in a poor attempt at Lao. 'Why do you not give food to the soldiers who protect you from your enemies instead of wasting it on these worthless people?' Turning to the novice who had received the food, he spat into his bowl and then knocked it out of his hands. 'Worthless Lao,' he taunted. 'Go on, lick the food up off the ground like the dog that you are.'

Seething with anger, Manophet helped the novice retrieve the scraps from the dirt. He travelled home to Muang Khoun with a sour taste in his mouth.

# FIVE

'What are you going to do with yourself when you finish at school?' his parents wanted to know. It was a question over which Manophet had been agonising privately for months. Surely a flash of inspiration would come to him before too long. But another eight weeks passed without any semblance of a breakthrough, and he could see it was only a matter of time before his father weighed in with some grisly proposal or other. This was the way of things in Laos. If you had a sensible vocation, like Jun, your family would encourage you to pursue it. If not, the decision would be taken out of your hands. The news, when it came, exceeded his worst fears. They had enlisted him in the army. 'Why are you looking like a chicken in a thunderstorm?' his father reproved. 'It isn't as though you will be going to war, as I did. The army has a peacekeeping role these days. There are no more than a handful of Hmong insurgents left in the jungle. But you will be able to learn fighting techniques and survival skills in case another foreign power decides to invade the country at some point in the future. It is no good ignoring the lessons of history because they are unpleasant. We are still viewed by half the world as nothing more than a buffer zone between the East and the West, and they will start interfering in our domestic affairs again the moment we let our guard down – mark my words. You will be trained at Vieng Xay.'

How would he ever be able to fulfil his dream of becoming a good person if he pursued a career as a soldier? A military life offered no scope for improving the lives of others. He thought hard about digging his heels in and refusing to go, but the plan had one redeeming aspect. He would be based at Camp Number One, the country's most notorious re-education centre, which had been taken out of commission a few years earlier and turned into a cadet training facility. Perhaps briefings would be held in the caves occupied by the Pathet Lao during the war, which lay close by. By asking around, he might be able to discover the truth about how the king had died in captivity. There was surely even a chance of getting across the border with Vietnam on a training exercise. The course would take at least a year to complete, during which time he would hardly see his family. Enrolling would be a big step. But it would not necessarily commit him to soldiering for the rest of his life. A stint with the army would be regarded as a useful qualification for a man with aspirations to rise up through the ranks of local government and become a senior Party official. This was presumably one of the possibilities that his parents had in mind for him now that an uncle on his mother's side had managed to land himself the lucrative post of Vice-Governor of Xieng Khouang. Deep down, however, Manophet could not see himself following in his uncle's footsteps. Sympathetic though he was towards the government in most regards, he had no appetite for spending his days buttering up the well-connected. There *must* be better ways for him to live his life. But where was the sense in rebelling when he had no counter-proposal to offer? Reluctantly, he packed his bags.

The worst thing was the food. He had not appreciated that rice could be cooked in such a way as to render it inedible, but the army's catering unit rose heroically to the challenge on a daily basis. If meat appeared on their plates, it tended to coincide with a sudden and unexplained reduction in the number of stray dogs skulking about the base. Vegetables tasted of diesel oil, and occasionally arrived coated in soot particles. Only fruit could be relied on not to scandalise the taste buds. The strict disciplinary regime to which they were expected to conform was another bone of contention in the ranks. While Manophet was no keener on having to obey orders bellowed out by high-handed officers than anybody else, he found the structured pattern of their day-to-day life more to his liking than most of his peer group. Other cadets retaliated by cultivating louche army habits. A few would slip out of the base after dark to hunt for girls and return bragging in the coarsest language about their conquests, while others stayed up late playing cards and drinking alcohol. But Manophet could not forget his reaction to the conduct of the Russian soldiers on his final day as a novice monk, and he was determined not to fall victim to the same malaise. If he was going to be a soldier, he was going to do it properly. Stumbling onto the parade ground at the crack of dawn in a crumpled uniform, unwashed, unshaven and too befuddled to concentrate, having snatched no more than two or three hours sleep, was not for him.

Several of the instructors were Vietnamese. They kept themselves to themselves, eating at a separate table, and enjoying the use of a private shower room that was off-limits to cadets and always kept locked when not in use. These were men from the army that had defeated the great American war machine. They exuded an air of irresistible confidence, underpinned by the knowledge that they had outwitted their mighty foe, withstood every crushing blitz that had been launched against them, ultimately enabling justice to triumph over evil. Their purposeful, professional lectures were in a different league to those given by most of the Lao instructors. Manophet gravitated towards them, doing his best to impress them without drawing undue attention to himself. Perhaps, if he played his cards right, they might invite him to spend a few weeks training at the Vietnamese facility just across the border. But when the group of cadets to which he had been assigned fell flat on its face during a night exercise he began to realise that ingratiating himself would not be easy. 'It is always the same with you Lao,' one of them exploded. 'You are too lazy to pay attention when you are being briefed, so you reach the field of battle without any clear idea of what you are supposed to be trying to achieve. You start out by putting on a great show of bravery, but as soon as somebody fires a gun in your vague direction you turn tail and run away as fast as your legs can carry you. What do you imagine would happen if you ever had to defend this country on your own?'

After this, it was difficult not to see the Lao instructors through jaundiced eyes. They could bark out orders convincingly enough, but they possessed none of the inner ruthlessness of the Vietnamese. They also had a weakness for fraternising with the cadets, which exposed their human sides. When fortified with drink, they were prone to become over-familiar and indiscreet. One told a story about a former cadet from a village in Oudomxay province, many miles to the west, who had enrolled even though he was betrothed to his childhood sweetheart, with the idea of progressing through the ranks as quickly as possible and securing a commission before they married. The couple would be unable to see each other for three years, but the cadet arranged for a friend to carry letters back and forth between Vieng Xay and his village so that they could continue to exchange declarations of love. At last, the cadet managed to pass his final exams and set off home, resolving as he walked along the road travelled so often by his messenger-friend to reward him generously for his troubles. But when he reached the village, there was no sign of his fiancée. Weary of waiting for him, she had married the messenger.

The story set Manophet thinking about My. She was to be married the following month. Much as he would have liked to accept his invitation to attend the wedding, it would take too long to walk to her village and back. She was eighteen. One moment, she had been a child; the next she would be raising children of her own. Did the cycle of life have to turn so quickly? The last time they had met, she had told him a story about a girl who had been deceived into becoming engaged to a man she did not love. The man she had hoped would ask for her hand in marriage had come to serenade her at the dead of night, as required by tribal custom, enticing her out of her hut to spend the night with him in the forest. But when morning came, and there was light enough to see by, she found she had been sleeping with a cruel deformed fellow hated by all the village girls, who had paid the object of her love a handsome sum of money to switch places. By spending the night with the imposter, she had consented – according to the customs of her village – to become his wife. Deciding there was only one course of action open to her, the girl had made her way to the remote forest clearing where the suicide tree grew. Having consumed four of its poisonous leaves, she had sat down alone beneath its branches and waited for death to release her from her bond. Misunderstandings were not uncommon when Manophet and My conversed, since neither was fully fluent in the other's language. For a moment, he had feared *she* was the one in the unbearable situation, the one on the brink of committing suicide. But then he remembered that the Khmu did not follow the betrothal customs she had described. The girl must have belonged to one of the other tribal minorities and, while the story was probably authentic, it had nothing directly to do with My.

Not so long ago, he had resented knowing so little about what had taken place during the war. Now the glut of detail to which they were made privy began to get on top of him. Each military initiative was analysed. At Mount Phou Pha Thi the key to the patriotic forces' success had been the element of surprise. Making the natural assumption that the cliffs were too sheer to be scaled, the enemy had concentrated on defending its positions against rocket fire and ground force attacks from along existing jungle trails. As a result, all its troops and equipment had been facing the wrong way when the assault commenced. Once the formidable cliffs had been conquered it had been a simple matter to overrun them from behind. At Long Chieng, the first incision had been made by a small band of commandos, who had sabotaged the enemy's ammunition dump. All night long, random howitzer explosions had pulverised the *falang* base, leaving the enemy unable to monitor the progress of the patriotic forces' ground assault or scramble any planes. The Plain of Jars had been the toughest nut to crack. Mistakes had been made the first time it had been captured, resulting in many casualties. Lessons had been learned, and an entirely different strategy had been employed when it was finally retaken from Vang Pao's forces many months later. On and on the litany of slaughter went, until the narratives blurred into a terrible continuum of lost lives. Manophet could not help thinking about the corpses. How many bodies still lay stranded on the inaccessible slopes of Mount Phou Pha Thi, mown down by gunfire as they climbed? What had happened to the remains of the heroic sappers who had mined the ammunition dump at Long Chieng after their captors had executed them?

A few instructors remained resentful that their country should have been set upon by an enemy boasting such technological superiority. What possible justification could there be for dropping so many bombs on a nation of two and a half million undefended peasant rice farmers? Never before or since in the history of warfare had a nation been at such a financial advantage that it could afford the luxury of constructing a fully operational airport in the heart of the very country it was ravaging. When desperate families had started taking refuge from the aerial bombardment in caves, the *falang* had responded by developing guided missiles with the ability to fly sideways, allowing them to commit still more egregious atrocities – most infamously, the annihilation of hundreds of villagers sheltering in the cave at Tham Piu. In the main, however, the levels of bitterness were controlled. There was a feeling that the average westerner was probably not as barbarous as the political masters who pulled his puppet strings. Difficult though it was to believe, US politicians had apparently managed to conceal the fact that America was conducting a war in Laos from the general public for more than five years. Some commentators even argued that it was public opinion in America that had been responsible for bringing the "Secret War" to an end when the government's illegal activities were finally exposed by the media.

Living in Vieng Xay yielded none on the incidental benefits for which he had been hoping. Cadets were rarely allowed access to the Pathet Lao caves. There was little or no reliable information to be had about the fates of the old king and queen – or, indeed, any other aspect of life inside Camp Number One, which was a taboo subject at the base. As for engineering a chance to enter Vietnam, his dreams were in tatters. The Vietnamese instructor to whom he had mooted the idea now suspected him of being a foreign agent, and he had been obliged to tread with extreme caution ever since. But the training itself was more satisfying than he had anticipated. Courses in jungle survival and self-sufficiency had taught him how to live off the land for extended periods. He knew which forest plants were nutritious and which to leave alone, how to find water, where to set a fire if it was important to avoid detection by the enemy. Trekking into the beautiful countryside that surrounded the base was always a restorative experience – not least because the threat from unexploded ordnance was significantly lower than at home. Most weeks, his life was bearable, aided by the surprising regularity with which meritocracy managed to hold its own against nepotism. It was not merely a question of who you knew. If you excelled, your efforts could sometimes be noted and you might be rewarded. After twelve months, he was offered a lucrative transfer to the base at Ban Penh in the Phoukut district of Xieng Khouang. He was the only cadet from his year to receive such an accolade, and it was enough to convince him to continue pursuing his career as a soldier.

Ban Penh was a sophisticated complex equipped with hangers full of military hardware – tanks, helicopters, combat vehicles fitted with rocket launchers – much of it Russian, as were many of the instructors. There were assault courses, climbing walls and rifle ranges, not to mention a primitive medical facility where casualties or, more commonly, victims of exhaustion were sent. Manophet was delighted to discover there was even a soccer pitch with proper goal nets. As the weeks went by, however, it became apparent that the equipment was largely for show. Rockets cost money. Even bullets were jealously rationed. Opportunities to fly helicopters or participate in tank exercises fell exclusively to a select band of cadets chosen by the instructors, a surly bunch, who turned the air blue with their expletives and picked on the trainees at the least excuse. It was difficult to be certain what the favoured few had done to gain the approval of their superiors, but there was a widely shared suspicion that several had connections to prominent Party members. Manophet was careful to avoid joining in with the resentful gossip that swirled about behind the instructors' backs. One or two of the more blatant chatterers were almost certainly junior Party members placed there by the authorities to see if they could provoke indiscretions from disgruntled trainees. It was less risky to trust a stranger than when the Party had first come to power in Laos, so people said, but in Manophet's judgement this was an environment in which mistrust was an indispensible defence mechanism.

And yet he was reluctant to think the worst of every soldier at the base, and he risked striking up a friendship with a cadet from the year above named Bounyong who had grown up in a village just outside Phonsavan. They shared a strong, if seldom articulated, conviction that the army was not where they belonged. Bounyong had plans to become a barber as and when he returned to civilian life. 'People will always need their hair cutting,' he would aver, nodding vigorously as though trying unsuccessfully to overcome a suspicion that his argument contained a fatal flaw. 'Whether they like it or not, their hair will keep growing even when times are bad.' The fact that he had no haircutting experience to speak of was a minor drawback, he was willing to concede, but how difficult could using a pair of scissors be? Taking pity on him, Manophet volunteered to be a guinea pig, and was relieved when the results brought no more than a mild reprimand from the parade officer. From time to time, Bounyong would cajole him into joining the other cadets on their evenings out. 'You can't spend your whole life in this dump,' was a typical gambit.

'You mean, you want me to keep you company if Saub doesn't show up?' Manophet gave a good-natured sigh.

'You can never tell with her,' Bounyong chuckled. 'But what about you? *You* could meet somebody.'

'With half a dozen other soldiers breathing down my neck and listening to every word I say? I don't understand how the two of you can stand being together in that tiny place. It's impossible to carry on a private conversation.'

'A man has eyes that he can use to tell a girl she is lovely,' he rejoined, 'and a smile to dazzle her. What is the point of having these deadly weapons if you fail to use them and concentrate all your energy on talking? If you ask me, words are for men who cannot manage without them.'

'Well, I believe in words,' Manophet insisted. 'What is the point of becoming intimate with a girl if you're not going to talk to her?'

Bounyong narrowed his eyes conspiratorially. 'I'll tell you what I think,' he said, reaching into his pocket. 'Ten kip says you have a girl waiting for you back at home in Muang Khoun.'

'Ten kip,' Manophet laughed, examining the small twisted coin. 'Well, what if I have?'

Every Saturday afternoon there was a soccer game. Opportunities to play the sport that he adored had occasionally fallen Manophet's way in the past, but they had only ever left him frustrated. Without goals, nets, proper footballs or painted lines to define the playing area, the exercise had usually been a lottery. There had seldom been enough players to make up two complete teams, and few of the other participants seemed to understand the offside rule or appreciate that they were not allowed to pass the ball backwards to the goalkeeper. And then there was always the issue of where to play. There were few flat spaces large enough to accommodate a full-sized soccer pitch, and never any boundaries capable of preventing the ball from flying yards out of bounds every now and again. Was it safe to go and retrieve it? Had the surrounding undergrowth been checked for bombies? But at last he was in an environment where soccer was taken seriously. The games were hard-fought and often skilful. He would troop off the pitch exhausted but exhilarated at the end. On one occasion during the rainy season, when the pitch was underwater and it was impossible to play, a film of the 1960 European Cup Final was screened on an old projector in the training theatre by way of recompense. Even by Lao standards, the grainy black-and-white footage left a good deal to be desired, but what a breathtaking spectacle the match was: ten goals in front of a crowd estimated at a hundred and twenty five thousand spectators! Manophet was agog at the artistry displayed by both teams. They were so clever with their passing interchanges, so aware of one another's movement. And what thunderous roars the crowd let out each time a goal was scored. Imagine smacking the ball high into the back of the opponents' net and provoking an outburst like that. How elated the scorer must feel. He emerged into the pouring rain with his head full of dreams and ambitions, as glad to be alive as he could remember.

Without warning, the base was placed on its highest state of alert. Instructors hurried from briefing to briefing, their faces taut, scarcely pausing to hurl insults at the bemused parades of waiting cadets. It was plainly not an exercise. Had the Thais invaded? Was Vang Pao back on Lao soil? Late in the evening, stories began to circulate that the Berlin Wall had been breached. Apparently East Germans were flooding gleefully across to the West. Manophet weighed the implications with a couple of the more cerebral cadets from his year. So the capitalists had won the propaganda war. Even the East Germans believed communism was a failure. But would their foray across the Iron Curtain reveal streets paved with gold, as they hoped, or would it show them they had been duped? This was the acid test. It was disturbing that they should have been so ready to discount the warnings about the perils of living a materialistic existence that had doubtless been drummed into them from an early age, since this suggested not only that they were convinced that living standards in the West were significantly superior to those in the East, as had long been rumoured, but also that the gulf was so vast that moral arguments ceased to have any relevance. Perhaps the instructors were right to be panicking, for it was not inconceivable that right-wing opportunists would now jump on the bandwagon and start stirring up trouble in other parts of the world. He went to bed depressed. If communism, for all its conceptual superiority, worked so much worse than capitalism in practice, as its detractors claimed, a terrible number of people had given up their lives for a worthless cause.

Unsurprisingly, there was no civil unrest in Laos. Only a handful of Lao had regular access to newspapers, and those who kept abreast of events by word of mouth had more pressing concerns. As far as ordinary people in Savannakhet or Phongsaly were concerned, the forthcoming rice harvest was infinitely more important than events in a partitioned State thousands of miles away. Tensions eased at the base, but the Russians treated the cadets with more suspicion and contempt than before. They made no secret of their bitterness towards the East Germans for betraying them, and little pretence that they viewed Laos as a reliable or worthwhile ally. 'You are as useless as the bluebottles that feed on buffalo shit,' an instructor with a face like an artichoke informed his class on discovering that less than half of them could name the Russian president. 'You swarm down on any country prepared to put a bit of Foreign Aid your way and suck all the juice from it – irrespective of whether the donor is principled or decadent. Then, when the Aid dries up, you are unable to fly away because you are too full of shit to get airborne, and you find yourselves splattered across the ground, writhing about in your own blood and demanding to know why you are always the unfortunate victims of history. Why do you imagine your country *deserves* a good outcome when you never make the effort to stand on your own two feet and look out for it?'

Manophet boiled with rage. How was a country the size of Laos supposed to stand up to a superpower? These Russians did not deserve his respect. He let his anger get the better of him and laughed out loudly when he heard about an incident in which they had completely lost face. A cadet had been surprised to hear his name called out by the instructors in charge of helicopter training. There had been no indication that such a coveted opportunity was about to fall his way. Reasoning that he was probably being taken up as a navigator, he donned a helmet, collected a map from the store room, and climbed into the seat beside the pilot. Ten minutes into the flight, one of the instructors gestured to him to take the controls. Nervously, the cadet did as he was told, wondering if it might not have been more sensible to start with a few lessons in the classroom to familiarise him with the instrument panel and operating procedures. Pandemonium broke out in the cockpit as the helicopter rolled over onto its side and plummeted a couple of hundred feet, the pilot wrestling to regain control. After a moment or two, the stricken machine righted itself, whereupon the instructors set about the unfortunate cadet, beating him on the helmet with their clipboards, shouting insults and jabbing him in the arms with their fingers. Once the pilot had landed safely, the cadet removed his bulky helmet – at which point, the Russians realised he was not the man they were supposed to be training, but one with an identical name.

He could not fault his family's logic in thrusting him in the army's direction. It was gaining influence all the time. A number of the Party's most senior officials were army officers, and it was almost a foregone conclusion that Khamtay, the Commander-in-Chief would succeed Kaysone as Prime Minister. But Manophet had no more desire to rule over his compatriots than he had to go off killing people of other nationalities, and he did not want to spend years of his life scaling the slippery rungs of the Party ladder. Little by little he grew more disillusioned with his lot. His parents would groan with disappointment if he threw in the towel now, having come so far. They would try and persuade him to reverse his decision by insisting that dreams did not put food in a person's mouth. And he would have no coherent reasons to give them for walking out, no alternative plan with which to defend himself against their jibes. He had nothing but his instincts to guide him, and his instincts told him he would never thrive in the army. He needed a challenge that involved riding on the coat-tails of the exciting changes that were taking place across the world. Even in Laos, the ground was already beginning to shift. Without explicitly acknowledging that the economic policies that it had pursued during the eighties had been a disaster, the Lao government had effectively consigned them to the scrap heap by announcing out of the blue that market forces would be permitted to operate in many areas, catching everybody on the hop. And, further afield, there were signs that the West had finally woken up to the possibility that waging war on innocent civilians might not be the smartest way of trying to convert them to alien ideologies or religions. Were these not hopeful indicators?

In response to the tumultuous events in Germany, the Russians brought in a new counter-espionage course. Areas where the nation was thought to be vulnerable were flagged up and analysed. The opium trade came in for special scrutiny. The CIA had purchased opium from the Hmong during the war as a means of bolstering the Hmong-US alliance, the instructors explained, selling it on to American troops in Vietnam for recreational use. Now that the right-thinking, highly principled Communist Party was in control of Laos, the growing of opium was illegal, but this had made the task of bringing about a reconciliation with the Hmong more difficult because it deprived them of a vital income stream. It went without saying that the devious Americans had found a way to exploit the situation. They were circulating rumours that the Lao government had resorted to making clandestine purchases of opium from the Hmong through third parties in order to keep the peace. By trafficking this on to US drug dealers, the authorities were raking in a handsome profit while at the same time weakening America by turning it into a nation of heroin addicts, much as the British had manipulated China in earlier times – so the allegations went. They were utterly untrue, of course. The Lao government had categorically denied them on several occasions. But the instructors were keen that the cadets should be aware that such stories were circulating because they were a perfect illustration of the sort of low cunning to which the enemy would resort in its ongoing efforts to destabilise Laos.

'You should never fall into the trap of imagining that, because the American imperialists have no morals, they also lack brains,' the instructor hectored. 'Make no mistake: they are clever. Take their "Missing in Action" programme. They have gone to great lengths to make it look authentic. Most Americans believe that some of the US pilots who went missing over Laos during the war are held in captivity somewhere in the jungle to this day. Where did they get this absurd idea? From a high-budget movie that has been watched by just about every American alive. How did the moviemakers get them to swallow the bait? By giving the screenplay a deliberate anti-establishment flavour. There is nothing Americans fall for quicker than anti-establishment messages. And the US government has kept the myth alive over the years by periodically denying there are any US prisoners in Laos. Every time it opens its mouth, the conspiracy theorists grow more certain it is trying to cover up the truth. It is painful to have to say it, but those cynical bastards have played their psychological game to perfection. The upshot is that Laos is always getting requests to admit parties of Americans wanting to hunt for missing relatives. Most of the people who show up are genuine, if completely deluded. But in every group there is *at least* one CIA agent masquerading as a bereaved relative. So be on your guard. If you are approached by a stranger – particularly somebody who is not Lao, ask yourself whether that person has a *genuine* reason for wanting to get to know you. If they spin you a story that sounds too good to be true, that is probably because it *is* too good to be true – even if you can't immediately spot the catch. Think very carefully before agreeing to do whatever bloody shit it is they ask you to do for them.'

At last Manophet's chance to venture onto *falang* soil arrived: he was to take part in a secret reconnaissance mission. They had orders to slip across the border into Thailand on a moonless night and gather intelligence on a village where the Thais were reportedly stockpiling military hardware and amassing troops. It would involve travelling hundreds of miles across the country. But at the last minute he was told to stand down. His place would be taken by the nephew of a senior Party official, a cadet remarkable only for being possessed of a rare eye condition that made it difficult for him to see in the dark. It was the final straw. Manophet gave notice that he would not be re-enlisting, and a few weeks later packed up his meagre assortment of belongings and started the long walk home. Four years of his life had been wasted. The few friends that he had made, he was unlikely to see again. The only thing he would miss was the weekly Saturday soccer game. Ahead lay a future that held no discernible promise. To make a living, a man needed an occupation, but having an occupation immediately crushed the life out of him. Once you had a steady job, your existence became monotonous, pointless. Before long, your life was controlling you, rather than the other way around, and that was the end of the road for your dreams. There seemed to be no place in Lao society where Manophet fitted. He was not usually given to dawdling, but he dreaded the thought of being back under his parents' roof, surrounded by the family's accusing eyes. Every passer-by became an excuse for an extended halt by the wayside. Aimless conversation succeeded aimless conversation. A night passed on the floor of an old crone's hut after he volunteered to patch it up, then a second night.

The following afternoon, he fell into step with a man who described himself as a travelling minstrel, a charismatic, long-haired fellow of about thirty who had many stories to tell. Manophet found himself caught up in a state of delicious confusion where he was precariously balanced on the cusp between credulity and scepticism. *Could* these tales be true? One concerned an ethnic minority group in the north of the country. This tribe, so the man claimed, subscribed to a morbid superstition that any woman who gave birth to twins was possessed and must be cast out of the village with her progeny and left to die. Against this background, it was customary for a woman to slip away to the forest when she was due to give birth. In the terrible event that she was delivered of twins, she would immediately murder one of the pair as violently as possible – preferably by smashing its skull against a tree – to deter the malevolent spirit responsible for the multiple birth from trying the same mischief again in the future, and then bury the corpse. Secrecy was of paramount importance, since the house of any woman found to have concealed the birth of a twin would be burned down by the other villagers. Another tale involved a woman caught in an open rice field during the war by a lone aircraft that dropped down suddenly from the sky. Wrapping her baby hurriedly in a shawl and heaving it onto her back, she made a dash for the nearest wood, calling out to her other children to run after her as fast as they could. Earth flew up as bombs crashed into the ground. Rocks whistled past her head. On instinct, she zigzagged to make herself a more elusive target, and miraculously reached her goal unscathed. Panting feverishly, she turned to look round. Thirty yards back, the corpse of her son lay face-down in the mud. Another thirty yards, and the remains of her two daughters could be seen jumbled together in a lifeless heap. The baby on her back was strangely silent. Bringing the shawl round to the front, she found that it no longer had a head.

As it turned out, the travelling minstrel lived no more than a few minutes away. The only travelling that he undertook was the journey to and from the next village to buy opium. He invited Manophet to stay for a few days, and it was soon apparent that the "minstrel" part of his job description was also spurious. He had won the khean that he carried on his back in a wager, and had no idea how to play it or sing in tune. He worked hard as a farmer during the rice-growing season, but at this time of year there was nothing to do in the fields, and he would spend his evenings smoking opium and passing himself off as an entertainer. What an accomplished showman he was. Village children would crowd around when he performed tricks with cards or coins, or made objects pass through pieces of cloth and then disappear. He had the gift of knowing how to hold his audience captivated, and Manophet warmed to him and felt more at home in his vibrant company than for many months. The key to his destiny lay hidden somewhere in this alternative lifestyle – he was sure of it! A week went by. If he could just make the right connection, everything would fall into place. He tried smoking opium, but this left him none the wiser and played havoc with his bowels. A second week passed, and the novelty of living a hedonistic existence began to wear off. For much of the day, his host was morose or asleep, and there was no companionship to be had. The evenings grew predictable and began to drag. Manophet found himself listening to stories he had already heard. If an opportunity to find answers to the questions that plagued him had existed, it was gone. He could not justify delaying his return to Muang Khoun any longer. It was time to head home and face the music.

# SIX

'Well, if you are not going to be a soldier, you had better get married,' his father said, as though producing the instructions for fixing a leaky roof or tracking down an escaped pig. 'Nothing focuses the mind on the business of earning a living quite like having a couple of extra mouths to feed. Uncle Monh has a cousin he is trying to find a husband for. I will go and have a word with him.'

Thong, Lar and Phanh hooted mercilessly in the background as Manophet staggered away. He had a hazy recollection of Uncle Monh's cousin from his school days. If he was thinking of the right person, she was a perfectly amiable girl without any calamitous defects. But marriage! He had returned with the expectation of being manoeuvred into an unsuitable job. Instead, he found himself under sentence of being harnessed up to a woman he hardly knew, with all that that entailed. Why was his family so determined to snuff out any lingering hope that he might have of becoming more than a conventional cog in the big machine of life? If he allowed himself to be frogmarched into becoming a dependable breadwinner, his chance of finding his true destiny in the world would surely perish like a dream at the dawning of the day. He pictured himself lying beside the girl on a sleeping mat night after night, a prisoner of convention, defeated, inadequate and without recourse, and hastily thrust the image to the back of his mind.

The idea met with the instant approval of his uncle's family. What could Manophet do to avert the catastrophe? He knew he should voice his objections straight away, before the two families could start drawing up plans, but how was he to justify himself? He procrastinated, hoping a solution would occur to him. But the longer he delayed, the further the preparations advanced. A date on which the prospective spouses could be introduced was agreed. His family was to travel to the girl's parents' house and, supposing there were no last-minute hitches, the engagement would be announced forthwith. His mother was already ankle-deep in recipes, finalising her contributions to the wedding banquet. His father was busy consulting every relative he could think of as he tried to ascertain how large the dowry should be.

Manophet felt wretched as the party set out. Because he had been too cowardly to speak out, everyone was expecting a happy outcome. He clung to a forlorn hope that the girl might privately be as unenthusiastic about the whole idea as he was, but there was every likelihood her hopes were sky-high. When his unwillingness to become betrothed was finally communicated to her, she would assume it was a judgement on her looks or character, and suffer an appalling loss of face. It would be kinder to be truthful with her from the beginning, but if he confided in her she would undoubtedly share the information with her family, and from there it would find its way back to his parents. He would then have the impossible task of trying to explain why he had been stringing them along. What sort of worm raised a girl's hopes like this? Was there not a terrible irony in the fact that he was following this course because he believed it was his only chance of keeping his hopes of becoming a genuinely good person alive? The day passed in a blur. Toasts were drunk. Speeches were made. Mechanically, he said and did whatever protocol required him to say and do. But eventually he was allowed to go home and reflect for a day or two before announcing his decision. His family was less exasperated than he had anticipated. It was almost as though they were already resigned to being let down. 'What of it?' his father grunted, shrugging his shoulders stoically. 'At least no bride money changed hands.' Two years later, the girl married a good-looking farmer from the east of the province.

Within days of the plan to marry him off collapsing, one of his other uncles came up with a suggestion that he should rejoin the army. Apparently they were short-handed in Pakse, the capital of the country's southernmost province, Champasack – to the point where they were prepared to make him a Captain if he re-enlisted. Why had fate seen fit to curse him with so many improvident uncles? Every damaging episode in his life seemed to have been precipitated by one or other of them. And yet, on consideration, the idea of putting three hundred and fifty miles between himself and the rest of the family seemed to have a good deal to be said for it. Champasack was a militarily sensitive region that shared a long border with Thailand and jutted out precariously into Cambodia. But, with Cambodia finally at peace, the chances of being packed off to a war zone were remote, and the army's command structures in the south were reputed to be less dominated by the Russian military than at Ban Penh. He would have liked to talk the idea over with Jun before committing himself, but she was away in Vientiane, studying to be a doctor. Part of him sensed this was the moment to steel himself and make a determined stand against the cycle of tradition into which the family was shoehorning him. And yet resistance was surely futile without a coherent plan of his own to pursue. Besides, if he spurned this opening, there was no knowing what gruesome fate the family might suggest in its place. Bowing his head, he packed his bags once more and set off on the longest journey of his life.

Pakse was lower-lying than the Plain of Jars and the two military bases where he had served previously. Temperatures here could exceed forty degrees for days on end. Sweat poured off Manophet's body whenever he was called upon to exert himself, blotching his uniform and leaving salt encrustations when the moisture evaporated. He was permanently dehydrated. Most of the other soldiers were local to the area and accustomed to the conditions, but on windless days even lowlanders struggled to complete their physical assignments. At night, it was too hot to sleep. The best policy was to lie as still as possible, since the slightest movement could trigger an outbreak of perspiration. Days and nights started blurring into each other. More than once, Manophet almost fell asleep on his feet. He would notice his eyelids growing heavy. The sounds of the outside world would fade into the background, and his mind would fill with half remembered images from the refugee camp in Vientiane, trekking through scrubby brown tundra towards the Mekong with handfuls of sweat-saturated clothes to wash. How odd, that he should have dreamed as a child of floating off downriver and over the border into a foreign land – for now, in an ironic twist of fate, he was charged with the task of guarding that very border and preventing would-be fugitives from reaching Thailand. By some estimates, more than ten percent of the population had fled the country by crossing the Mekong since the war – some four hundred thousand people. Escape attempts had tailed off steadily over the years, but the tide had never been completely stemmed, and the authorities liked to keep a close watch on the situation.

When he could not sleep at night, his mind would return to the problem of how to find his rightful place in the world. Was it possible that defecting to the West was the answer? Had his childhood dreams about the Mekong been a portent? Nobody would be suspicious if a soldier waded into the water. It would be assumed that he was intercepting a fugitive. If other soldiers came rushing to assist, he could simply turn back and say it was a false alarm. The river was poorly lit. It was easy to make mistakes on moonless nights. It would mean taking his rifle into the water, but he could always ditch it if he was lucky enough to reach half way without the Lao guards noticing. How would the guards on the Thai side of the river react if they spotted a swimmer in uniform? They would probably want to capture him alive in order to identify him and establish whether he was on a spying mission. That should reduce the risk of them opening fire before he reached the shore. Once they had interrogated him, however, he would either be left to languish in a Thai gaol, or forcibly repatriated, thrown out of the army and locked up as a deserter. Perhaps it would make better sense to jettison his uniform while in the water and take his chances like any other common fugitive. The timing would be critical. By the end of the rainy season, the river would be too wide. The night of the first big thunderstorm of the year would be ideal. With the moon hidden behind dark clouds and thunder rumbling in the background, it would be difficult for the guards to see or hear what was going on. If the storm passed overhead at the right moment, the Thai guards would scurry for cover, and he would be able to clamber ashore without anybody noticing. Or perhaps he could drift downstream undetected on the steady current, as in his dream, until he reached a point where the far bank was unguarded.

Subconscious reflexes had taken over the running of his day-to-day life – to the point where he could daydream without compromising his ability to carry out his duties proficiently. If a decision was required of him, a sixth sense would summon him back from whatever fantastic adventure happened to be playing out in his head. His mind conjured up extraordinary fantasies. One moment, a tiger would be leaping insouciantly into a derelict jeep that had been abandoned on the trail ahead, the next it would be swimming out through the exhaust pipe, transformed into a stripy carp. Processions of monks bearing alms bowls would come drifting down the Mekong in longboats fashioned from cluster bomb casings before floating gracefully up into the air like soap bubbles and vanishing. Then, with a violent shudder, his senses readjusted and he grasped the seriousness of his situation. He was in a cave that he had no recollection of entering. Silent figures lurked in the shadows. It was impossible to make them out clearly, so fierce was the glare from the circle of light at the entrance. Try as he might, he could not move his head, which seemed to be wedged into a divot of spongy rock. Squinting out of the corners of his eyes, he could descry the uniforms of other soldiers. What were they doing here? Was it a training exercise? Sweat was trickling off his body, and yet he was shivering. Was it hot? Cold? He could no longer tell the difference. From out of the reverberating hush, a slight sound caught his attention, a woman trying to smother her own weeping. It was his mother. He was lying in her lap.

The army was used to dealing with malaria cases. More than half the soldiers based in the south contracted the disease at some point, and deaths were not uncommon. Anti-malarial drugs were beyond the cash-starved government's resources – though the official line was that they could not be issued to soldiers because they caused undesirable side-effects if administered over extended periods, and the men were better off without them. Like most victims, Manophet survived the attack, but he emerged severely weakened, and with a heightened awareness of his own mortality. Had he not been promptly treated, his unremarkable life might by now be no more than a fading memory in the minds of those who had known him. He was in wretched physical condition. None of his faculties worked properly. How was he to function effectively as a solider if he could not run without growing breathless or shoot straight? Weeks went by. Little by little, he regained his strength, until he felt almost whole again. But then the recurrence that the doctors had predicted knocked him back to the bottom of the slope, and he found himself in the infirmary once more. He felt utterly dejected. There had been one relapse. Another would surely follow, then another. He was a useless deadweight. He could wait for the army to push him out, or he could take the more honourable course of resigning.

The doctors advised him not to travel until he was stronger, but he could see no virtue in enduring the heat for any longer than was necessary. His family would be as dismayed to see him back in Muang Khoun as he himself would be at having to become dependent on them again, but he was left with no alternative. After bumping along a succession of atrocious roads for two days and a night in overcrowded buses, he was in a pitiful condition when he reached the house. But his parents recognised the seriousness of his plight and responded generously. His mother pampered him and cooked all his favourite dishes. His father, meanwhile, rather than making summary arrangements to have him launched on some other undesirable trajectory, told him not to worry, put on his walking boots and left the house. He returned four days later clutching a small bottle. Manophet did not like to ask how much of the family's meagre savings had been expended on procuring the medicine. He dosed himself according to his father's instructions, rested when he was told to, and paid the sorrowing Buddha a visit once a week for good measure. Sometimes his mother would find the time to sit with him as he convalesced. He was not used to having her to himself. Usually she had too many household chores to get through to be able to afford the time.

'Tell me about the cave that we lived in during the war,' he suggested one afternoon. 'How big was it?'

She took her time before answering. 'Big enough for five families,' she said eventually.

'Was the Vice-Governor's wife in the same cave as us?'

'You know, I don't really want to talk about those days. They are behind us now.'

Jun came home for a few days. She sniffed the contents of the medicine bottle, shrugged her shoulders, and admitted she had no idea what it contained. 'All I can tell you is that it isn't what a doctor would prescribe,' she said. She and Manophet had the same determination to make their lives count. Both felt the weight of the family's expectations on their shoulders – expectations that conflicted to an extent with their own desires. The family would be delighted to see Jun qualify as a doctor, but only if this did not get in the way of her marrying a suitable husband while she was still young and having plenty of children – the traditional and, in their eyes, more appropriate course for a Lao girl to follow. 'How will I ever have time to cure sick people if I have half a dozen little ones to look after?' she complained. 'They don't seem to understand that being a doctor is hard work.' For a long time, her principal ally within the family had been her elder sister Kone, but now that Kone was married Jun had become more isolated. Manophet found he could talk to her about subjects that he felt uncomfortable raising with other members of the family. She instinctively took his side. Unlike the rest of them, she understood precisely why he had fought so hard to avoid being adopted by Uncle Athakhanh in Vientiane, and why he had wriggled out of the arranged marriage. The special bond that they had shared as children was re-establishing itself.

'So you are glad now that you didn't kill me all those years ago?' he teased.

Her chin trembled, the memory still raw. For a long time they sat silently together, arm in arm.

He awoke one morning knowing the parasite had finally been purged from his bloodstream. He was cured. His family had succeeded in nursing him back to health. Now he owed it to them to fit in with their wishes – indeed, to embrace whatever plan they had waiting in the wings with genuine enthusiasm. They were only trying to help. But his heart sank when he learned what his next assignment was to be. They had decided he should try his hand at farming rice. He would be apprenticed to Kone's husband, who had moved in with the family and was now in charge of the rice fields. He did his best to block out his instinct that this was another wrong turning. Only the most unreasonable man could keep on finding fault with proposal after proposal. It was time to put his shoulder to the wheel. A successful rice farmer could make a prosperous enough living if he was blessed with fertile land. He faced none of the perils to which a soldier had to expose himself – provided of course that he could manage to avoid disturbing any unexploded bombs while he was hoeing. But none of these admirable justifications could disguise the bleakness of his situation. This was surely the dead-end existence to trump all dead-end existences. As humankind inched its way inexorably up the ladder of progress, he would be marooned in an enclave of bygone time, beating the track trudged by generations of Lao before him, at the mercy of the elements, consigned to work that demanded brawn, sweat, an affinity for mud and the brain power of an ant. All hope of joining the great march of progress would be extinguished. His chance to make a difference would be gone.

He applied himself as best he could. Although the rains were still some weeks off, there were furrows to be ploughed, culverts to be mended and rerouted, banks to be built up. Every feature of the land that could be shaped or enriched or otherwise readied in advance was attended to so as to lessen the workload during the planting season. The family now owned a water buffalo, a placid creature that relinquished its air of lugubrious resignation only when the heavens opened and it could lie almost concealed beneath the flooded paddy fields, blowing desultory bubbles up through its nostrils. Manophet's roster of duties required him to spend more time in the company of the buffalo than any other living thing, beast or human, and he could not help identifying with it. Both he and the buffalo were gregarious creatures, he reflected, isolated against their wishes from their own kind. A spirit of camaraderie grew up between them as the weeks went by. And yet the buffalo's habits were at the same time a never-ending source of frustration to him. It had no objection to following when he walked in front of it, but as soon as he darted round behind to straighten up the plough its instinct was to stop. Once it had come to a standstill, he had only a brief window of opportunity in which to retrieve the situation, since it construed any pause in the proceedings of longer than a few seconds as an invitation to lie down in the puddles under its feet for a breather.

Even on the rare occasions when he felt they had done a good day's work, his brother-in-law was dissatisfied. Why had he not built up the bottom corner of the field before ploughing it? Could he not see that as soon as the rains came the banks would be washed away and the water would empty out into the field below? And why were the furrows so crooked? Where they converged, the rice plants would be too close to one another, and to either side there would be gaping spaces where nothing would grow. What impact was that likely to have on crop yields, did he suppose? As for the culverts, had he not been explicitly instructed to move the bunds before starting work on those? What was the point of clearing a culvert that was not going to be used again? And why had he not prevented the buffalo from scratching its bottom against the pear tree? Young pear trees were not designed to withstand the onslaughts of a twelve hundred pound buffalo. Was it any wonder it had keeled over and died? Manophet felt minded to defend the buffalo. It did not seem fair to deprive it of its one great pleasure in life. But he knew it would only make relations with his brother-in-law more awkward. This was the lot of the inexperienced – to be pilloried for making mistakes they were not yet in a position to be able to anticipate and avoid. His first year of army training had been the same. But it made the reprimands no easier to endure.

He could spend hours at a time on his own. Although his brother-in-law also devoted most of his day to manual work, he usually assigned himself to a separate task on a different part of the farm. If Manophet was ploughing, his brother-in-law would be seeing to the ducks or the chickens. When one of them was down at the river, the other would be taking his turn to irrigate the turo crop or clear weeds from the bean sprout beds. Occasionally, a neighbour would come walking along one of the paths that marked the farm's boundaries, and Manophet would seize the chance to relieve the monotony by accosting them. Passers-by of his own generation seldom dallied long. If they did, the subject of conversation was generally a mutual acquaintance, somebody from his school days who was getting married or expecting a child, topics that only heightened his sense of isolation. All around, his contemporaries were pairing up and starting families. He was being left behind. Older wayfarers were better value. Their interests were wider-ranging, and they did not mind if it took half an hour to tell a story. However, his favourite distractions were children, on whose insatiable thirst for knowledge he found he was adept at capitalising. Rarely were they allowed to go on their way before they had added a few new facts to their store of learning. He loved their openness to unlikely possibilities. Without warning, you might find yourself invited to enter their private imaginary worlds, and your own supernatural hopes – the ones you had half forgotten with the passage of time – would come flooding back as you listened.

Tensions built as the rainy season approached. Through sheer boredom, Manophet regularly lost concentration, resulting in hours of work going to waste. If he carried on in the same vein when the time came to plant out the fields, yields could be gravely jeopardised. His brother-in-law no longer trusted him to carry out simple instructions unsupervised. Time and again, he ran over the procedures they would need to follow when the rains came, until Manophet wanted to scream with frustration. But the tedious preparation paid off. When the clouds finally arrived with their precious cargo, the operation went without a hitch. Every bund and culvert functioned exactly as it was supposed to. None of the banks collapsed. The correct measure of rice grains plopped into each seedbed, and the process of thinning out the seedlings ran like clockwork. As his workload finally began to subside, he was buoyed up by a sense of satisfaction. In every direction, healthy rice plants were climbing purposefully towards the sky. For six months, he would have the luxury of not needing to spend half an hour after work each day cleaning mud out of his hair and ears and removing soil from under his finger nails. But all too soon the period of respite was over. A host of pressing jobs proceeded to land one after another on his plate. Day after day, he would be caught in the open by a deluge as he mended a fence or shifted boulders, while the rest of the family pottered about contentedly indoors, out of the elements' reach.

The buffalo came into season towards the end of October. He found it difficult to adjust to the idea that his leathery accomplice had a sexual dimension. She was normally a silent beast, but muffled grunts and bellows could be heard from the paddock where she was tethered during the night, and by day there was no mistaking her longing for the herd in which she belonged. She would pull her hooves laboriously up from the mud when she moved, as though to indicate that more than the usual effort was required, and at times seemed so dispirited as to be almost unequal to her workload. How long did buffaloes live, Manophet wondered? How many more times would she have to endure such reminders of her enforced solitude? Before, he had hardly noticed the sound of her breathing. Now, when she exhaled, each breath seemed to have its own character. A long resigned sigh would follow a sequence of irregular rushes of frustrated air. Heaves of exhaustion would take their turn with forcefully vented snorts that told of an existence of utter futility. A life of drudgery could be bearable, he reflected, as long as a creature had nothing better with which to occupy its time – perhaps even a blessing. But if all its instincts called it in another direction, in the end it became impossible not to be overwhelmed by the burden it was expected to carry.

Evening was his favourite time. Sinking lazily towards the horizon, the sun would set the heavens aflame, transforming the hillsides to the west, the fiery circle bathing the valley in golden light, dipping eventually beneath the horizon to leave the firmament a deep pulsating azure. Birds would shake off their afternoon lethargy and swoop away in pursuit of insects. Frogs would croak greetings to one another. It was the signal that work was over for another day. Weary, and usually nursing a few aches and pains, he would trudge back towards the house, where a hot meal would be waiting for him and, after that, a good night's rest. As he walked, the pleasing smell of burning wood, still a little green, would drift across on the breeze, and he would watch the blue-white wisps floating up from the smoke stack. In due course, his ears would catch the murmur of voices – perhaps the first of the day – and he would quicken his stride. Who could tell what entertaining diversions might lurk just around the corner? Maybe his parents would decide to throw an impromptu party to celebrate the new moon. A few relatives and neighbours would gather, and out would come a bottle of his mother's rice wine. A stranger might turn up unannounced, somebody with the power to change his life. Perhaps this would be the evening when something monumental finally happened to him. Or there was always the chance that a parcel might have arrived from Sing bringing new photographs of his life in Russia, candles, sweets, mysterious objects that he hoped they might be able to sell for a few kip.

Another means of keeping his spirits up during the long days was to think ahead to harvest time, and the companionship that it would bring. The harvest ritual was always one of the highlights of the year. Folk would appear from the surrounding countryside like a swarm of locusts to help in the fields, laughing, chattering, launching into the occasional song. The school would close for a few weeks to leave the local children free to lend a hand. He could still remember the excitement of racing up and down the rows of fully grown rice plants as a boy, chased by Jun or Thong. Dozens of exuberant children descended on the farm when the time arrived. They were liable to flatten half the crop with their games if he did not distract them. He took them to one side on the pretext of teaching the younger ones how to make sheaves out of the plant bundles left by the cutters, showing them how to knock the stalks level before tying them together. The sun beamed down and, one by one, the sheaves – some neatly tied, a few looking more like mangled birds' nests – were loaded onto wooden trestles and left to dry. Two sisters from a family that lived across the valley came up to ask if he could sharpen their knife. How old were they? Eighteen? Twenty? Mischievous eyes scrutinised him as he felt the blade. Smiling awkwardly, he handed it back with an assurance that there was nothing wrong with it.

Once the sheaves had dried, the winnowing began, and the valley echoed with the sound of threshing. Husks collected in the furrows, and a fine dust rose above the fields, dancing and glittering on the slant of the sun's evening rays. This was women's work. Manophet's role was to heave away the baskets of rice when they were full and transfer the contents to the barn. The two girls were a perpetual distraction. Every time he came within earshot, they seemed to be giggling or bringing attention to themselves by cavorting about rather than getting on with their work. They had knotted their skirts at the knee to keep them from catching on the rice stumps, and were revealing more of their legs than was customary. 'Perhaps he's shy,' he heard one of them whisper loudly. Manophet applied himself to patching up a hole through which rice had started leaking out of one of the baskets. The past four years of his life had been spent in the company of men, and he had not had much to do with the opposite sex. These girls were very different to the women who frequented the hostelries where soldiers drank when they went out for the evening, but they too played games with rules that had not been explained to him. They seemed intent on luring him into their shimmering web. Could some kind of bet have been placed behind his back? While he did not wish to appear rude or become the subject of malicious rumours, he was wary about letting himself be drawn in. The worst mistake that he could make would be to give the impression he was leading them on.

The barns were full, and the volunteers had dispersed, leaving Manophet surrounded by stubble-strewn fields. To his brother-in-law's dismay, the lapses in concentration that had marred his work during the run-up to the harvest returned, until he was even more unreliable than before. Flashbacks from his malarial attack reduced him to a state of semi-permanent mental disarray as he staggered from task to task. Some of the hallucinations had been so believable that he now had difficulty distinguishing the fictitious experiences from the real ones. Had he really attempted to swim the Mekong? He had clear memories of making his way in to the cool water in his uniform, but no recollection of turning back. The river was said to be traversable in Vientiane – by strong swimmers, at least, when the water levels were low, but at Pakse it would surely have been too wide to cross, even at the end of the dry season. What could not be explained away as the feverish ravings of a malarial victim was his desperation to escape the country and find a better life in another part of the world. The impulse had been skulking at the back of his mind for some time, growing stronger with every passing month. Crossing the river was dangerous. It would be naïve to pretend otherwise. But the gamble *must* be worth taking. Why else would so many have risked their lives attempting it? Laos was a backwater. It offered no crumb of succour to a man with an entrepreneurial spirit. Suddenly he was certain of his course. It was as though the difficulties and disappointments of his life had all along been signposts towards the path that he needed to take. He *belonged* in a different country. That was the coded message that he should long ago have deciphered and acted on.

And for once he was in the thrall of a dream that seemed genuinely viable. It did not matter that the plan in his head was still vague and ill-researched. This was a challenge that required him to take one step at a time. First he must cross the border. And, since Thailand was the only other foreign country in which he would be able to make himself understood, it was the Thai border that he must find a way to negotiate. Now that he was back in the northern part of Laos, where the Mekong was narrower, he stood a sporting chance of making it safely to the other side. Once across, he would be in a better position to assess the options available to a refugee and decide what his next priority should be. His understanding of how the outside world functioned was limited, and it was difficult to know quite what to expect in the West, but he was realistic enough to recognise that, if he set out with a specific goal in mind such as reaching Australia or becoming an air steward, his bid would almost certainly end in failure. All he could do was shut his eyes, take a deep breath and plunge into the unknown. He might need to find his way to Bangkok, learn a new language, or perhaps strike off in some entirely unanticipated direction – there was no telling how the enterprise would unfold. It would doubtless be difficult, if not impossible, to obtain a work permit in Thailand, but there must surely be ways forward if you had enough determination. He could start by inviting himself to stay with his sister, Boun in Phon Hong, twenty-five miles outside Vientiane. From there, he could hike south and cross the river to the west of the capital, where the border should be less heavily guarded. It was the dry season. The water would be low. What was he waiting for? The time had come to act.

His heart thudded violently beneath his ribs as he surveyed the black, slow-moving water. This time, there could be no doubt that his bid for freedom was real. There was more cloud than he had dared to hope – enough to prevent the moon from making even the briefest of appearances. The far bank was a dark formless mass in this light, but it seemed reassuringly close. Then he remembered the powerful current that had threatened to sweep him off his feet as a five year-old. The river would carry him far downstream before he reached the opposite shore. Was he strong enough to make it? He had been secretly exercising his swimming muscles at a sequestered lake near his parents' home, but the Mekong was a far cry from the still shallow waters in which he had been practising. This would test him in a way he had never been tested before. His tongue was gummed to his palate. He tried to swallow, but his mouth was dry and unresponsive. At last the dog that had been barking since he had stolen through its territory a few minutes earlier fell silent, and there was peace. Cautiously, he eased himself down the bank, testing each foothold, dislodging little showers of stones into the river below, until he was standing on a narrow platform of shingle at the edge. Discarding his shoes, he stepped into the water and waded noiselessly away from the shore. But then a sudden outbreak of shouting tore into the stillness. He could hear heavy boots thudding along the path, three or four pairs at least, closing rapidly. Moments later, a searchlight cut through the darkness, probing the bank, sliding inexorably towards the place where he stood half-immersed. He knew the drill. If he continued to advance, they would open fire. He shouted some words of surrender and immediately started back towards the Lao shore, his hands raised high above his head.

The soldiers tied his hands and feet and dragged him along the river bank like a sack of rice to an isolated building, where they thrust him through the door of a cell and slammed it shut. The small dark space smelt of sweat and urine. He lay prostrate on the floor, aching from the kicks and bangs that he had received along the way. At length he worked himself gingerly into a sitting position. In Pakse, army policy had been to let unsuccessful fugitives off with a roughing-up and some angry words of warning not to try repeating the offence, but procedures here could be harsher. Vientiane had been the Royalists' stronghold during the war. They would be used to dealing with hard-liners. However vehemently he swore allegiance to the Party, there was a danger they would assume he was lying and treat him as an enemy of the State. He had taken this gamble believing the quality of his life could not deteriorate any further. Could he have miscalculated? Fighting back his exhaustion, he heaved a despairing sigh and tried to order his thoughts. What a fool he had been. If whoever made the decisions in this district took a dislike to him, he could easily be served with a jail sentence. He might even be despatched to a remote outpost to do a few months' hard labour. His best hope of receiving a lenient hearing would be to grovel like a dog. It would not be pretty. Only a complete loss of face would satisfy them. His head lolled forward onto his knees as he contemplated the humiliation ahead. How quiet it was. And suddenly a tiny spark of hope flickered in the gloom. He ran back over the sequence of events in his mind. Absurd though it seemed, he could not remember hearing his captors lock the heavy door. Hesitantly, he levered himself up onto his feet and felt about for the catch. It was not even engaged. Moving with the utmost stealth, he eased the door ajar and poked his head through the gap. The guard post outside was unmanned. The place was deserted. They had left him to work out for himself that he was free to go.

When he arrived back home, it was as though the fabric holding his soul together had been torn from top to bottom. The will to continue going through the motions of being a farmer deserted him. He could do nothing right. His brother-in-law grew angrier by the day. The farm would be ruined if he did not pull himself together. The family no longer troubled to conceal its disappointment in him. He had never pulled his weight. It would have been better if he had been handed over to Uncle Athakhanh at the age of five, as they had intended. It could only be a matter of time before matters came to a head. The end arrived on a dismal day when Manophet lost control of his threshing knife and inadvertently gouged a lump of flesh out of the unfortunate buffalo's leg. His father shook his head slowly as he surveyed the ugly wound. 'This is not working,' he said. 'You will never make a competent rice farmer. The sooner you leave, the better.'

# SEVEN

By Xieng Khouang standards, the government-owned Vietnamese Friendship Hotel – more commonly known as the Phu Doi – was a formidable institution. Its foursquare outline dominated the intersection between the road along which the provincial government's imposing offices were concentrated and the access road to Phonsavan's main highway, Route Seven. The rooms were fitted with basins set with pairs of metal taps, one dispensing cold water, the other a spluttery rust-tinted liquid whose temperature could vary from lukewarm to scalding, depending on the mood of the boiler. Staircases – which, like multi-storey buildings, were something of a novelty in northern Laos – led triumphantly from floor to floor. There was even a telephone at the reception desk. More remarkable still, a disco was permitted to operate at weekends in the large function room on the ground floor so that the military pilots stationed in the town could let their hair down. When President Khamtay visited Xieng Khouang, it was at the Phu Doi that he stayed. So too every Vietnamese, Chinese or Russian statesman. Their only alternative was a collection of log cabins on a small hill to the east of the town known as *L'Auberge de la Plaine des Jarres*, a complex recently constructed at great expense by a Frenchman. His plan, if hearsay was to be believed, was to corner the tourist market – a notion that had prompted much hilarity among the locals, who would have been happy to inform him that no tourist had ever visited Phonsavan, had he bothered to ask.

Manophet's uncle, the Vice-Governor of Xieng Khouang, had arranged for him to be employed at the Phu Doi as a janitor. Delighted though he was to be able to give up working as a rice farmer, he was under no illusions about what lay in store for him. His new life promised to be even duller than the one he was leaving behind. No salary would be payable. He would be expected to put in brutally long hours in return for nothing more than board and lodging. Nor were his parents taking the trouble to conceal the low regard in which they held the assignment. They had done all that they could to launch him on the road to respectability, but he had frittered away every opportunity they had crafted. Now he was on his own, a work-shy freeloader who seemingly cared nothing for the family's good name.

Their one remaining hope was that he should not embarrass them by drawing unfavourable attention to himself during the course of his employment. A solitary ray of sunshine filtered through the air of gloom that hung over the house as he left: the prospect of living in an urban environment. Phonsavan was hardly Vientiane, but more than a thousand people inhabited the town. Perhaps that would make a difference.

Mopping floors and sweeping courtyards were straightforward enough tasks, and he was offered no formal training when he reported for duty. This placed him at a disadvantage when he was called in to cover for the clerk at the reception desk. How was he to answer the questions that the guests fired at him? They came in frantic clusters. At what time did the bus depart for Luang Prabang? Where was the bus station? Were there any taxis in Phonsavan? Was it going to rain? Why was there no hot water? Did the hotel accept Vietnamese Dong? Who was responsible for watering the plants in the reception area? How much would it cost to make a telephone call to Savannakhet? There never seemed to be anybody to consult. The girls who cleaned the rooms were useful information sources, but they were seldom on hand when he needed advice. With their help, he sketched out a plan of the town on the back of a large stiff-card envelope retrieved from a guest's waste paper basket. One by one, he added the important streets, landmarks and buildings as he learned where they were located, so that he could show the map to anybody who needed directions. In due course, he discovered that the lady who laundered the hotel's sheets was proficient in the dark art of weather forecasting, and he would seek her counsel when she arrived at work each morning. Persuading the telephone to function was an altogether trickier skill, one that even the reception clerk himself had not fully mastered.

As the weeks went by, he began to feel more settled. He had almost no free time, and the work was tiring – particularly when he had to man the reception desk overnight, which meant sleeping in uniform on the uncomfortable couch in the lobby in case it was necessary to unlock the door to let a guest in or out. But he no longer suffered from the terrible sense of isolation that had afflicted him during his days in the rice fields. Even though it was no clearer to him where his destiny lay, for perhaps the first time in his working life he was not weighed down by a conviction that he was travelling in the wrong direction. The men and women who stayed at the hotel were big cheeses. He could not have wished to be among more interesting people. Not that a mere janitor could expect a big cheese to deign to talk to him, of course. But even the biggest of cheeses had little option but to sit in the hotel lobby waiting for transportation to arrive after checking out, where they would often resort to reading the previous day's

*Vientiane Times*, a copy of which was always prominently on display. If Manophet was covering for the reception clerk and had already read the paper, something he was permitted to do discreetly behind the counter if there were no guests to be attended to, he could sometimes use one of the articles as a pretext to strike up a conversation.

On Sundays, the laundress brought her three children with her to the hotel, two boys and a girl, an arrangement that was tolerated by the manager on the understanding that they would remain out of sight in the laundry room. Sunday was also the day when the reception clerk took a half day, leaving Manophet in charge. In due course, the children discovered they could fit underneath the counter behind the reception desk without anybody other than Manophet realising they were there. The first time they appeared, he made the mistake of ignoring them, and carried on reading the paper in the hope that they would take the hint and go back to their mother. Ten minutes later, he fell flat on his face when he attempted to get to his feet to serve a couple of guests, not realising that his shoelaces had been tied to the legs of his stool. But he found it impossible to remain cross with the children for long. It was not as though he had never been naughty himself as a youngster. He made up stories as a way of keeping them occupied – to which they would listen open-mouthed, clinging nervously to one another as they sat at his feet if the narrative became frightening, or rolling about on the floor when it amused them. There were always questions when he reached the end. 'Why did the elephant's wings fall off?' they would demand indignantly, or 'Did the little girl *really* turn into an aubergine?' Rarely could the three of them agree on what was likely to be true. But this did not prevent them from being exacting listeners. There would be uproar if he re-told a story and muddled up any of the details. The dog had had two tongues last time and now it suddenly had three. The tale was *clearly* a lot of old nonsense.

When the chance came to take an hour or two off work, he would explore the town. Much of the time, it was no more entertaining than being at home, but at least there was usually some traffic on Route Seven to provide a distraction if nothing more interesting caught the eye. A motor car might bump by, or a lumber-laden truck on its way to Vietnam. Convoys of military vehicles occasionally rattled past, stirring up clouds of dust as they made haste to investigate the latest rumour of a Hmong uprising to the west. Exaggerating the seriousness of this threat was one of the government's favourite methods of keeping citizens on their toes. In reality, the situation was less precarious than the breathless reports in the *Vientiane Times* implied. There were plenty of Hmong in Phonsavan, particularly on market days, easily distinguishable in their distinctive tribal costumes. They mixed freely with the ethnic Lao, neither group showing any sign of antagonism towards the other. Evening was the best time to wander round the town. The generators came on at six and, for a few hours, shafts of golden light would spill out through chinks between the wooden shutters. Sometimes he strolled up to the old airport as dusk was falling. Was it here that his family had come to be airlifted off the Plain of Jars? Such had been state of chaos in 1970 that there was no real consensus about where the airfield had been. Phonsavan town had not existed in those days, and the only maps of the region had belonged to the *falang*. Further down the same path was the patch of open land where he had watched his first soccer match as a ten year-old. How he missed playing football. If only he could find some other players and organise a game.

The hotel was thrown into confusion by the arrival of a *falang*. His passport contained a recently issued visa surrounded by a cluster of immigration stamps, indicating that the authorities regarded him as *persona grata*, and revealed that he was from Sweden. He spoke no Lao at all, and responded with the word "English" whenever an attempt was made to establish his intentions. Fruitless efforts to communicate had been carrying on for half an hour when the hotel manager surprised everybody by racing out of the building to accost a passing cyclist. Moments later he returned, leading the reluctant youth by the hand. 'This is the nephew of Mr Chantha Seng,' he informed the uncomprehending Swede triumphantly. 'Mr Chantha Seng is the first man in Phonsavan to speak in English!' The cyclist, whose name was Kong Keo, had been making his way home from school, where he was in his final year. To the astonishment of the assembled hotel staff, he was able to establish that the Swede had travelled from Vientiane on a bus and wanted a room for a week. The hotel manager named a steep price, expecting to be negotiated down in the customary fashion, and made an inept job of trying to conceal his delight when the Swede agreed to his terms without a murmur. Manophet could scarcely believe his luck when a 500-kip note was pressed into his hand as a gratuity for carrying the man's suitcase up the stairs to his room.

Kong Keo called at the hotel every afternoon that week in case the Swede required further assistance. Manophet was at a loss to understand his uncle's bizarre decision to learn English 'What possible use did he think English could be in a place like this?' he asked.
'It is the universal tongue,' Kong Keo replied with a knowledgeable flourish of his hand. 'Everybody else in the world learns English as a second language. If you learn English, you can talk to *anybody*.'
'Did the Swede tell you what he is doing here?'

'I can only understand some of what he says,' Kong Keo replied, 'but it has something to do with bombies. When I told him I had been in an accident, he kept asking me for more details. He is obviously very interested in them.'

'You had a bombie accident?'

'When I was about nine. I avoided getting killed by the skin of my teeth. Some friends and I found one near the schoolyard. We didn't realise what it was, and started kicking it around. Luckily I went inside to drop my bag off. When I came back out, two of them were dead and one of the others was badly injured.'

They paused the conversation out of respect for the victims, as was customary.

'Why should somebody from Sweden have an interest in cluster bombs?' Manophet said presently. 'It smells suspicious to me.'

'Do you think he could be a spy?'

Manophet pondered. 'They taught us to mistrust people like him when I was in the army, he said. 'But it's difficult to see how he could get hold of any information worth having if he can't understand a word anybody is saying. Besides, the authorities wouldn't have let him in to the country unless they were certain he posed no threat to our security.'

'My uncle believes we should allow foreigners to visit our country. He says there are *falang* who have more money than the whole of Laos put together. Why not let them spend some of it here if that is what they want to do?'

'Tourists, you mean? Why would anybody want to come to a place like this?'

'*Falang* go to Thailand all the time,' Kong Keo countered. 'Why not Laos?'

'Tourists do not visit communist countries,' Manophet said. 'They think they are dangerous. It is the same in Russia, where my brother has lived. Anyway, there is nothing for them to do here.'

'Well, the Swede is as happy as happy can be that he is one of the first westerners ever to visit Phonsavan.'

Manophet scratched his head. 'Perhaps your uncle is right,' he said. 'If they *want* to pay hundreds of thousands of kip to stay in the hotel doing nothing...' His imagination began to whirl. 'Maybe there is an opportunity.'

'He tried to explain why,' Kong Keo said. 'I'm not sure that I understood correctly, but I think it is because Laos is different to what he is used to.'

'Is there something we could do to help him enjoy his visit more, I wonder? If he goes home believing he has rediscovered Shangri-La, he might encourage other *falang* to come and stay.' An idea flashed into his mind. 'Do you know if anybody is getting married this week? They say it is very lucky to invite a *falang* to a wedding. Perhaps the Swede might like to be a guest – he could see everybody dressed up and watch the dancing.'

'That would be magnificent,' Kong Keo exclaimed. 'I will ask around.'

A minute or two later, a still more inspired scheme occurred to Manophet. 'Maybe westerners are secretly fascinated by communism and have a hankering to find out for themselves what communist countries are really like,' he postulated. 'Perhaps more and more will be allowed to come to Phonsavan for a few days. Well, most of them will come by air, presumably. What do you suppose happens when such a person arrives at the airport?'

Kong Keo shrugged his shoulders.

'He probably asks a taxi to take him to a hotel.'

'So?'

'Where do you think the taxi takes him?'

The hotel manager took a little persuading, but the idea of stealing a march on the Frenchman who ran the *Auberge* proved too alluring to resist, and the following day Manophet and Kong Keo were despatched to the commercial airport in the hotel's transit van to meet the daily flight from Vientiane. Manophet had created a large sign bearing the hotel's name, which he held above his head as the disembarking passengers filed through the arrivals hall. Their efforts were in vain. No *falang* arrived. For ten days in a row they repeated the exercise, their entrepreneurial aspirations dwindling with each setback. But on the eleventh day they ran across a dishevelled Australian badly in need of a shower, who was under the impression that he had just landed at Luang Prabang. It took several minutes to convince him that he had in fact boarded the wrong aeroplane and was now in a province of which he had never heard. They did what they could to let him down gently. Most regrettably, they informed him, there were no direct flights from Phonsavan to Luang Prabang. Nor would there be any flights back to Vientiane until the following day. Under normal circumstances, he would have been able to extricate himself from his predicament by catching the overnight bus from Phonsavan to Luang Prabang, but unfortunately Route Seven was closed to traffic beyond Mouong Soui, as it had been for the better part of a year. However, all was not lost. The Phu Doi Hotel would be delighted to come to his assistance if he would care to spend a night in Phonsavan.

'You will have to teach me English,' Manophet said to Kong Keo after they had installed the Australian in his room. 'He will want to ask questions.' Kong Keo, who was already late for school, had time to teach him two words before hurrying away: yes and no. Manophet practised the curious little sounds assiduously under his breath, and it was not long before he was put to the test. The Australian had been fortunate enough to arrive at the hotel at a time when the hot water system was functioning smoothly, and he came down from his room freshly scrubbed, in much improved humour, and keen to talk about his adventures. Manophet listened attentively to the torrent of incomprehensible verbiage pouring from the man's mouth, smiling every so often to assure him he was following every word. All was well until the monologue came to an abrupt halt, and the Australian fixed him with an expectant gaze.

Apparently some kind of feedback was required. Manophet weighed up his limited options. It was time to take the plunge. 'Yes,' he declared with a forceful nod.

The thrill of realising he had been successful in making himself understood lasted only momentarily. Rather than looking satisfied or disappointed, the Australian burst out laughing. Had he mispronounced the word? Could "yes" have different meanings in English and Australian? The man's laughter was infectious, and Manophet could not stop himself joining in. Fancy being able to crack a joke in somebody else's language without having any idea why it was funny. For a good few seconds, the two of them cackled away like a couple of drunks, but eventually the stream of gibberish resumed. As soon as it dried up for long enough to invite an interjection Manophet was ready with his salvo: 'Yes,' he exclaimed, with a conspiratorial grin. This time, however, the word had an altogether different effect. The Australian remained grave, stroking his chin thoughtfully while he considered the implications of the response. 'Yes?' he repeated a couple of times, eying Manophet quizzically. The charade continued for a while, until Manophet's fifth or sixth 'yes' sent a look of consternation surging through the other's features. 'No,' Manophet corrected himself hastily, 'no, no – *no!*' Perhaps it had not been such a clever idea to conduct this exchange in a part of the hotel that was commonly assumed to be bugged. For all he knew, the Australian might be interrogating him about national security. The police could make his life very awkward if they took it into their heads that he was consorting with the enemy.

Their forays to the airport brought a slow drip-drip of *falang* into the hotel over the months that followed. Every encounter with an incoming stranger was scrutinised by the police from the privacy of a glass booth in the corner of the arrivals hall, and they would sometimes follow the transit van back to the hotel when a passenger had been signed up as a guest, though they never intervened. Foreigners with advance bookings also checked in to the Phu Doi from time to time, amidst rumours that Sweden had agreed to fund a bomb disposal programme in Xieng Khouang province that would be overseen by a British outfit with an unpronounceable name generally commuted to MAG. There had been attempts to make inroads into the hateful legacy of unexploded ordnance before. The Chinese, the Vietnamese and, most prominently, the Russians had all chipped in with clearance operations since the end of the war. Once the scale of the problem had become apparent, however, their enthusiasm had waned. During the past twelve years only the Mennonites had shown any interest in helping out. But the Party was no more enthusiastic about having Canadians roaming around militarily sensitive regions of Laos than Americans, and their initiatives had been doomed from the outset. Proposal after proposal had become fatally ensnarled in red tape. Now, at last, a compromise with which all parties were comfortable had apparently been hammered out. In due course, a party of four bomb disposal consultants arrived at the Phu Doi, along with a huge consignment of equipment, which sat in the lobby for several days while they worked out where to store it.

Manophet wrestled with his old prejudices. Why should the Scandinavians or the British wish to involve themselves in his province's affairs? It was not as though they bore any responsibility for dropping the bombs. These consultants must have a hidden agenda. And yet there was no getting away from the fact that making bombs safe was dangerous work. In the evenings, they would sit slumped in the big rattan chairs in the lobby after completing another harrowing day in the field, drinking quietly to soothe their frayed nerves. What could be motivating them to put their lives on the line like this? According to the authorities, westerners were only ever driven by self-interest, but this group belied the stereotype. On the face of it, they were not generously remunerated. Their clothes were worn through, and they owned no flashy accessories according to the girls who serviced their rooms. Nor was their behaviour furtive. They would always respond with a friendly smile if he tried to communicate with them. He lapped up every morsel of English that Kong Keo could teach him in the hope of learning more about the strangers, but his vocabulary never seemed equal to the task of constructing the questions that he wanted to put to them.

'You want to learn English?' Bo, one of the consultants, enquired after a particularly frustrating encounter.

Manophet nodded vigorously, unsure whether he was serious.

'I could teach you.'

'Teach English? Very much yes please,' Manophet replied, wondering if he had understood correctly.

'One hour a day. And in return you will do my laundry – OK?'

'Laundry?'

'Clothes. You clean my clothes for me. Does that sound a fair deal?'

At a stroke, Manophet had sacrificed almost all his free time, but he had no regrets about his decision. He was itching to understand more about these *falang* and their strange ways. Private English tuition was exactly what he needed to try and make sense of them. Over the course of the next few months, he grew close to his instructor, who never seemed to mind what questions he asked. Bo encouraged him to stick to mundane topics while he was learning the basics of the language, but Manophet had never been shy about trying to run before he could walk, and he started to construct a picture of how Laos appeared to outsiders. People the world over knew about the Korean War, Bo explained. They knew about Vietnam. But they were hazy about Laos and its history – to such an extent that large numbers of Europeans seemed to be under the impression that Laos was in Africa. As for the communist regime, it was not really taken seriously at all, being seen as hopelessly out of touch with reality. Not that this damning verdict was as offensive as it seemed at first blush, since Bo was just as scathing when giving opinions about Western politicians. In his eyes, none of the world's leaders were up to the job, apparently.

'Why did you come to bombies in Xieng Khouang?' Manophet asked, being careful to put half the verb before the preposition, as Bo had been teaching him.

'To blow up bombies,' Bo corrected. 'Why did I come to *blow up* bombies in Xieng Khouang? That's a good question. Well, I didn't want to be an insurance salesman like my father, you see, or a lampshade maker like my mother. I wanted to do a job that would make a difference to people's lives. And I came to Laos because, the more I read about what happened here during the war, the more unfair it seemed. Laos was neutral. It did nothing to provoke the bombing. And yet nobody was prepared to lift a finger to clear up the mess.'

'Who is paying for the money?'

'A Swedish group named Diakonia raised some money from private individuals,' Bo answered, 'and the Swedish government then contributed an equal amount. Governments and private donors in the West like to give money to projects like this if they can afford to. But there are huge numbers of programmes around the world that deserve funding, and the problem Laos has is that the bombing here happened twenty-five years ago. Laos is never mentioned by the media these days. It's what you might call "old" news. When people watch their televisions, they hear reports about the disasters that are taking place today, and those are the ones they tend to give money to.'

'There is many bombies here for blowing up,' Manophet pointed out.

Bo nodded. 'I'm afraid we shall only be able to make a small percentage of them safe. But we also have another idea for saving lives. At least half the bombie accidents in Laos affect children. Children from ethnic minority villages are particularly at risk because they don't go to school, so they don't learn how dangerous bombies are. When they find one, they may start playing with it because they think it is a toy. We want to teach those children not to make that mistake.'

Manophet never revealed how much he detested having to do laundry work, which he found more demeaning even than mopping floors. The envious glances that Bo's crisply starched shirts drew from his colleagues were no compensation for the loss of face that came with having to scrub away at his mentor's socks and underpants in a tub of soapy water while the laundress's children fell about laughing. But he endured the indignity patiently and without resentment, for the rewards from the deal that he had struck were profound. At last he had a window through which to see how men and women elsewhere in the world lived their lives – and it was just as he had dared to hope. In the West, you did not spend all your days in the place where you were born, doing the job decreed by your family, and marrying the spouse chosen by your parents. Like an eagle, you soared above the panorama until you spied the niche where you belonged, and there you settled and flourished and were able to develop into a good person. Not that *he* was any closer to having this luxury, of course. With no passport and no money, he was as firmly consigned to the lot to which he had been born as ever. But now at least he had the reassurance of knowing that that his ambitions were legitimate. You *could* travel. You *could* help other people. You *could* make the world a better place. And these *falang* were surely the key to discovering how to turn his dream into reality. If he could learn to think as they thought, perhaps his eyes would be opened and he would be able to identify the path that would lead him away from the pointless existence in which he was trapped.

One evening Bo asked him whether he spoke Thai.
'You want to learning Thai from me?' Manophet queried.
Bo shook his head. 'But I have an idea.'
Two weeks later, Bo presented him with a parcel wrapped in brown paper.
'For me?' Manophet stripped off the paper to reveal the thickest book he had ever seen. The title on the glossy cover was printed in Thai script. 'Learn to Speak English in 79 Hours,' he translated.
'It comes with tapes,' Bo explained, producing another package from behind his back, 'so you can hear how it ought to sound. You can play them on my cassette player.'

Manophet was beside himself with excitement. He could think of nothing in the world more desirable than such a learning aid. 'How much for me to paying you?' he asked nervously, determined to raise the money by whatever means it took.

Bo waved away the offer. 'It's a birthday present,' he said.

'It is not my birthday,' Manophet objected.

'You will have had at least one birthday by the time you finish it,' came the riposte. Both men were aware that it would take many weeks for seventy-nine hours of free time to come Manophet's way. To make matters more complicated, he would first need to translate the text from Thai, a language in which he was only moderately fluent.

'You are teaching the hill-tribe children about bombies now?' Manophet asked Bo a few weeks later.

For a moment Bo looked confused. 'Oh *that*,' he said, when he had worked out what Manophet was talking about. 'Well, that idea turns out to be harder to put into practice than we had anticipated. For one thing, there are more tribes here than we thought. We've been told there are at least ten in Xieng Khouang alone, and of course they all speak different languages. But there are no maps to show where villages are located, or which tribes live where. If we're going to mount an operation like this, we will need to take an ordnance disposal expert, a local Lao guide who knows the area, somebody who can translate from English to Lao, and at least one other person to translate from Lao into whatever language the various tribes speak. We just don't have the contacts or the manpower at the moment.'

Manophet pondered the problem. He could speak enough English to make himself understood now, and his Khmu was passable. Although living in Phonsavan had done little to enhance his grasp of Hmong, he had learned the general principles of the Tai-Kadai language family from a Phouane cadet at the army base in Ban Penh, and he also had a smattering of Akha to his name. He knew from his army training how to locate and identify villages, how to find the way from one to the next, how to look after himself in open terrain. And he had first-hand experience of the damage that a cluster bomb could inflict on a child. Was he not as good a man for this job as anybody? The trouble was, it would take days rather than hours to walk out to a village and then back again. The hotel would never be prepared to release him for such an extended period.

'If the war was secretly, how did you know about some bombing in Xieng Khouang?' he asked Bo.

'I read about it in an extraordinary book,' Bo replied. 'You probably haven't heard of it – I don't think it was ever translated into Lao: *Voices from the Plain of Jars*?'

Manophet shook his head.

'Throughout the sixties, it was more or less impossible to get hold of reliable information about what was happening in the north of Laos because it was dangerous for reporters to leave Vientiane and travel into the area under Pathet Lao control. But when the displaced villagers from the Plain started flooding into the refugee camps around the capital in 1970, the press finally had an opportunity to discover the truth. None of the journalists could speak Lao, but there was an American based in Vientiane who offered to translate. Fred Branfman, he was called. US newspapers ran the story, and suddenly the Secret War had ceased to be a secret. After that, Branfman got the refugees to write down their stories and draw pictures of what they'd witnessed, and that was how this book came into being.'

It took Bo six months to track down a copy of *Voices from the Plain of Jars*, but eventually a battered second-hand paperback arrived at the Phu Doi. Manophet gazed down at the horrifying sketch on the front cover. Drawn in primary colours by a nameless twenty-seven year-old, it had something of the inadvertent caricature about it. Lakes of red blood lapped across the landscape. The hills were a bilious green, the bombers black. A horse, upside down, in blue, was prominent in the foreground alongside a disembodied head blown violently into the air, the features frozen in an expression of bewilderment. These were the awful recollections of the villagers who had been his family's neighbours in Muang Khoun, the stories that his parents had always refused to share. The descriptions were rough and raw, the narrators' experiences too recent, too appalling to be distilled into neat palatable sentences. It took him many days to translate them back into Lao. Even Bo could not work out what some of the words meant. But Manophet was determined to see the task through, for the book reconnected him to that part of his history from which he had always felt irreparably severed. This body lying on the ground in the picture could have been his brother, that blazing timber heap the house in which they had lived. And it was not that the *falang* did not care about what they had done, as he had imagined. It was that they had no memory of having done it. The book had been out of print for years. Having floated briefly on the surface of the great ocean of global tragedy, visible for all to deplore, the Secret War, with its arresting capital letters, had sunk beneath the waves and become merely another forgotten tiff between power-hungry ideologues.

# EIGHT

Manophet froze. A bend had come into view a few yards ahead. Apparently the path along which he was heading was about to veer left. Something about the turn gave him a bad feeling. A

Red Helen looped silently by. That could hardly be a good omen. Without moving his head, he ran his eyes across the jungle floor, then scanned the canopy overhead. Silence: an unnatural stillness – as though the creatures of the forest were holding their breath to listen. Liana tangles crowded the gaps between the trees, shutting off the view to either side of the path. Now a notch in the bark of a nearby pine caught his eye. No tribesman would risk angering the forest spirits by carving such a mark. But how else could it have been made? It was not recent. An arrow graze? He contemplated the unsettling curve. Could there have been a fork here at some point, with another path continuing straight ahead? The jungle was capable of swallowing up a disused trail in no time at all. At last, a long way off, the chortle of a frog broke the spell. Up above, the birds that had been quarrelling before the lull resumed their spat. Normality was returning. But his uneasiness would not let go. Padding forward a couple of paces, he squatted down so that he was at eye level with the ground cover. Yes, here were the branches, now long since grown over, that had been placed across the old path to show that it was no longer in use. Judging by their state of decay, they had been here two or three years. Perhaps the village towards which he was heading had been relocated, and a new path had been cleared to replace the old one.

He took a sip from his water bottle. This raised the chances that it was Hmong. Most of the tribal minorities stayed put once they had built a village, but the Hmong seldom remained in the same place for longer than ten or fifteen years. Land that had been used for cultivating opium could take decades to regenerate after it became exhausted. It was simpler to abandon it and make a fresh start elsewhere. On the other hand, the path to the left might lead to a different village altogether – in which case it could be Hmong, Khmu, Phouane, even one of the more obscure tribal sub-groups. You could never be certain what you might find when you were so far into uncharted territory. Nobody in the Hmong village from which he had set out that morning had been able to come up with a name for the settlement towards which he was now heading. Not that that was, in itself, any great surprise. Names had limited significance in Hmong culture. They did not name their villages, or their cats, and it would not necessarily occur to them that other tribes might have different customs. But it was unusual for villagers – of whatever tribe – not to be able to identify the ethnicity of the next village along the path. All the Hmong had been able to agree on was that it was a very long way away. And now he had the added complication of this path junction to factor into his calculations. This was unsettling terrain. He would need to keep his eyes peeled.

His body tensed. Something had moved. And there it was again – a slight trembling beneath the tangle of low vegetation edging the path ahead. But this was not where the danger lay. It was the clump of jungle debris on the opposite side of the trail that drew his attention. The pattern of light and shadow followed a suspicious contour. Stems had been pressed aside and flattened by a stealthy presence. The snake was masterfully camouflaged. Even after he had realised it was hiding there, it took him a couple of seconds to trace its sinuous outline. Not the sort you would choose to cross swords with. All pit vipers could be dangerous, but the green ones had the worst reputation. They were hard to spot from a distance, and unsuspecting passers-by would often stumble over one before it had time to beat a retreat, resulting in a potentially fatal confrontation. It was said that a pit viper could remain in the same place for hours after biting a human, as though waiting for a chance to inflict the same fate on anyone rash enough to stop and help the victim. He counted the chevrons, trying to estimate its length. Twenty inches? Probably longer.

The rustling continued, but the snake appeared content to bide its time. For whatever reason, it was holding out for a better moment to strike. The stand-off could be over in seconds or last for minutes. He could not afford a long delay. It seemed unlikely he would reach his destination much before nightfall, and he wanted to spend as little time in the jungle after dark as possible. He knew better than to make a detour through the undergrowth. Straying off the beaten track was never a good idea in Xieng Khouang. Another option was to drive the snake away by throwing sticks at it, but this could be just as risky. If the village towards which he was heading had the trail under surveillance, the lookout would report his actions to the elders, and they would accuse him of having provoked the forest spirits and refuse to cooperate. Almost all the different ethnic traditions embraced the existence of forest spirits, even if they could not always agree about how numerous or powerful they were, or how best to avoid upsetting them. Like most Lao, Manophet had nothing against a good legend as long as nobody took it too literally. It was only when superstitions were carried to extremes that they became problematic. He stood pondering. In all probability, there was nobody else within miles of this isolated spot. On the other hand, there was little to be lost by erring on the side of respectfulness.

Before long, the snake spared him the decision by slithering away, and he began the slow descent into the next valley. It was a good day for walking: not too hot, not too sticky. The climb had been rough in places, and the going was now deteriorating – probably because this section of the trail was not much used. No doubt it would improve again once he was within striking distance of his destination. Was he guilty of discounting tribal belief systems too lightly? Creatures like tigers kept themselves hidden deep in the jungle. Why not forest spirits driven by the same desire to live undisturbed by humankind? The fact that you had never encountered a particular creature or spirit was no guarantee that it did not exist. On the other hand, where were you supposed to draw the line? The existence of ancestor spirits was not so difficult to accept, but what about the belief that they could only travel in straight lines? Or the Hmong notion that they had difficulty crossing water? He had noticed an exquisite little bridge on his way out of the village that morning, expertly crafted, too fragile to bear the weight of a child, let alone an adult, a contrivance that must have taken hours to fashion. And why was it there? To help ancestor spirits cross the little stream over which it had been constructed. Surely attributing spirits with such peculiar behavioural traits could only detract from their credibility. And yet to refuse to engage with the spirit world on the grounds that spirits were elusive and difficult to fathom was just as illogical.

He paused to examine a tiny orange flower. All his life he had been coming to the forest, and still he could discover plants that he had not encountered before. The tribesfolk would know what it was, and whether it had any medicinal value. He counted the petals and memorised the leaf structure so that he could describe it to them. The war must have been doubly terrifying for the hill-tribes, with their animist beliefs, he reflected. Presumably they had been convinced, as bombs rained down from the sky on their villages, that they were experiencing retribution from a spirit they had unwittingly enraged. Events had taken a diabolical turn in a village inhabited by one of the more elusive minorities, according to the head man of a settlement that he had visited earlier in the year. Like many other ethnic sub-groups, the tribe involved subscribed to the doctrine that the way to appease an angered spirit was to sacrifice an animal. The larger the beast, the more effective the sacrifice. But the villagers had gone as far as sacrificing their only buffalo, and bombs were still falling on their huts and crops. What were they to do? Guided by the shaman, they had reached the conclusion that it would take a still more substantial sacrifice to bring about an end to the destruction. But it was possible that the story had grown in the telling over the years, and was no more than a myth. It was always difficult to know how far to trust villagers who relied on word of mouth and never wrote anything down.

The path finally met the stream that splashed along the valley floor. From here, it began to wind its way up the thickly forested flank of a mountain crag, the gradient gentle at first but becoming ever steeper as he climbed. For two hours, he concentrated on the stony trail beneath his feet. Ground creepers reached across it from either side, suffocating it with tapestries of leaves and thrusting tendrils, squeezing it to a narrow ribbon. Here and there the vines knotted themselves into cables or webs that were passable only if he crawled underneath or hacked them down. Leeches attached themselves to his legs, but he had learned how do defend himself against their hungry mouths in the army, and one by one they dropped off unsatisfied. Animal traps were his primary concern. Though crude, these were capable of inflicting a life-threatening injury on a man, and often craftily concealed. To stumble into a snare in a place like this could be a bad mistake. It might be days before anybody found him. He passed a ghostly clearing carpeted with ruined cindery branches through which nothing green penetrated. Ash-grey tree skeletons poked up at oblique angles, waiting for their turn to tumble in and join the wreckage. Even mould could not gain a foothold here to do its natural work, such was the level of contamination. Ordinary bomb craters the jungle could take care of, but something deadly had been contained in the payload that had created this one.

Pausing to catch breath after reaching the summit of a ridge, he contemplated the patterns made by the rays of sunshine filtering between the treetops. What a joy it was to be out in the open instead of mopping dusty floors all day. The Phu Doi had agreed to allow Kong Keo to cover for him from time to time so that he could make expeditions of this kind, and one of Bo's successors at MAG had even been kind enough to give him a few kip with which to purchase some provisions for the long journey. It was the closest thing to a holiday that he would get. A sudden branch crack in the distance disturbed his reverie. He stopped to listen. At first, he could hear only the whispering of the tall branches in the breeze and the spasmodic buzz of insects. But then a muffled thump echoed back from the forest below, as though two heavy objects had collided. If a tribesman was coming the other way along the path, Manophet had little to fear. But the path seemed to run down the left side of the ridge. The disturbance had come from the right. Gingerly, he padded forwards, moving slowly to avoid snapping twigs or dislodging stones. A moment later, the distinctive grunt of a wild pig told him he had nothing to worry about. He would have alarming crashes and howls preying on his senses all night if he failed to reach the village before dusk. Perhaps it would be prudent to keep an eye out for fresh animal droppings. If you were forced to sleep out in the jungle, your chances of remaining undisturbed were considerably improved if you could avoid making the mistake of hunkering down hard by a predator's lair.

There were those who maintained that the minority tribes had always been treated as second-class citizens in Laos, even arguing that it was this that had encouraged some of the Hmong clans and others to side with the French against the patriots during the First Indochina War, and then with the Americans in the sixties. During Manophet's lifetime, every Lao national had had the same battle to fight, whatever their ethnicity: long hours toiling away at one form of drudgery or another in return for a few grains of rice. And yet, even in the dismally harsh conditions in which they all had to exist, there was a pecking order. There were ethnic Lao who had no qualms about letting it be known that they considered themselves to be derived from superior stock, referring to the Hmong as *Meo* and the Khmu as *Kha*. Educated Lao, like Manophet, knew better than to use these derogatory labels. But he could not pretend that he did not feel relieved from time to time about belonging to the "right" social group – even if this sentiment brought with it a sense of guilt. Imagine having to be bound by some of the primitive courtship rituals that existed amongst the hill-tribes, for instance. In one tribe, you were expected to go late at night to the hut where the girl who had caught your eye lived, crawl underneath and poke her with a stick as she slept to announce your interest. What kind of romantic gesture was *that*? The ground underneath a house was hardly the most sanitary of places. Even if the girl welcomed your overtures and stole out of the hut to be with you, you would probably smell revolting. And what would happen if you inadvertently poked the wrong member of the household?

He had been walking almost nine hours when the first signs that he was nearing a village appeared. The trail broadened as minor paths fed into it and, through a break in the tree cover, he spotted smoke rising over the jungle ahead. The roar of a far-off waterfall floated back on the evening air. Before long, he could hear the barking of dogs. The tins of tuna that he had purchased with the money that the MAG consultant had given him clanked together in his pack, reminding him how hungry he was. He was also carrying a small bag of rice and a few plants that he had picked up along the way – in short, the ingredients for a satisfying meal. Here and there, small objects – presumably sacred – dangled from tree branches on thin cotton cords like the ones used in *baci* ceremonies. There were also a couple of dilapidated shrines beside the trail of a design that he did not recognise. It began to look as though this might be a minority tribe that he had not encountered before. The moment of arrival after a long journey was always nerve-wracking. All manner of factors might prejudice the villagers against him, from the colour of his boots to the time of day at which he appeared. He had brought a small bottle of rice whisky as a gift, but there was no guarantee they would regard this as acceptable. Before the war, the arrival of a stranger in a remote village would have been cause for general excitement, it was said. Where had the man come from? What stories did he have to tell? But these days the first instinct was one of suspicion. Was this another tax collector? What business did he have demanding money? What had the government ever done to help the village?

Rounding a bend, he found himself at last at the entrance to the village. His spirits plummeted. The gate was closed, and there was a taleo bound to it, daubed with blood and chicken feathers. A second taleo was staked out directly in front of it. He had seen taleos on individual houses before, but never on a gate. The latticework was crude – a rough interworking of bamboo and dried grass, but the message could not be clearer. The village had an emergency on its hands. Nobody was to enter. Manophet groaned out loud. To the left lay the tattered carcase of another village gate angled against the ground, presumably the predecessor of the one now in use. This was very bad. Village gates were replaced only if they were deemed to have proved ineffective at keeping malevolent spirits at bay. If the tribespeople were in a state of deep anxiety, as this suggested, it could be challenging – if not impossible – to gain their trust. Breaking their taboo would immediately put paid to any chance he had of accomplishing his mission. But he could not turn round and walk back. It would be dark in an hour. He contemplated the prospect of spending a night in the open. Jungle predators would probably leave him alone provided he stayed close to the village. If he was lucky, the villagers might lend him a rug to throw over himself while he slept, and perhaps a pot in which to cook. And yet they might equally well drive him back into the forest. Nor was there any certainty he would be permitted to enter the village the following morning. If funeral rites were involved, it could be several days before the taboo was lifted.

Presently a dog sniffed out his presence and came to bark, followed in rapid succession by several others – surly, scrawny animals glad of an excuse to kick up a hullabaloo. Before long, a small grubby girl arrived to see what was going on. Her shapeless once-white garment, which was many sizes too large, gave no clue to the ethnicity of the village. Beautiful as the dawn, she stood and considered him through the gate with grave eyes, as though contemplating some exotic creature from the forest. There was no sense in bidding her *sabaidee*. She would not understand. Keeping one eye on the dogs, who looked ready to run riot at the first opportunity, he tried the effect of a cheery wave, but it brought no response. At length a villager appeared and set to work shooing away the dogs. Manophet hailed him in Lao, to show there were language barriers to be negotiated. The reply was agitated and unintelligible. Here and there Manophet caught a word he thought he recognised. It was probably an obscure Tai-Kadai dialect. But there were ways around such obstacles. Neighbouring tribes often knew a smattering of each other's languages as a result of bartering with each other for goods. He repeated the greeting in Hmong, in which he was now reasonably fluent, having spent numerous evenings in Hmong villages on other missions. Gesturing to him to stay where he was, the villager turned and headed back the way he had come, aiming a kick at a recalcitrant dog as he left.

He returned accompanied by three more villagers, including an elderly man with a rudimentary knowledge of Hmong. The other two, the Hmong speaker explained, were the head man and the shaman. Both wore loosely buttoned tunics and faded black calf-length trousers, but the shaman's jacket had a red trim, and his belt was hung with accoutrements – pouches on drawstrings, metal artefacts, a length of carved wood that resembled a blowpipe, underlining his status. He also sported several tattoos, and frequently interrupted the head man when he tried to speak. Manophet began to state his business, but the elder motioned to him to be quiet. Apparently this was not relevant. In the shaman's eyes, the arrival of an unexpected visitor at such a late hour was evidently an ominous and troubling portent. He had come equipped with a short gnarled stick, probably ceremonial, which he swished dramatically, either to lend authority to his pronouncements, or in a calculated show of aggression designed to intimidate any watching spirits. In one of the villages in this area, there was rumoured to be a fearsome healer-cum-occultist who fell into trances and cast magic spells. Could this be him, Manophet wondered. In due course, an argument broke out. Even without being able to understand the insults being traded, it was not difficult to get the gist of the disagreement. The head man was making the case that visitors who had walked all day to reach the village should not be refused a welcome and left to fend for themselves in the jungle overnight. The shaman was insisting that if the forest spirit saw a stranger pass through the gate it would be emboldened to do the same, and all manner of havoc could be let loose on the village.

Dusk had fallen by the time the dispute was resolved. Laboriously, the interpreter explained that Manophet was not to enter the village until the following morning. However, if he walked around the perimeter to the other side, he would find an outhouse where he could spend the night. In the event, there were three structures in which there was room for a man to sleep – two rice barns and a small hut without a door. In one of the barns there was a cooking pot, and a patch of burnt earth nearby showed that fires had been lit here before. He began to feel more cheerful. Things were working out better than they might have done. He stumbled off in the direction of the river, using the sound of the water as his guide. Here, having filled his water bottle and the cooking pot, he washed. Children's laughter rang out from the village as he made his way back. On the breeze, he could smell yams frying in a tantalising blend of herbs. He gathered some fallen branches, and soon had a smoky fire going. Next he manufactured a tripod so that he could fix the cooking pot in position. In went the rice and, when it had almost boiled dry, the herbs, the plant leaves and one of the tins of tuna. His mother would not have approved of his recipe. There were too many conflicting tastes for a single dish, but the plants would not keep, and it seemed a pity to waste them. At last, the mushrooms that he had been toasting on skewers around the fire were ready to be added. It was delicious! Was there anything more satisfying than tucking into a good meal after a long day's walking?

At the end of his banquet, he lay back and gazed up at the stars. What an enchanting soul the little girl at the gate had been. It was impossible to lose hope for a nation that could produce such inspirational children. Perhaps his parents' generation had judged more wisely than he had realised in deciding not to talk about the war. By keeping their hatred and bitterness bottled up, they had allowed the wheel of healing to turn more quickly. The past had no hold over these little ones. Because they had been allowed to retain their innocence, they had the freedom to dream and could now infect the rest of the population with their hopefulness. But was it right, allowing children to dream visions of a better world when they had so few opportunities to realise them? How could the nation hope to take advantage of this store of positive energy if it refused to let go of the old dogma that free enterprise was a western ideal that led only to the betterment of the rich at the expense of the poor? Only a fool would try launching ground-breaking initiatives in Laos when the golden rule of enjoying a quiet life was to avoid bringing yourself to the attention of the authorities – so conventional wisdom would have it. But somehow the nation's children needed to be encouraged to challenge conventional wisdom. And yet they would need to be taught so many new skills if they were to have any realistic chance of reshaping the world in which they were growing up.

Eerie howls and cries reverberated around the jungle as he climbed a rickety ladder to the upper storey of one of the rice barns. It was all very well rehearsing lofty philosophical arguments like this, but what about the practicalities? How was he, a hotel janitor, ever going to be able to help bring about any of these fantastic changes? He hollowed out a space in which to rest, and in no time it became impossible to keep his eyes open.

The taleos were taken down at dawn, and Manophet was allowed into the village. As usual, it took several hours to explain to the villagers what he needed to do and persuade them to cooperate. His request, though straightforward, was out of the ordinary, and custom required that a council of village elders be convened to debate it before any preparations could begin. By the time they gave their blessing, the sun was high, and half the children had disappeared to the fields with their families. It was late afternoon before they were finally all assembled in a big circle around him in front of the head man's house. Dozens of inquisitive adults had also turned out, so that there were perhaps two hundred in all gathered for the presentation. Manophet had three villagers with him in the circle: a young man who could understand his broken Hmong and was happy to act as interpreter, and two reluctant volunteers. The children's eyes were on stalks. This was the most exciting thing to have happened to them for months! But Manophet knew their attention spans were short. He needed to drive his message home quickly. Like a conjurer, he whipped away the mat beneath which he had concealed his exhibit. 'Who has seen one of these before?' he asked. There was jostling and pushing as they tried to get a better view. Necks craned. The tinier ones stood on tiptoes. 'It is called a bombie,' he continued, 'and it is very, very, *very* dangerous.' The group standing behind him, which had been creeping steadily closer, thinking he could not see them, backed hurriedly away. The device had been made safe so that it could be used in demonstrations, but he preferred to create the illusion that it was live. 'You can come and have a closer look when I have finished talking if you like – providing you do not touch it. As long as you do not touch it you will be safe.'

Cluster bombs came in many shapes and sizes. This was one of the more seductive varieties – alluringly spherical, inlaid with fascinating grooves and precise circular depressions, bronze-coloured, burnished, giving out an irresistible metallic gleam – exactly the type of object you would expect a child to seize on if they came across one in the forest. 'This is what can happen if you are working in a field and your hoe strikes a bombie buried under the soil.' He pointed to the volunteer with only one leg.' A bombie is powerful enough to blow off your leg. 'And this is what can happen if you pick one up, or if you light a fire in a place where one is buried.' He pointed to the other volunteer. 'If you are unlucky, you may lose both your eyes. If that happens, you will not be able to see any more. It is also possible for a bombie to kill you. That happened to two of my friends when I was nine years old. So you must be very careful. Most bombies are buried underneath the ground, but rain can wash away the soil lying on top of them, so you should keep a special lookout if it has been raining hard. If you ever find anything that looks at all like this, there are three rules that you must follow. Rule number one: leave it alone. Never touch it – even if it is in a place where somebody else might tread on it. Never, *never* play with it. Rule number two: make a pile of branches somewhere close by to remind you exactly where it is. One piece of jungle looks very much like another, and you can easily forget where you found a bombie if you do not mark its position. Rule number three: as soon as you have done that, go back to the village, find a grown-up and show them where the bombie is.'

That was the important work done. There were questions, and a moment of panic when a boy took it into his head that the device was about to explode. The children formed themselves into a crocodile and trooped nervously round the tree stump on which it was displayed. One by one, the older villagers came up to shake his hand, their faces lit with broad grins, and stood chattering away, undeterred by the knowledge that he could not understand a word they were saying. As the meeting was breaking up, he felt a tug on his trousers. It was the small girl from the previous evening. Reaching for his hand, she uncurled his fingers and pressed a smooth blue pebble into his palm. He looked around for the interpreter, wanting to know the word for thank you, but she was already scampering away.

Late in the afternoon, as the shadows were beginning to lengthen, he caught sight of a throng of villagers gathered beside the river. Had something happened? He hurried along the winding path to get a better look. They were watching a circular object floating lazily on the surface of a wide pool slightly out of the current. It was the tin of tuna fish from the previous evening, now lid-less and empty. He had left it lying in the long grass near the rice barn, intending to dispose of it later. Dozens of pairs of eyes followed as it wobbled atop the ripples. 'What are they doing?' he whispered to the interpreter, who he had spotted amongst the group. 'Catching a fish,' the interpreter answered. Manophet suppressed his curiosity for as long as he could. 'How are they going to catch a fish with a tin?' he asked eventually. 'Spirit magic,' the interpreter explained. 'The shaman says the tin must possess a spirit because a fish has jumped into it in another place. He says that, if that happened before, it can happen a second time.'

These excursions were eating up a lot of time, he reflected as he was walking home the following day. He had already visited all the communities within easy walking distance of Phonsavan, and now needed to spend at least four nights away from the hotel to reach villages that had not already heard his talk. Before long, it would be six nights, then eight. Undertaking missions that might save children's lives brought infinitely more satisfaction than scrubbing floors or standing in for the night porter, it went without saying. But how much longer could they continue? To earn four nights' leave, the hotel required him to work eight weeks without taking any other time off. If only he could hire a vehicle to drive him the first few miles and then pick him up at the end of each trek. He chuckled to himself. A fine aspiration *that* was for a man who not only had no money, but lacked even the spare time in which to scrape any earnings together. It was a conundrum as old as the hills. Half the people in Laos asked themselves the same question every day: what can I do to earn a few more kip? The irony was that it was because nobody *had* any kip to give away to employees that it was impossible for anybody to earn any kip. As he pondered the depressingly circular argument, however, he saw that it contained one conspicuous flaw. The *falang* who stayed at the hotel always had kip to spare. Furthermore, if the bombie consultants were any guide, they were also generous by nature. Surely the question that a smart Lao entrepreneur should be asking himself was: how can *falang* be parted from their money? What was it that they desired? Or, to be more exact, for what sort of goods or services would they be willing to pay?

# NINE

He was sitting one afternoon, as so often, on the high stool behind the reception desk, trying not to nod off in the drowsy air, when the hotel door swung open and three men shuffled in off the street. For a moment, he thought he must be hallucinating. Had his malaria returned? Khmu came to Phonsavan on market days to trade goods, but at other times they were a rare spectacle, and a landmark establishment such as the Phu Doi was about the last place you would expect them to put in an appearance. The subtlety of the stitching of their tunics marked them out as hailing from distant parts, and their trousers were also shorter and baggier than those worn by the Khmu who lived locally. The three tribesmen were covered in dust. Evidently they had been journeying for a considerable time. Manophet shook himself awake and made an effort to collect his senses. The leading man looked vaguely familiar. Was this not the head man of one of the remote hill-tribe villages to which he had trekked a few months earlier? When people came calling like this, it was traditional to invite them to sit down, give them tea, enquire whether they would care for some food. But the hotel would not appreciate it if he tried offering hospitality to three shabby-looking tribal elders in its lobby. For want of a better plan, he took them outside to the courtyard where there was a low wall against which they could lean and rest. There would need to be at least half an hour of small talk before they got around to stating their business. Anything less would be considered rude. Keeping one eye on the reception desk, he set about exchanging pleasantries.

At length, the head man handed him a square of soiled yellowing paper, frayed at the edges. 'White men came to our village many months ago and gave this to us,' he explained. Manophet unfolded the crumpled offering, which turned out to be a leaflet produced by the American organisation Missing in Action, usually known as MIA. Lucrative rewards were promised to any person who could provide information that helped identify the whereabouts of any US airman reported missing over Laos during the war and still unaccounted for, or the recovery of relics. Neither the Lao script nor the English translation that followed would have been comprehensible to his guests. 'They said they would give us money if we assisted them,' the man continued. 'At that time, we could not assist them, but now we have found something.' After glancing round to satisfy himself there was nobody watching from the street, he delved under his clothes. When his hand reappeared, it was tightly clutched. Slowly, he uncurled his fingers, allowing the contents of his fist to drop with a tinkle onto the wall. Manophet picked up the bracelet and held it against the sky, letting the light reflect off the metal. It was an identity tag. Presumably it had once belonged to a US pilot. Now he understood why the man was nervous. *Falang* would pay a fortune to get their hands on such an article.

'Where was this found?' he asked.
'A boy picked it up.'
'Has anything else been discovered? Other objects made from metal?'
The man gave an ambiguous shrug of the shoulders. War scrap did not survive for long in the countryside. Uses could generally be found for the leftovers – bomb casings could be pressed into service as structural supports. Twisted oddments could be beaten into shape and sold off. Metal was like money. It always carried a scrap value. But a dog-tag was different, and the tribal elders were canny enough to know they could not process it through the usual channels.

'Did you search the area?' Manophet persisted. 'This is important. The *falang* will want the bones of the man to whom this belonged, and they will need to know if there is also an aeroplane wreck.'

The men conferred amongst themselves, using a dialect with which he was not familiar. 'His brother found it,' the head man said eventually, indicating the man to his left. 'They went back together the next day to see if they could find anything else, but his brother was not able to remember exactly which part of the forest he had been hunting in.'

They were probably working on the basis that the less they revealed the harder it would be for interested parties to back them into a corner, Manophet decided. Besides, the bones would almost certainly have been scattered by animals after all these years. He tried a different approach. 'Why did you bring this to *me*?' he asked.

'We trust you,' the head man said. 'We know you will not cheat us. You speak Khmu. You also speak English, so you can talk to the Americans.' He jabbed a finger down on a number printed at the bottom of the flier beside a picture of a telephone. 'And you have a magic speaking machine.'

Manophet glanced towards the hotel telephone, wondering how they would take the news that speaking to an office in Vientiane was a magic trick that needed several thousand kip to pull off.

'You have reasoned well,' he said at length. 'But unfortunately there is a problem. We are not supposed to deal with the MIA *falang* directly. Everything has to go through the authorities.'

'That is not what the piece of paper says,' the head man objected. 'We had it translated.'

'It will be a serious loss of face for the authorities if you go behind their backs,' Manophet said. 'It makes them look weak in the eyes of the *falang*. And they are bound to find out sooner or later, however hard you try and keep them in the dark. The Americans will apply to bring helicopters and recovery teams and search equipment to your village, and then it will be obvious to the authorities what has happened. When they eventually catch up with you, they will be angry.'

The men discussed the idea. 'At least we would have the money,' the smallest and quietest of the three observed.

'If we hand this over to the authorities, we will never receive any money,' the head man concurred.

'Oh, I imagine you would get *some* money,' Manophet said. 'Just not as much as if you dealt with the *falang* directly. My guess is that the authorities would treat the reward as taxable and retain part of it for the benefit of the State. But I'm afraid I have no idea what percentage they tend to keep in situations like this.'

'Then it is a simple decision,' declared the brother of the treasure finder.'

'It is not so simple,' the head man countered. 'If they know we have money on which we have not paid tax, they will get back at us in other ways.'

'They will come after the money whether or not we have paid tax on it,' the short man argued. 'Once they know we have money to pay them off, they will find some pretext for making a nuisance of themselves. One way or another, they are going to take some of this money away from us. But it seems to me we are likely to end up keeping a bigger share if we make it difficult for them to grab it than if we make it easy.'

'How are you going to negotiate with the *falang* if you try and deal with them directly,' Manophet asked, 'once they arrive in the village?'

'When they came before, they brought an interpreter.'

'But how will you know they are negotiating in good faith? Are you sure it is safe to trust them? Maybe the authorities would be able to negotiate a bigger reward for you. It would surely be in their interests to do that if they were going to receive a cut.'

'We do not trust the *falang*,' the head man said. 'But we trust the Lao authorities even less. Besides, our negotiating position with the *falang* is stronger. We have something they want. And the interpreter told us you can sometimes say they offered you a million kip when in fact they offered only a hundred thousand. He said that, if you hold your ground, they will eventually conclude that the original translator must have muddled up the number of noughts, and cave in. It is going to be very difficult for the authorities to be certain exactly how much money we received if we keep them on the outside.'

Late that evening, an official presented himself at the reception desk. The lapels of his uniform were braided, and there was piping down the sides of his trousers, implying that he held a position of some significance. 'Your shift ends at ten o'clock,' he announced. It was a statement of fact rather than a question. Manophet nodded. 'We would like to invite you to call at the Ministry of Affairs at that time,' the man continued. Without waiting for a response, he turned crisply on his heel and headed out into the street. Manophet sat contemplating the seriousness of his position. Invitations to visit the Lao police were not the kind you could decline. While it was possible they wanted nothing more than to establish why the Khmu had come to visit him, his instinct was that they already knew this. Assuming the hotel telephone was bugged, they would by now be aware of the call that he had made to the MIA office. In that eventuality, it was crucial that the statement that they would now require him to make contained nothing that conflicted with what he had told the *falang*. He went back over the phone conversation in his head. If the police caught him lying, they would list him as a troublemaker, and he could be placed under surveillance for the rest of his life. Even if he succeeded in satisfying them that he had acted in good faith, a dossier might already have been opened in his name. His precious anonymity was probably gone forever.

He sat down in the chair indicated by the orderly who showed him in, trying to conceal his nervousness. There was one other chair in the dingy room, a table, on which there was an ashtray, and in one corner a hooked wooden pole for opening and closing the high-set window, which had heavy bars across it. Presently the official who had come to the hotel earlier in the evening strode through the door and seated himself on the opposite side of the table. He had a file in his hand, which he proceeded to consult, holding it at such an angle that the contents were just out of Manophet's view. Slowly he turned the pages, giving away nothing in his expression.

At length he closed it and placed it carefully on the table. 'Thank you for accepting our invitation to come to the Ministry,' he said.

'It is my pleasure,' Manophet replied. 'How can I help you, sir?'

'You have been at the Phu Doi hotel for how long now?'

'For two years.' If the man knew when his shifts ended, he obviously knew the answer to this question already. But there was nothing to be gained from trying to look clever.'

'And before that?'

'Before that, I was a farmer in Muang Khoun. And before that I served in the army.'

'And yet you speak English.'

'I have been learning English, yes.'

The man fixed him with intense eyes. 'Why is that?'

Manophet made a pretence of brushing away an insect. 'There was a bomb disposal consultant staying at the hotel who offered to teach me.'

'I see. But it is still not clear to me why you should want to learn English when there is nobody in Xieng Khouang who understands it.'

Manophet took a couple of deep breaths. 'It was difficult for the cluster bomb clearance team to communicate when they were here. Although they stayed in Phonsavan for many months, their Lao was very limited. I considered it would be rude not to make the effort to speak to them in their language.'

'From what country did the man who taught you come?'

'From Sweden.'

'And yet you chose to learn English from him rather than Swedish.'

Manophet swallowed. 'The team came from various different countries,' he said, 'so they used to speak to one another in English.'

The man seemed satisfied with this explanation. 'You will appreciate, I am sure,' he said, 'that we have a difficult job to do here. The majority of the people in this province are aware of what the Party needs them to do to ensure that the benefits of prosperity are fairly shared, and to guard against the possibility of hostile forces destabilising the country or compromising our interests. However, there are also small numbers of people who are ignorant of the guidance that the Party has issued, and others again who choose to ignore it. Unfortunately, it is not always possible to identify the individuals who fall into the latter two categories without asking questions, and that can sometimes mean inconveniencing ordinary law-abiding citizens.'

'I fully understand, sir,' Manophet said. 'It must be very challenging work.'

'Through no fault of their own, the tribal minorities are often ignorant of their duties as Lao citizens, for example. The necessary information does not always reach them because they are effectively cut off from the rest of society.'

'Yes, I see.'

'You would be in a good position to understand this, since you have trekked to some of the remotest settlements in the province in order to educate the villagers about the dangers posed by unexploded ordnance.'

Manophet's palms were damp with sweat. He had been naïve in imagining he might still be an unknown quantity as far as the police were concerned. Of course he was already a person of interest to the State. He had had dealings with *falang*. He had visited far-flung hill-tribes. They had probably been watching him for months.

The lower half of the man's body was concealed by the table, onto which he was now leaning. Manophet's chair, by contrast, was out in the open, so that every movement he made was visible to his interrogator. He concentrated on trying to remain still, while at the same time giving the impression he was at ease with the questions that were being fired at him. There was no point in stalling. He might as well broach the topic himself. 'The head man from one of those villages came to visit me today,' he volunteered: 'a Khmu village.'

'Is that so?'

'He brought two fellow tribesmen with him. They wanted advice. The villagers had found a war artefact in the forest. They were hoping it might be of some value.'

'Were you able to identify it?'

'From the description I was given, it sounded to me as though it might be a dog-tag.'

'A military identity bracelet? How did you reach this conclusion?'

'I was shown pictures of American dog-tags when I was in the army, so I know what they look like.'

'What advice did you give the head man?'

'They had brought a flier issued by the US MIA office with them.'

'*They* had a flier?' For the first time, the man appeared wrong-footed. 'Surely it was you who provided them with information about the MIA office.'

'Oh no,' Manophet insisted, relieved that he did not need to worry about editing the truth for the moment at least. 'I was aware that such an office existed, of course, but no more than that.'

'But how had they come to be in possession of this flier?'

'They said it had been given to them by an American team that had come to their village a year or two ago as part of a programme to spread word that they were looking for lost pilots.'

'What language was it in?'

'The flier? It was in Lao.'

'And what would be the point of giving a flier printed in Lao to a tribe that speaks Khmu?'

'That is an excellent question, sir,' Manophet replied, 'and one that I have been considering myself. But I suppose this MIA team must have visited many villages belonging to many different ethnic minority tribes, and perhaps they decided it was not worth the effort to try and print fliers in every different language that they might encounter. Particularly when so many of the tribesmen are illiterate.'

The officer drummed his fingers on the table as he pondered. 'You have never had any direct contact with US MIA personnel yourself?'

'A team once came to stay at the Phu Doi, I believe, but that was several years ago – before I started working there.'

'You are telling me you have never had any contact with MIA personnel.'

Manophet took a deep breath. 'Prior to today, none whatsoever.'

'Prior to today,' he repeated in a neutral tone.

A heavy reverberating silence descended over the airless room. 'There was a telephone number at the bottom of the flier,' Manophet said at length, deciding he had no alternative, 'for the MIA office in Vientiane.'

'A telephone number?' The mild surprise in his voice was adroitly feigned.

'The Khmu wanted to speak to them. They asked me if I would make the call because they knew that I spoke English.'

'So you telephoned the MIA office in Vientiane on their behalf.' The man leant back in his chair. 'Do you consider that to have been an appropriate course of action?'

Appropriate was a word with specific connotations when used by the police. Manophet knew he now needed to tread with extreme caution. 'Can you be more specific?' he asked apprehensively.

'It is understandable for Khmu villagers living in remote areas to be ignorant of their duties to the State, as I have already observed,' the man said. 'But it would be surprising for there to be any doubt in the mind of a well-connected man with extensive army experience behind him as to what is expected of him.'

'It seemed to me,' Manophet said carefully, 'that my duty to the State was to make contact with the *falang*. It struck me as suspicious that they should have been circulating fliers to the tribal minorities which made no mention of the Lao government, and I felt it was important to try to establish whether there was a subversive element to their activities. I was also concerned that, if I refused to help the Khmu, they would walk away and find somebody else to act as their intermediary. That could have resulted in them being tricked or cheated, because not all Lao are as fair-minded as they might be when it comes to dealing with the hill-tribe people.'

'And you thought you would be better suited to playing this role than the State authorities?'

Manophet shifted uncomfortably in his chair. 'I felt there was one significant advantage to an ordinary person such as me making the first approach – namely, that it offered a better chance of uncovering any plot that existed. It seemed to me that, if the MIA staff in Vientiane were approached by the Lao authorities, they would be certain to give nothing away. But if they thought they were dealing with an ordinary citizen, somebody interested only in the reward money, they might be lulled into inadvertently revealing any hidden agenda that they might have.'

The man pulled a packet of cigarettes from his pocket. Carefully, he extracted one and lit up. Smoke drifted across the naked bulb hanging from the ceiling. 'What did you discover as a result of your telephone call?' he asked eventually.

'I'm afraid that I may in fact have taken the wrong approach,' Manophet said, adopting an apologetic tone. 'I thought they would be more open if I talked in English, but it is possible that this aroused their suspicions. I would probably have done better to speak in Lao.'

'They did not attempt to undermine your commitment to being a dutiful Lao patriot?'

'No. They were not as forthcoming as I had expected.'

'You were not subjected to any subversive propaganda?'

'No.'

'Inducements?'

'There was nothing specific. There were suggestions that they would make it worth my while if I let them know the number on the identity bracelet. But the Khmu had not given me that information as they did not want it passed on immediately.'

'So you do not have the dog-tag?' The message could not have been clearer. The man was aware that Manophet had seen the bracelet, but was prepared to tolerate this minor deception as long he was straight with him on the larger issues.

Manophet shook his head emphatically. 'The Khmu know they will be in a much weaker negotiating position if they let it out of their sight.' How much of the phone conversation had been translated back into Lao and reported to his interrogator, he wondered? How swiftly were they able to process such information?

The man transferred the file deliberately from one side of the table to the other. Several times, he drew on his cigarette, letting the smoke drift in slow agonising trails from his nostrils. 'Would you say that you are in the habit of assuming the State authorities lack the competence to do their jobs properly?'

'Absolutely not, sir,' Manophet hastened to assure him. 'This is not something I would ordinarily do. I'm afraid I may have made a serious error of judgement.'

'It did not occur to you that the State authorities are themselves capable of testing the soundness or otherwise of organisations such as the MIA by masquerading as villagers who have come into the possession of war relics such as identity tags?'

'No, sir. I regret that I failed to anticipate that possibility. I feel very ashamed of myself.'

'Let me remind you what is at stake here. You are clearly an intelligent man, and I am sure you grasped these arguments many years ago, but allow me to refresh your memory. The first point is that the CIA has an ongoing mission to try to destabilise communist countries such as ours by whatever means it can. We know from experience what can happen if the CIA is allowed to bribe the ethnic minority tribes. Last time it was the Hmong. Who is to say that next time it will not be the Khmu? The second point is that we are a poor country, and it is right that the little wealth that we have should be fairly distributed. If there is a bonanza somewhere, the proceeds should be shared out, not retained in their entirety by the individuals who had the good fortune to be in the right place at the right time. The third point is a political one. Historically, foreign powers such as America have been contemptuous in their dealings with this country, treating it like a counter in a board game or a casino chip. They have entered into solemn undertakings with us at international conventions, only to renege on the promises enshrined in the treaties before the ink is even dry. Americans need to get out of the habit of acting as though the Lao government does not exist, or trying to bribe it if this approach does not yield what they want, and learn to deal with us in the same way that they deal with other sovereign nations.' He stubbed out the cigarette, grinding the butt forcibly into the ashtray. 'Having said this, the Americans, together with the rest of the outside world, can only be expected to take the Lao government seriously if it is clear that it speaks for the Lao people. How are we to convince outsiders this is the case if the Lao people routinely go behind the government's back and deal with the Americans directly?'

They had reached the endgame. Manophet could sense that the man had decided not to take the matter further. As long as he grovelled for long enough, he would be let off with a caution.

Kong Keo's fortunes had taken a miraculous upward lurch. By some inexplicable quirk of fate, he had managed to net a rare butterfly while wandering in the forest, for which a Japanese collector had been prepared to pay an astronomic sum of money. Transformed at a stroke into one of the richest men in the province, he had resigned from his menial position at the Phu Doi, and was busy calculating how to make the most of his windfall. His dream was to build a guest house. Once or twice a week, he would arrive in the lobby to pick through the possibilities and pitfalls with Manophet. Another hotel had recently opened in Phonsavan, the Maly, but there was still nowhere catering for tourists on tight budgets. Was this not a tailor-made opportunity for a fledgling entrepreneur? The government had begun to mention tourism in official communiqués, which implied that any application to start a tourist-related business would be approved without a fuss. Suddenly *falang* were welcome again, for the simple reason that they brought money in to the country. On the other hand, there were plenty of thorny issues with which to wrestle. Why should any right-minded foreign tourist *wish* to visit Phonsavan? What could induce them to make this desolate frontier town their destination in preference to the Taj Mahal or the Great Pyramids of Egypt? And how would they find out that there was a competitively priced guest house in town where they could stay? The first clue came when a *falang* walked in off the street and enquired what time the Phu Doi's disco opened. How on earth had he managed to find out about the disco, Manophet wondered, given that it was never advertised? The man obligingly fished out a weather-beaten volume from his rucksack and showed him the paragraph where it was mentioned.

The book's title, *Lonely Planet – Southeast Asia on a Shoestring* was a conundrum. Why was the planet lonely? What did shoestrings have to do with anything? And yet he and Kong Keo shared an instinct that it could be an important resource. Kong Keo sourced a copy through a connection of his father's, and he and Manophet worked their way through it. Although it contained numerous terms and allusions that they could not understand, Manophet's English was now good enough to allow him to grasp the publication's *raison d'être*. The brief chapter on Laos described it as primitive and backward: the telephones did not work; the mail service was unreliable. Perplexingly, however, the editors appeared to believe that their readers would find these defects attractive, even endearing. By studying the tiny print, intrepid souls could discover how to reach Phonsavan, the provincial capital of Xieng Khouang, where they could sample the delights of the Phu Doi hotel's diabolical disco. The more he read, the more convinced Manophet became that the sort of westerners at whom the book was targeted were not in search of convenience or luxury. They were explorers with hankerings to tread unpredictable paths that had not already been beaten flat by a million other tourists before them. Why a person who could afford a comfortable living should be filled with such desires was not explained. It seemed to be assumed that readers would already know the answer to this question. Whatever the rationale, the guidebook would surely not have reached its ninth edition unless there was a genuine and continuing demand for the information that it contained. Because its borders had been closed, Laos had not been mentioned in the previous eight editions, but here it was, rubbing shoulders with Hong Kong, Malaysia and Thailand, no longer an international pariah.

For a few days, Kong Keo talked as though success was assured. He started assessing potential sites for his grand enterprise, spent long alcohol-fuelled evenings trying to decide what to call it, obtained quotations from building materials contractors. Then, without warning, he called the whole project off and slumped into a depression. 'We cannot get round the fact that there is nothing for tourists to do in Phonsavan,' he said disconsolately. 'If you look at the other destinations that they describe – even the ones nobody has ever heard of – there are activities or places of historical interest or local beauty spots for them to visit: waterfalls, stupas, elephant trekking to see animals in the jungle.'

Manophet opened the book at the well-thumbed page. 'Tham Piu gets a mention,' he said, shaking his head slowly. It was their insensitivity that made westerners so difficult to relate to. To *falang*, there was apparently nothing untoward about slaughtering a few hundred villagers in a missile strike, and then jetting in, paying an admission fee to visit the cave where the massacre had taken place, and taking photographs of themselves, surrounded by the bones of their victims.

'Tham Piu is too far away. It must be fifty miles there and back.'

'The hotel has guests who go there. They travel in jeeps.'

'But low-budget tourists are not going to be able to *afford* to hire a jeep,' Kong Keo pointed out gloomily.

Why was it beyond westerners to grasp how unsavoury their attitudes were, Manophet wondered? Why did they not seem to be bothered by the damage that their "Me! Now!" ideologies had done to other countries, future generations and the planet as a whole? Generation after generation, the happy powerful few made rich by capitalism had taken it upon themselves to declare it a universal panacea that must be rolled out across the rest of the globe regardless of any collateral damage that might result. Western logic trumped all other types of logic. Christianity was the only valid religion. Anybody who disagreed was either an idiot or a terrorist. Time and again they had poured money and military might into initiatives designed to impose *falang* culture and values on societies that did not share or want them – even though it could not be clearer from the history books that such exercises were self-defeating. If they would only step back and contemplate the results of their meddling over the decades. There was such an obvious lesson to be learned. And yet Manophet knew from personal experience that there also existed magnificent westerners such as Bo, who were determined to redress the wrongs done during the course of these imperialistic rampages despite being native to countries that had played no part in perpetrating them. How could he reconcile these conflicting perspectives? Was it possible that the tyrannical *falang* who caused all the trouble were simply brainwashed? Could they be under a passionate yet calamitous misapprehension that they were fighting evil rather than dancing to its tune?

'What about the jars?' he suggested to Kong Keo. 'There was an Italian staying last week who wanted to see them.'

'As a visitor attraction?' Kong Keo scratched his head dubiously. 'How would you stop tourists wandering off and treading on a bombie?'

'We could try and find out if there are any areas the *falang* have already made completely safe. The UNESCO team from New Zealand that stayed at the Phu Doi last year is coming back next month to clear another section at Site Two. Perhaps they would tell me if I asked them.'

Kong Keo's Guest House was suddenly a going concern again. If a picturesque waterfall was enough to attract tourists to an unknown destination, surely a plain littered with prehistoric stone jars, the likes of which were to be found nowhere else in the world, would pique their curiosity. Crucially, several of the principal jars sites were within easy reach of Phonsavan. Manophet and Kong Keo cycled out to an area rumoured to be ordnance-free following the UNESCO team's earlier visit, and surveyed the unlikely panorama. Barrel-shaped megalithic urns strewed the hillside, massive overturned structures leaning at obtuse angles, all with perfect circular openings at one end. Being too heavy for pilferers to carry away, they remained embedded in the positions in which they had been deposited two thousand years earlier. To Manophet's eyes, the spectacle had nothing of the haunting magic of the ruined Buddha at Muang Khoun, but perhaps they could devise a few stories to enhance its mystique. He climbed inside one of the largest jars and squatted down so that he could no longer be seen. There was no smell, no aura. How had the stonemasons fashioned them? How had they brought them here? What were they for?

'The thing is,' Kong Keo said, 'I cannot do this by myself. I will need a partner to take charge of the guest house when I am not there – somebody to attend to any guests who arrive or want helping out.'

'It would be useful to have a driver who could transport them to and from the airport or the jars,' Manophet reflected.

'It needs more than that. It is essential that this person is a fluent English speaker. The guests will all be *falang*. They will be unable to make themselves understood if they cannot speak in English.' He shifted uncomfortably from one foot to the other. 'Not many people have the necessary skills,' he finished hesitantly.

It had been apparent to Manophet for many weeks that the venture would require an arrangement of this kind if it was to succeed. And yet it came as a shock to learn that the moment of decision was already at hand. Construction work on the guest house had not even started, but he realised now that this was because Kong Keo needed to be sure he could count on his support before giving the builders the green light. Manophet's job at the Phu Doi was leading him nowhere. It had been losing customers to the Maly and the Auberge for months, and could no longer count on securing the patronage of every VIP who passed through town – and yet no measures were being taken to halt the slide in its popularity. Leaving to become Kong Keo's business partner would be a risky career move. The enterprise could easily fall flat on its face. But his hours would be shorter, and there was a chance of receiving a worthwhile salary if the guest house took off. Besides, it would be an adventure. Every day would be an opportunity to spend time with *falang* and discover more about their strange habits and thought patterns. There was no telling whether he would be inspired or disillusioned by being so much in their company, but one thing was certain: it would not be dull. Things always happened when there were *falang* around.

# TEN

Now that he had a bicycle – a battered specimen procured with Kong Keo's help – he could cover the distance from Phonsavan to Muang Khoun in less than two hours. He grew into the habit of paying his parents regular visits, something that had not been possible when he was in the army, and an amiable Sunday afternoon routine developed. They could not see where his life of drudgery at the Phu Doi was leading him, but on the whole they refrained from labouring the point, and it seemed prudent to keep the news that he had decided to throw in his lot with Kong Keo to himself until the last possible moment, since there was every prospect that they would only view it as another step in the wrong direction. A second reason for wanting to avoid a scene was that he was privately concerned about their wellbeing. An erratic streak had entered their behaviour. Pauses interrupted statements that should have been automatic. Abrupt changes of topic threw conversations off in incomprehensible directions. He would pose a question, and receive a reply that bore no relation to what he had asked. Kone seemed to be in on the secret, but relations with his sister were delicate as a result of the tensions that had sprung up between him and her husband during his time as a rice farmer, and he was reluctant to seek her counsel. Arriving at the house one Sunday, he was taken aback to hear the sound of raised voices from within. Just as he reached the door, it burst open and his father came marching out wearing a look of undisguised irritation. 'I am not listening to this nonsense again,' he thundered over his shoulder. 'I have better things to do with my time.' Pausing only to acknowledge Manophet's arrival with a cursory wave, he stormed off towards the orchard. Manophet was even more surprised to find most of the rest of the family already gathered in the main room. Six of his siblings were present, including his eldest sister, Boun, who he had not seen since his ill-fated trip to Phon Hong. What was *she* doing here? His mother had an arm around her. 'Do not worry about your father,' she said. 'He will sort himself out. It is time for the others to hear your story.'

Boun had been on the brink of rising to her feet, but thought better of it. With regular customers, it made no odds how quickly she stood up. They would return to her stall week after week because her prices were reasonable, and they knew they would get a fair deal. But tactics could be important when it came to dealing with strangers. Some would turn and walk away if you moved too suddenly. They liked to be given time to pick things up and inspect them, feign interest in pieces of merchandise they had no intention of buying, with the idea of confusing you about which items they were considering seriously. In their heads, meanwhile, they would be calculating how much they could afford to spend, how dismissive to appear when a price was first suggested. And then there were others, usually women, who preferred you to engage them straightaway, people who wanted to talk about everything under the sun before getting down to business. They were not here to hunt down the keenest bargain. They would deal with whomsoever made them feel welcome. What did it matter, whether the same goods could be bought for a few kip less at a stall across the street? Everybody buying and selling knew the going rates; the difference would be nominal – that was how they saw it. The longer the young man dallied at her stall, the more she suspected he had no real interest in the wooden bowls over which he was poring. It was *her* that he was surreptitiously eying up. Cheeky fellow. He looked about twenty-two. She made an elaborate show of playing with her wedding ring.

The day dragged on. Trade was slack – not that that was unusual. She rearranged her wares periodically to keep herself occupied. Half the stall was exposed to the sun, which burned down with its accustomed ferocity. Housewares occupied the sunny side, leaving the shaded half for the clothing and the limes. It was not the most cohesive selection of goods, but in this part of the world you sold what you could. Any chance to make an extra ten kip was worth taking. She had bought the limes that morning as a job-lot from one of the other stallholders who had too many to sell on her own. Desultory passers-by were picking them off in ones and twos, and she was quietly hopeful of being able to turn a profit by the end of the day. In the meantime, they were doing a splendid job of brightening up the display. The sun crawled across the sky. It would be so much better if she could have the stall next to her friend Soupaphone on the other side of the market. Then they would be able to chat whenever neither of them had customers to serve. But those stalls were highly sought after as they were near the entrance to the marketplace, where trade was brisker, and the quality of her merchandise did not really justify the extra cost.

Late in the afternoon, a group of Hmong appeared. Having nothing better to do, she kept half an eye on them. They seemed to be stopping at every stall in the marketplace but making no purchases. Some of the other stallholders looked uneasy. Could they be government inspectors? She checked her pocket to make sure she had her Permit. Yes, here it was. There was nothing to be concerned about. When they finally reached her stall she could see immediately that they were not local. One was flourishing a packet of cigarettes covered with slogans in a foreign language. Another was wearing an outrageous pair of reflecting sunglasses. It was Hmong New Year in a couple of days. Most likely, they had come to their ancestral home to enjoy the celebrations. The man in front reached into a bag and pulled out a photograph. 'Excuse me,' he said, in passable Lao, 'I'm sorry to trouble you, but I wonder if you might recognize this person?'

Her family possessed a couple of photographs, but nothing as vibrant or as glossy as this. She was afraid to take it from him in case her fingers made a smudge. Deftly intercepting a couple of limes that had started rolling towards the edge of the stall, she gave it the briefest of glances. 'No, I'm sorry,' she said, 'I don't think I've seen him before.'

'Actually, it's more complicated,' the man said. 'It's more a question of whether you might know anybody who looks like him. Here, please, take it – we have copies.'

She took it gingerly in both hands. The words "Main Lee" were scrawled in ink on the reverse. 'I don't understand,' she said. 'He looks Lao.'

'He *is* Lao.'

'But Main Lee is a Hmong name.'

'It is a complicated story,' the man said.

Boun was having difficulty taking her eyes off the photograph.

'He was born on the Plain of Jars,' the man said. 'But he became separated from the rest of his family during a bombing raid.'

'What year was this?'

The Hmong argued amongst themselves. 'He was too young to remember exactly,' they said eventually. 'Maybe 1969.'

'Why is he called Main Lee if he is Lao?'

'A Hmong soldier rescued him from the battlefield and he and his wife looked after him while he was recovering. It was them who gave him that name. Eventually he emigrated to America, and that was where we met him. We live in America now.'

'So he is a war orphan?'

'Nobody knew who his real parents were,' the man said, 'or what might have happened to them. They might have perished. They might still be alive.'

'Did he never try and find out?'

'He wasn't told that his Hmong parents were not his real parents until just before he left Laos, and by then it was too late to do anything about it. Besides, he had no real idea whereabouts on the Plain his real parents had lived or what they were called. There was nothing that he *could* have done.'

Her antennae were quivering with suspicion. Why should Hmong from America be spinning such a fantastic yarn?

'Do you think you might recognise him?'

'It's just that –'

'Does he look like somebody you know?'

He had been twelve the last time she had seen him. Twenty-five years had gone by since that terrible day. And yet Manophet had hair like his, and Sing had almost identical facial features. 'I don't know,' she said. 'I suppose –'

Excitement rippled through the group. They pressed in closer, creating a feverish crush around her stall. 'He could be a nephew,' one of them suggested. 'Did you have a nephew who went missing? Or a cousin?'

Boun began to feel intimidated. This was stupid. She should have kept her mouth shut. Now they would go back to America and raise the unfortunate man's hopes. 'All my cousins and nephews are accounted for,' she said. 'We are not looking for anybody. How old is this person anyway?'

A few seconds went by while they conferred. 'I don't think he really knows,' one of them answered. 'A lot of Hmong don't celebrate birthdays over here, apparently.'

'But isn't his date of birth on the licence on the notice board back home,' one of the others interrupted, 'outside the hall?1964, I think it says.'

117

She tried to hide her disappointment. He needed to be much older than that. But perhaps it was better not to be left with the uncertainty. 'In that case, I don't think he can be anything to do with our family,' she said.

'Why not take the photo anyway,' said the man who had done most of the talking. 'Perhaps one of your friends will be able to work out who he is. His address is written on the back. You could always write to him and see what he has to say.'

She hid the photograph. She did not want her children stumbling on it accidentally and asking awkward questions. What was she to do? There must be hundreds, if not thousands, of orphaned Lao casting about for lost kin. It could not be right to open a dialogue with one of them when there was so little prospect that it would end happily. She had told the truth: they were not looking for anybody. Besides, the story did not ring true. The Hmong had been their enemies during the war. Why should they have taken pity on a Lao child at that terrible time? And then there was the question of why these émigrés should be handing out photographs in Phon Hong, a little town situated miles from the Plain of Jars. The chances that a member of Main Lee's family was living *here* must be ridiculously small. On the other hand, what if destiny had taken some incomprehensible swerve, and Bua, by some miraculous chance, had survived his accident? Even if it *was* only a tiny chance, was it not at least worth investigating? And, while there was always a risk that she would get into trouble with the authorities for communicating with an American, there was a reasonable hope that her letter might evade their prying eyes if she used a PO Box address, as Main Lee had.

Six months went by. She wrote the letter a hundred times in her head. In the end it was very simple:

*Dear Mr Lee,*
*I was given your photograph by some Hmong who were visiting Phon Hong. I think it is unlikely that I will be able to help you find your family, but I wonder if you could tell me about yourself in case there is a clue that I could follow up.*
*Yours sincerely,*
*Boun (née Athakhanh)*

She tried not to brood on the possible outcomes while she waited for an answer. As the weeks went by, she began to wonder if the letter had even reached him. Perhaps the famously erratic Lao postal service had allowed it to blow away into the forest or delivered it to the wrong country. But at length a blue air-mail envelope plopped onto the floor of her Post Office box.

*Hello Boun,*

*I was astonished to receive your letter. Thank you so much for taking the trouble to write to me. Some of my dance students talked me into letting them take that photograph to Laos as they were going back to celebrate Hmong New Year, and they thought it might be worth showing it around. I never dreamed it would lead to anything.*

*Main Lee was the name that was given to me by the Hmong who rescued me from the battlefield. I must have had a Lao name before that, but I don't know what it was. I have no memory of my early childhood.*

*I was found in a cave not far from the old capital. My family had probably given up hope that I could survive a serious shrapnel wound in my back and left me for dead. (I say this because, as well as a big hole in my back, I have a scar on my right ear lobe. People tell me that, back then, the way to find out whether somebody close to death would recover was to slash their ear lobe and see if any blood flowed out.) But somehow I survived. A soldier found me and he and his wife nursed me back to health over the next three or four months. After that, they...*

The letter dropped from her hand and fluttered to the floor. It had not occurred to her that there might be physical evidence by which to identify him. Surely this could not be a coincidence. So many years had gone by since the family had lamented his passing. Could they have been mourning an empty grave all this time? And yet the authorities were forever warning of the dangers posed by sinister plots of this kind. Nobody in their right mind would take such a letter at face value. How could you trust a man who claimed he could remember nothing about his childhood? Besides, any number of wounded Lao had probably been abandoned on the Plain of Jars as their families fled from the bombers. It was exactly the sort of story a spy would concoct. The photograph could easily be a fake. In actuality, Main Lee was probably as Hmong as his name implied, a dissident loyal to Vang Pao who wanted to re-enter the country on a bogus pretext. And yet she so wanted the story to be true. How could she prove or disprove it? What questions could she put to him?

A drawn-out correspondence ensued. It was not uncommon for a letter to take as long as three months to negotiate its tortuous passage to or from America. Fresh photographs arrived, descriptions of the life that Main Lee now led, stories about the community in which he had grown up before leaving Laos. An aching loneliness pervaded his writing. He was a man who had lost not merely one set of parents but two, his adoptive parents

119

having passed away many years since. He now had not a solitary relative to his name. Through circumstances beyond his control, he had wound up in a big city thousands of miles from where he belonged, where people worked in skyscrapers and snow froze your feet into your boots if you went out of doors. He was part Lao, part Hmong, part American, a man with no proper sense of identity. Her heart was passionately convinced that this was her lost brother. But her head was equally certain she was being manipulated. It was nothing more than an elaborate hoax, a web of lies spun with the intention of inveigling her into pitying him. There were many questions that she was reluctant to ask for fear of forfeiting his confidence. Why had he left Laos? What had he been afraid of? Had he committed some dastardly act? Was he sure he had not been older than five when he was adopted? And why was he consorting with Hmong now that he was in America if they were not related to his adoptive parents? The idea of telling her mother and father that their son might still be alive filled her with dread. To put them through the trauma of re-opening a place for him in their hearts, only to discover subsequently that it had all been for nothing, was too awful to contemplate. But what else could she do?

After three years, she decided she could keep the secret from them no longer, and made the long journey to Muang Khoun. It turned swiftly into the bitterest of homecomings. Her father received the news with undisguised scorn. 'I am ashamed of you,' he said quietly, pushing back his chair before she had even finished narrating. 'I cannot believe that a child of mine could be taken in by such a crude trick. How many times have I warned you not to be deceived by appearances?' Turning his back, he trudged off towards the room where he and his wife slept.

'Oh, Father, please –' Boun had never felt so small. It was like being seven years old again, in disgrace for frightening the carp away when he was fishing, or spilling sticky rice into his shoes. 'I have a picture. You could at least take a look at it.' She rummaged in her bag for the largest of the photographs and laid it timidly on the table.

'I am not interested in your picture,' he growled, without breaking step. 'I am too old to be bothered with this kind of infantile rubbish. I am going to bed.'

'And there are letters,' she called after him, desperate to retrieve the situation. 'You might be able to recognise his handwriting.' It was to no avail. The door to the bedroom had closed. Fighting back her tears, she clambered to her feet with the idea of following, then slumped back down, realising it was hopeless.

Her mother had picked up the photograph. Without speaking, she studied the thoughtful intelligent face, the small ears, the long articulate fingers.

Boun's heart started pounding. 'Mother?' she whispered.

Her mother tilted the photograph so that the light came off it at a different angle. She covered the chin with one of her hands, then the forehead.

'Do you think it might be –?'

'That is my son,' her mother exclaimed. Tears were pouring down her cheeks. 'That is Bua – I am sure it is.'

It was as though an enormous cloud was starting to lift. The state of irresolution that had settled over Boun on the day the Hmong had accosted her in the market and dominated her life ever since finally seemed to be clearing away.

Her mother mopped her face on her sleeve. Then, blowing her nose defiantly, she rose unsteadily from the table and made her way to the door that her husband had just closed. 'You can hide in there like an old woman or pretend to fall asleep if that's what you want to do,' she shouted through it. 'But tell me one thing first. Which of Bua's ear lobes did you cut? The left one or the right one?'

Now, a few weeks later, it was the turn of the rest of the family to hear Boun's tale. 'Main Lee is talking about coming to Laos,' she said when she had finished. 'He believes the government will let him back into the country now it is opening up to foreigners. That means we have to decide what to do – as a family.'

Nobody spoke. The idea that their lost brother might have been making his own lonely way through the world all these years was too difficult to grasp.

Manophet's mother put a hand on his arm. 'You always said you were sure he was still alive.' The two of them smiled. She had remembered his childhood instinct.

'They almost killed him with their bombs, and now he is living there,' Lar mused, slowly shaking his head.

'But Father is right to be cautious, of course,' Manophet said. 'When I was in the army, the Russians warned us about situations of this kind. He could be an imposter. It would be the perfect cover story if you wanted to enter the country with a false identity and stir up trouble.'

'You must understand that this is very difficult for your father,' his mother said. 'He cannot accept that a Hmong soldier – one of the men he was fighting against – saved his son from dying and then looked after him until he had made a full recovery.'

'How is Main Lee going to get here?' Manophet asked.

'He says he can fly to Bangkok and get a connection to –'

'Yes, but who is going to pay for the ticket?'

'He has a job that pays him many kip each month, at a hospital. He can afford to pay for the ticket himself.'

'He is a doctor?' Thong queried. 'Like Jun?'

'No. But he has some specialist medical knowledge and speaks many languages, so he is an important link between the doctors and their patients,' Boun explained. 'It is a big hospital. They see hundreds of patients every day, and not all of them speak good English. These are the sorts of thing I have been able to learn from his letters. But I have been writing letters for three years now, and I still cannot be certain whether or not it is Bua. I think it is time to find out the truth, and there is only one way to do that. I believe we should agree to meet him.'

Manophet had lost count of the number of times he had driven out to Phonsavan airport to meet the Vientiane flight. Day after day, he had stood here in the arrivals hall, grinning like a cat in the hope of making a good impression on an arriving passenger, the Phu Doi's garish purple sign thrust high above his head. But this morning it was as though he was seeing the worn wood-slat benches and the faded posters on the walls for the first time. Even the hills beyond the end of the runway seemed unfamiliar, the weak sunshine struggling ineffectively to clear a blanket of stifling shadow from their broad slopes. The uncertainty of his position was intolerable. Within the next few moments, he was to experience either the most uplifting event of his life, or possibly the greatest disappointment. Other members of the family stood close by, gazing intently at the plane, which was parked about a hundred yards away. Passengers were dribbling out from the rear door in ones and twos. Down the steps they came, and onto the tarmac. There could not be many left inside now. For the first few yards of their short walk to the arrivals hall, they could be seen through the glass, still quite small, but after that they disappeared behind a pillar. There was no sign of his mother. She had travelled to Vientiane two days earlier to join up with Sing, Boun and Jun and meet the traveller off the flight from Bangkok. If he had managed to satisfy them that he was who he claimed, she would be bringing him back with her to Xieng Khouang this morning.

Two of Manophet's young cousins were dancing excitedly up and down beside the baggage dump, convinced that a happy outcome was inevitable. Neung transferred his weight silently from one foot to foot to the other, and motioned to them to calm down. Manophet watched the baggage handler manoeuvre the last suitcases out of the hold and onto the truck below. Why was this taking so long? Perhaps his mother had sent his brother on ahead to introduce himself to the family under his own steam. Was it conceivable that he was already here in the arrivals hall? Carefully though Manophet had studied the pictures that he had been shown, there was a nagging doubt in his mind. People liked to display themselves in the best possible light when they had photographs taken. After a long flight and an emotional reunion, his brother might appear very different in the flesh – exhausted, confused, exhilarated. He held the sign as high as possible, a lovingly crafted placard bearing the words "MAIN LEE" in black stencilled letters, scanning every passing face, looking for the slightest flicker of disorientation. None of the passengers filing by bore any resemblance to the man in the photo. He shifted his gaze back to the plane. The trickle of disembarking passengers had all but dried up.

Another possibility now occurred to him. Might the authorities have ordered his brother to remain in Vientiane so they could keep him under surveillance during his visit? And yet what purpose would confining him to the capital serve? It would surely be much easier for them to keep tabs on him up here in Xieng Khouang. The baggage truck shuddered into life and began trundling towards the arrivals hall. Lar's shoulders slumped. 'It wasn't him,' he whispered. 'They have sent him back to America.' Like dumb animals, they continued staring towards the dark opening at the rear of the aircraft, not willing to accept the evidence of their eyes, as though hoping that, by an act of collective willpower, they might be able to suck out another two passengers. More seconds ticked by. A stewardess appeared and placed her hands on the big door, as though preparing to close it. But then, at last, a dim figure became visible in the shadows behind her, a man. Slowly, he advanced into the daylight, seemingly stunned by the scene that greeted him, and stood motionless at the top of the steps, framed in the doorway, taking in the sweep of tranquil land, the grassy hills, the bomb craters. A moment or two later, a second figure had appeared beside him: his mother.

Manophet dropped the placard and started running towards the arrivals gate, dancing around the disorderly clusters of people waiting near the baggage collection counter, seized by an uncontrollable impulse to be the first member of the family to welcome him. The duty soldier made a half-hearted attempt to block his path, but Manophet was easily able to evade his sluggish lunge and burst through the outer doors into the open. The stranger saw him racing across the tarmac and broke into a run. 'Are you my brother?' he cried in a hoarse whisper. 'Are you my little brother?' Flinging their arms clumsily around one another, they fell into a bear hug, beyond words, beyond coherence, swaying like drunkards on the spot where they had collided.

Manophet had talked the hotel into allowing him to borrow the van for the occasion. It was early evening by the time they pulled up at the family home.
'Where are you, Moui?' his mother called. 'Did you not hear us arrive?'

The house was silent. She poked her head behind a couple of screens, then came to a standstill in front of a closed door. 'Your son is here,' she announced, putting her mouth close to the wood. 'He has flown eight and a half thousand miles to see you.'

There was a grunt from within.

'Well?'

'Is he for real?'

'It is as we never dared to hope,' she said. 'This is our lost son, Bua. We have seen the wound in his back and the cut on his ear. Come out and greet him.'

'I am tired,' the disembodied voice returned testily, 'and it is late. I am going to sleep.' There was a sound of a chair scraping along the floor. 'If he is for real, no doubt he will still be here in the morning.'

The door flew open, and Manophet's uncle stumbled in, his hair wild, his face written over with fear. 'It has started.' He panted for breath. 'We have to go.' Mother tore the burlap bag out from its place behind the wood basket. She knew what she had to do. She had been over it in her mind a hundred times. In went the silver ear-rings and bangles, the wrist-watch, the carved ivory, the *baci* thread, her lightest wok, rice, the chinese celery left over from the previous evening, the little wooden casket in which she kept her herbal remedies. In went the spare clothes. She had been storing them in bundles so they would be easy to scoop up at a moment's notice. So soon! They had hoped there might be days, even weeks left. Father raced out of the house. Where had he left the hunting knife? People were hurrying along the dirt road at the top of the bank dragging shapeless sacks, petrified children, the odd pig or goat. Above the hubbub he could just make out a low far-off whisper of aircraft. He doubled back into the house. '*Go*,' he shouted at his wife. 'Go *now*. They are coming already. Take the little ones. We will catch you up. Sing, come with me. And you too, Bua. We must find a couple of chickens. You round them up, and I will wring their necks. And get a sack to put them in. *Quickly*.' Mother dragged Jun out from under a length of coconut matting where she was pretending to be an anteater, ignoring her protestations. For two or three long seconds, she lingered on the threshold, breathing in the familiar smells. She had been born in this house, and in her turn she had borne seven children between its walls. All their lives, it had been their home. Shaking silently, she reached down and stroked the cat between its moth-eaten ears. Then, pushing the girls out of the door, she heaved Manophet onto her back and set off towards the dirt road.

'Aeroplanes!' one of the children screamed.

The shambling villagers broke once more into a laboured run, exhausted muscles somehow finding fresh energy. Lungs heaved. Hearts pounded. Legs pumped valiantly up and down. Grandmother hobbled along sideways with the aid of a gnarled stick, bent over like a crazed jungle creature, her face ashen. Mother focussed her attention on keeping the burdens on her back in balance as she moved. It was no good forcing the pace. Whenever she took too big a stride, the baby slammed into her spine, banging his face and hurting her knees as the weight lurched forwards. It was better to take small rhythmic steps, keeping her feet as close to the ground as possible. Glancing behind him, Father saw four tiny shapes separating out of the haze. At first, they hung at the horizon as though suspended on strings, noiseless ghosts. But soon their faint terrifying hiss became audible. A moment later, the specks had swelled to the size of locusts. Another moment, and they were as big as birds. The sky began to tremble with a harsh rasping din. It was all happening too fast. There had not even been time to dig new bolt-holes. 'Spirits of our ancestors,' he muttered. 'We are sitting ducks.' The aircraft powered towards them, their engines grinding out a shrieking roar. Larger and larger they loomed, hurtling in at impossible speed. Shedding their bundles, the villagers flattened themselves against the ground as the four gleaming thunder-clouds, each as vast as a metal house, screamed over their heads, shutting out the sun, disgorging heavy teetering cylinders from their bellies as they passed. Sing plunged off the dirt road onto the verge, clapping his hands tightly over his ears. '*Bombs,*' he shouted inaudibly against the shrill sinking whistle.

Time stood still. Then a series of monstrous thudding explosions rocked the earth. Mother braced herself for the impact of the shock waves as the ground trembled. Moments later a violent hurricane surge punched the breath out of her, flipping her sideways even as she lay on the ground, smashing into her ear-drums. Sand hailed down, stinging her eyes, followed by little stones, small rocks, chunks of landscape. The remains of a fence hurtled out of the sky and buried itself in the scrub grass a few yards away. A child came cartwheeling past, the muffled thud of its head hitting a tree stump faintly distinguishable above the abominable racket of the departing aircraft. The villagers lay where they had dropped, strewn across the dirt, uncomprehending, too weak to move. An unearthly sound was coming from Mother's back, a thin high wail that sounded at first like a tiny kitten's mew but soon grew more intense, more certain, more chilling. Groggily, she tried to work her arm through the sling so she could slide him round in front of her. It smelled as though he had been sick down her back. His distress set off the rest of the children. Hysterical crying erupted up and down the path. The baby in her good arm, she crawled towards her two youngest daughters. Kone lay slouched on the ground, her head buried in her lap, her hands still covering her ears. Jun, very small, was in the process of trying to stand up, her arms held out to either side as though somebody had just thrown a bucket of water over her.

The sound of collapsing timber could be heard in the distance. From the far side of the contour, a dense cloud of swirling black smoke billowed up. The air carried an evil stench. Something living was on fire. Sporadic pulses of energy coughed up bursts of smoke that swirled viciously above the hidden blaze until the sky was dark with ash. A myna burst out of the smog cloud, flying no more than a yard or two off the ground, and careered into the hillside, where it lay flapping like a fish washed ashore. Tears were now pouring down Jun's cheeks, carving streaks through the red earth caking her face, as she stood on wobbly legs howling at the injustice. Mother's mouth and throat were clogged with dirt. Her ears were still ringing. She made a weak attempt to brush the debris out of Jun's hair, then staggered to her feet and lurched a few paces towards Kone, only to fall down again, unable to keep her balance. And now she noticed the pain at the back of her head. Putting up a hand, she found blood running from a wound. Something had struck her, a small rock perhaps. On the other side of the ruined town, Father was lifting his face from a shallow depression in the dirt. Through the dust and smoke he could just make out the line of the path. Two deep jagged flame-breathing craters had appeared, and there were fires gobbling up the crops in the fields to either side. An uncanny stillness had finally settled over the wreckage. Bodies lay motionless. He looked about frantically for his children. Here was Sing signalling that he was unhurt. There was Neung. And Boun was beside him. But where had Bua got to?

Laboriously, he transferred his weight onto one arm and tugged his sleeping mat flat with the other, seeking to find a less uncomfortable position. Every ache, every sore that had ever afflicted him seemed to be baring its teeth tonight. His body had absorbed more than its fair share of hardship over the years, and it was wearing out. How much longer did he have? Two years? Three years? Could the fates not have left him to finish his life in peace? Surely he had earned the right to be spared this final indignity. There was no longer any room for doubt. His wife would not have brought the wanderer home with her unless she had been certain of her ground. It must be true. His son, Bua had returned from the grave. He should be ecstatic. What happier news could a father wish to receive? But it was not so straightforward when you were the one who had buried him – that was what the rest of them did not understand. Bua had been too heavy to carry, too badly injured to keep moving from shelter to shelter. If the others were to have any hope of outrunning the bombers, he had to be left behind. This was the choice that Father had faced on the battlefield. It had been his decision to abandon the boy in the cave. He had been the one who had signed his death warrant. And now the ghost of his dead son had returned to confront him.

Other relatives began arriving early the following morning. The shrill voices of excitable children penetrated to the remotest corners of the house, rousing the weary householders, most of whom had stayed up half the night talking. Main Lee did his best to get the names of each family group straight before the next one appeared, but it was a daunting task. For so long, he had been alone in the world, a parentless orphan without a relative to his name. Now, at a stroke, he had acquired two parents, nine siblings, and aunts, uncles, nephews, nieces and cousins too numerous to count. It was all too much to take in. And yet the person he most badly wanted to see, his father, was still holed up in his room. Why was he refusing to give him his blessing? Main Lee knew that he would never be able to embrace his alter ego, Bua unless his father was also prepared to accept him as his son. Was there some vital scrap of knowledge that he had withheld from the rest of the family, a piece of information that allowed him to be certain Bua had *not* survived his accident all those years ago? It was essential for Main Lee to hear his father's side of the story – even if this resulted in him having to return to America in the same orphaned state in which he had arrived.

'Father,' he called through the closed door, 'I'm here if you feel like talking. It would mean a lot to me to see you.'

For a moment or two, there was silence. Then, slowly, the door swung open, and he saw a stooping grey-haired septuagenarian not much taller than his mother. The old soldier, the strict disciplinarian accustomed to being obeyed by his children was today as vulnerable as a new-born calf. Tentatively, he smiled, and it seemed to Main Lee that he had never before seen a more beautiful expression.

'Why are you crying?' one of the innumerable nephews objected. 'You are supposed to be happy to see each other again, not sad.'

'This is gladness-crying,' Main Lee tried to explain, wiping tears ineffectively from his cheeks.

The four year-old scurried off, evidently not satisfied with the answer. 'Auntie Kone,' they heard an indignant voice complaining from the cooking area, 'Grandfather is crying like a baby.'

'Look, I have something for you.' Main Lee said, pulling out the sleeveless jersey that he had brought as a present. 'I hope it fits. I wasn't sure what colour you would like.'

His father held the primrose-yellow garment up against himself, turning it back and forth, clearly touched. 'I have never possessed such a precious piece of clothing,' he said. 'It is beautiful. But, my son, let me give you one piece of advice so that you know next time you visit. It can get very cold here. It was not a good idea to cut the sleeves off.'

# ELEVEN

His earliest reliable memory was of the cave in which he had been nursed back to health. It was not a clear picture, more a confusion of interleaving sensations – pain from the wound in his back, the roaring screams of prowling aircraft, thudding explosions that sent shivers through the rock on which he lay, musty air that never seemed to satisfy his lungs however deeply he inhaled. A shimmering image of the golden arc that would form around the lip of the cave opening at daybreak danced from time to time across the outskirts of his mind, dreamlike, half-believable. Sometimes he thought he remembered a silent woman sponging sweat from his body, but it was difficult to be sure where memory gave way to hallucination. He had been delirious for much of his early convalescence, dipping in and out of nightmares. Often the scene was a battleground. He would be picking his way into the thick of the action instead of running away, searching for other survivors. All around, bombs would be crashing into the forest and detonating with terrible violence, hurling rocks and branches into the air, sending him flying into ditches or craters. Each time, he would haul himself up and hobble on, desperate to catch up with the stream of fleeing refugees, but in the end his luck would always run out. A hail of shrapnel would strike him, and he would fall to the ground screaming. But amidst the nightmares there was also one recurrent dream in which there were no bombers or burning houses. A woman was trying to teach him to sew, a wise gentle woman with loving eyes, surrounded by a troupe of other boys and girls.

Three or four months passed before he was well enough to leave the cave. Other patients came and went without explanation. Each time he felt strong enough to take an interest in what was going on around him, the casualties occupying the spaces to either side of his sleeping mat seemed to have changed. The girl without an arm had become a man with a face wound round with bandages. A man who coughed all night had taken the place of the one who muttered in his sleep about a lost Buddha image. Suspended between life and death, he drifted in and out of consciousness, unable to make sense of his situation, aware only that he was being cared for. When the stabs of pain from his wound became too fierce, there was always a nurse on hand to help him find a more comfortable position or give him medication to dull the agony. He could be hurled from the savage embrace of a nightmare, shaking, sobbing, his mind still flooded with atrocious images, convinced that a bomb had just carved a chunk of flesh out of his body, and there would straightaway be a calming presence crouched behind him, pressing his hand, touching his arm, lighting the way out of the apocalyptic labyrinth. Was it opium, this soothing balm? In fretful moments, he tried to rise from his mat and escape from the cave, fearful that the injections were weakening him. But they became less and less frequent. Inch by inch, he was climbing out of the abyss into which he had tumbled.

His first days outside the cave were terrifying. The roar made by the bombers was ten times louder now that he was in the open, and he trembled with fear whenever an aeroplane approached. Pathet Lao soldiers had destroyed their village during the battle during which he had been wounded, and they had become a group of homeless refugees living from hand to mouth in the jungle. It was hazardous terrain. Unexploded bombs lay all around, and many of the plants had been killed by the yellow chemicals that had been dropped from the sky, making it difficult for them to find food. Main's wound was still painful, and he lived every day on the brink of agony, in perpetual fear of an ambush since it was impossible for him to move at any speed without tearing his flesh. Before long, the Plain of Jars had become uninhabitable, and they were left with no alternative but to make their way south towards the Royalist zone. He saw little of his father, who was usually in the vanguard, looking out for mines and enemy forces, but his mother was always at his side. She was overjoyed that he had survived, and her face would light up whenever he smiled or took her hand. To begin with, he could scarcely understand a word that was said to him and used sign-language to communicate. But she would sit with him at every opportunity and help him build up his vocabulary. Soon they were able to have proper conversations. He should not worry that he had no memory of life before his accident, she told him, or that he found it impossible to put his feelings into words. After enduring such a terrible ordeal, it was only natural that his brain should try to shut out the past in its efforts to come to terms with what had happened. The important thing was that he had turned the corner and was growing stronger and wiser all the time.

If there was one thing that seemed dependable in this bewildering landscape, it was his mother's love for him. He was her only child, and he relied on her for everything and clung tightly to her assurances. But it was difficult not to feel confused when you had been hit by shrapnel from a bomb dropped by somebody who was supposed to be fighting on the same side as your father. Or when you had nothing in common with your peer group, most of whom seemed to want to spend their days pretending to be aeroplanes. Or when you found you could understand languages that you had no business to be able to understand. There had been an evening when he had overheard a conversation between some Phouane through whose village they passed. Not all of it had made sense, but he had found certain passages almost as easy to comprehend as his native tongue. His mother did not like it when he tried to talk to her about such things. Any suggestion that he was struggling to come to terms with the world around him was liable to fill her with alarm at the thought that his recovery might be faltering, and he kept the incident to himself. He would do anything to avoid upsetting or disappointing her. It was obvious to him that he was receiving more food, care and attention than any other boy or girl in their party, and he saw it as his duty to pay back the love that she lavished on him by playing along with her cherished belief that she was raising a fine uncomplicated son.

What they could forage depended on whether the land across which they were travelling had already been stripped of its quota of edible flora and fauna by other refugees. Most nights, they went to bed hungry. As they dropped down from the Plain, their bodies began to struggle with the demands of living at lower altitudes, to which they were not adapted. The debilitating heat became a constant challenge. Diseases broke out and spread like wildfire, forcing the group to stop in its tracks, however inhospitable the surrounding countryside, until the crisis had passed. One epidemic claimed the lives of at least two members of the community. And yet Main did not regard himself as wretched or even particularly unhappy. At least there were no bombing raids to worry about now, and no chemicals raining down from the sky. Nor was he was the only person in difficult circumstances. It was the same for all of them. One day, they had the good fortune to run across the trail of a wild pig in the forest. Four or five young men immediately set off to hunt it down. A few hours later, they arrived back with a magnificent beast dangling by its feet from a thick branch. The group sat jubilantly in a big circle around the fire until late into the evening as the animal roasted. The elders kept them all entertained by telling stories of the heroic deeds of their ancestors and narrating ancient Hmong legends. After they had feasted, a bottle of rice wine was handed round, then an opium pipe. A wizened elder launched into a song, and one by one the rest of the group joined in as they picked up the melody, chanting in time even though most did not know the words, tapping out the beat or clapping. In due course, a few of the younger adults got to their feet and started dancing. This was the memory that stayed with Main the longest. The spectacle mesmerised him. To and fro the dancers glided, snaking out their arms and fingers, swaying towards their partners, then away again, even

1. The ten siblings (left to right) back row: Thong, Kone, Neung, Bua, Sing. Front row: Phanh, Lar, Jun, Boun, Manophet

2, 3. Manophet's parents, Moui and Douangdy

4. The family reunion with Bua (1997)

5. Bua (left) washing clothes in Chiang Kham refugee camp (1986)

6, 7. Bua as a performance artist in Minnesota (1990/91)

8. Visiting a hill-tribe village

9. On the Plain of Jars (Photo: Mark Steadman, 2009)

10. At work, surrounded by cluster bombs

11. War scrap (Photo: Paul & Linda Castleman)

12. Popular *al fresco* dining destination  (Photo: Paul & Linda Castleman)

13, 14. Wearing the uniform of the Japanese Mines Advisory Service (JMAS) in Phonsavan (left) and "at his podium" on the Plain of Jars (right) 2009. (Photos: Boon Vong [www.b-vong.com] and Patrick Clarkin)

15. Participating in a *baci* ceremony (Photo: Paul & Linda Castleman)

16. With Channapha Khamvongsa, Founder & Executive Director of *Legacies of War*, 2009. (Photo: Boon Vong [www.b-vong.com])

17. At his mother's house  (Photo: Paul & Linda Castleman)

18. With his players at a Lao football tournament

19. An EDS player surges past his Brazilian opponent at the 2010
Gotha Cup in Sweden  (Photo: Per Friske)

20. With some of his school pupils in front of his new house

while sometimes hardly seeming to move their feet, each moment a new expression dawning in their faces.

After several weeks, they reached the outskirts of the capital. Here they halted while the elders decided what to do next. After a day or two, his mother took him to one side and told him he was going to go and live in a camp.

'What sort of a camp?'

'A children's camp,' she said, 'where you can go to school.'

'With no grown-ups? Where will all the grown-ups live?'

'I'm afraid it will not be possible for us to be with you, Main,' she said. 'In fact, it may be some time before we can be together again.'

'You are going away? But I don't want you to go away.'

'We don't want to separate either,' she said. 'But I'm afraid we really have no choice. If our side wins the war, we can all go back home together and life will be easy again. But, if we lose, our lives may become very difficult, and you will be safer if they do not know you are our child. So we think it will be best for you if you pretend you are an orphan and live with the other orphans in the camp for the time being.'

At first he was miserable. He missed his mother and father, and hated being stuck in one place after the nomadic existence to which he had become accustomed. They had canvas over their heads at night, but the drab grassless camp had nothing else to commend it, and became more overcrowded by the week. Most of the other children were genuine war orphans. When they were occupied, they could be indistinguishable from ordinary children, but if there was nothing to distract them they would withdraw into themselves, sitting on their own staring listlessly into space, as though waiting for whoever had abandoned them to reappear. Lessons were ridiculously straightforward. Everything they taught in class, Main seemed to know already. But soon they moved him up a couple of classes, and now he began to find the work enjoyable. Numbers fascinated him. He worked out *pi* to eleven decimal places, and could recite the results from memory. Not bad for a six year-old! He found Lao easy to pick up, and before long he was having conversations with the Lao children in the camp. A few of the others resented the effortlessness with which he was able to outshine them in every field of endeavour, but most were glad to have a friend who displayed wisdom beyond his years and was also a good listener. Living without parents, they were reliant on other children for information and, with Main's help, they were at least able to make some sense of the confusing world in which they found themselves. For three years, he did not see his own parents, but a couple named Ly and Nhia called by periodically to let him know they were still safe and well. Then, just as it seemed a reunion might be on the cards, news came that they had decided to flee across the Mekong. They were distraught about having to leave Main behind, but promised to send messages from Thailand and were already longing for the day when he would be old enough to join them. Two weeks later they were gone.'

He had known from an early age that he wanted to be a nurse. It was because of the dedication of the nurses in the cave that he was still alive. What could be more natural than to follow in the footsteps of those selfless men and women? The first two years at nursing college flew by. Then, for the final stages of his training, he was posted to the Vietnamese border, cutting him off from the Hmong community within which he had grown up. The unfamiliar surroundings sharpened his awareness of how much they had been through together. Pegged down by the sclerotic economy, the country's ethnic Lao had faced a tough struggle to survive the past decade, but the battle to eke out an existence had been twice as arduous for the Hmong. Swathes of their ancestral territories had been confiscated in a crude attempt to curb opium production, and the marginal land that they had been given in exchange would not support their upland rice strains. Their livestock had languished in the fierce heat. There was nothing that could be sold for a profit. As for former Hmong soldiers and their families, even now, ten years on from the end of the war, they harboured a lingering fear that the Party was liable to come after them. Although people seldom complained, he knew many were secretly unhappy and longed for a better chance. And yet suffering was a way of life in Laos. He was continually moved by the plights of the patients that he tended during the course of his day-to-day nursing duties. These people's need was so much greater than his, and now he was in a position to make a tangible difference to their quality of life. The work was not glamorous. He moved the sick from place to place, took charge of delivering their medication, and performed a never-ending cycle of menial chores. But it brought him a sense of fulfilment that was worth as much as any financial payoff.

The compassionate efficiency with which he discharged his duties was well received by his superiors. When his placement came to an end, he was summoned to the Principal's office and offered a place at Medical School in Vientiane. At a stroke, his fortunes had been transformed. At first, he found the capital daunting, but new friendships quickly blossomed, and before long he began to feel more settled. Soon there were ten or eleven contemporaries to whom he felt a close connection. For the first time in his life, he was surrounded by people with interests and values that squared with his. Teachers and professors of sundry nationalities filled his head with stimulating ideas. But before long he found himself confronted by the biggest decision of his life. Six of his new friends had become obsessed with the idea of crossing the Mekong into Thailand. Weary of waiting for their lives in Laos to take an upturn, they had pooled their resources and were on the verge of purchasing a boat. It was notoriously difficult to get messages into Laos from the refugee camps on the Thai side of the border, but the news filtering back from those who had managed to secure onward passages to distant parts of the world suggested that living standards there were immeasurably superior. More and more of those who had chosen to flee were striking it lucky. His friends were convinced the risk was worth taking. Main was torn. On the one hand, he wanted to finish his studies. As a qualified doctor, he would be in a significantly stronger position when it came to mapping out his future – whether he stayed on in Laos to practise medicine or tried to defect to the West. On the other, his friends were everything to him now and, if he accompanied them, there was also the chance of being reunited with his parents.

He borrowed a bicycle and pedalled off to consult Ly and Nhia. 'You have still not heard anything from my mother and father, I suppose?' he asked.

'Nothing,' Ly answered. 'You?'

Main shook his head. 'Perhaps they are still stuck in one of the camps.'

They quizzed him about Vientiane and his studies. 'My professors ask me why I am called Main when I look more Lao than Hmong, he joked. 'They swear I could pass for a Laotian.'

'You used to get teased about that in the camp, didn't you?'

'Well, you expect it from children. But it is different when it comes from professors.'

'How long before you qualify?'

'Many years still. It is depressing to think how long. I am sure my parents would want me to finish my studies before I follow them, but it could all be a waste of time. There is no guarantee that the qualification that I receive will be recognised in other parts of the world. I might have to start all over again from the beginning. In fact, to tell you the truth, some friends and I are thinking of going across the Mekong within the next few weeks.' He watched their expressions apprehensively. 'I am here as much as anything to ask what you think.'

Nhia rearranged a few of the dishes on the table and gave her husband another spoonful of rice.

'You know it is dangerous,' Ly said.

Main nodded.

Ly glanced at Nhia. A silent exchange of information seemed to be taking place.

Nhia's eyes were fixed on her sleeve. She was tugging at a thread, as though concerned that it might be working loose. At length she said, 'Main, if you are really going, there is something we need to tell you first.'

'There is a reason your professors think you are Lao rather than Hmong,' Ly said.

Main sat back in his chair. This was not the response he had anticipated.

'Your mother and father,' Nhia started – 'well, there is no easy way of putting this, but they were not in fact your real mother and father.'

'You will probably find this difficult to comprehend at first,' Ly said. He was rocking back and forth in his chair now, his fingers running abstractedly through the stubble on his chin. 'But the truth of the matter is that you are not their child. They – adopted you – perhaps that is the best way of putting it.'

Main's mouth fell open. This could not possibly be right. 'I'm sorry,' he said. 'I think there must be some mistake.'

'Your father – your adoptive father – found you in a cave,' Ly continued. 'It was during the war. There had been heavy bombing all day. He was supposed to be flushing out the last enemy soldiers, but then he came across your unconscious body in a small cave. He knew you would die if you were left there, so he picked you up and carried you off the battlefield to the field hospital where you were looked after.'

'I really don't think this can be correct,' Main said weakly.

'For a long time, they were afraid you weren't going to pull through. But eventually you started to recover, and by that stage they had become attached to you. You were still very weak when you left the cave, and they thought it might be too much for you if you found out straight away that you were an orphan.'

'Have you ever wondered about the scar on your ear lobe?' Nhia asked.

He kneaded the familiar discontinuity with his thumb and finger, more confused than ever. What possible relevance could *that* old wound have?

'Whoever cut your ear was probably trying to determine whether you were likely to survive. If blood had flowed, they would have taken it as an indication that you were going to live, and they would not have left you behind.'

Main ran his finger back and forth across the faint but unmistakeable groove. 'So they had decided I was going to die.'

He pedalled back in a daze. Why had nobody told him this extraordinary tale before, if it was true? He found it impossible to grasp the idea that he might not be the person he had always believed himself to be. He felt Hmong to his fingertips. Every stage of his struggle to survive, he had shared with other Hmong – and yet now he was being asked to believe he had been a cuckoo in the nest, a member of the race that over the years had done all it could to make life unendurable for his people. His birth family, whoever they were, had probably fought *against* his father in the war – on the communist side. All his instincts told him the story was false. But his head was less adamant. From as long ago as he could remember, he had been more mature than other children of his age. According to Nhia, this had been down to an error of judgement at the camp. 'You were very skinny when you were enrolled,' she had explained. 'You looked about five or six, and they gave you a date of birth that fitted with that impression. Within a couple of years, it had become obvious that you were actually much older, but by that stage it was too late to do anything about it. It would have completely thrown you if they had tried changing it.' And Ly had reminded him that, while adoptions were common in Hmong culture, Hmong parents, by convention, never adopted other Hmong. The idea of a Hmong couple taking in a boy from a different ethnic background was not nearly as implausible as it appeared. Over the next few weeks, he sank into a state of morbid disconnection. His adoptive parents – if he could call them that – had long since disappeared to a foreign land. His birth parents, if they had ever existed, could still be in Laos but, if so, he had no idea where they might be living, and there was a good chance that they were dead.

He crossed the Mekong in 1986 with his six friends. Silently they paddled their flimsy coracle across the dark water, scarcely daring to breathe, terrified of splashing, straining for the sounds of guards, dogs, gunfire. But they had done their homework well, and their luck was in. On the other side, they knocked at the door of a Thai farmhouse and pleaded for a transfer to the nearest camp. The farmer was no stranger to such requests. He was prepared to take the risk of transporting them as long as he was suitably compensated. The guards at the camp gate would follow the same code. If offered the right money, they would allow the migrants into the camp. The friends sat up all night, weighing their chances. They were penniless. Their meagre resources had disappeared into the pocket of the man who had sold them the boat. Their only hope lay in finding friends or relatives in the camp who could be persuaded to lend them money. The following night, they were loaded into a tractor trailer, hidden under a tarpaulin and driven several miles south to the camp. Two of the seven were allowed in to try and raise the necessary funds. The rest were instructed to remain outside the perimeter fence, surrounded by armed guards who left them in no doubt as to their role in the transaction. They were now regarded as human collateral. If their friends failed to reappear, they would be shot. It was the longest wait of Main's life. But at last, after three hours, the emissaries reappeared and they were waved in through the gate.

His exhilaration lasted no more than a few hours. One of the other refugees in the camp came forward to give him the worst imaginable news. His adoptive parents had lost their lives while trying to cross the Mekong, shot dead by border guards as they swam. Main slumped into a dark depression. It was not as though he had failed to anticipate this terrible possibility. Deep down, this was what he had long feared. But there was a crushing finality to the revelation. He was now alone in the world, kinless and at the same time irrevocably cut off from the land from which both his families had sprung. Although living in Laos had been a perpetual struggle, he had managed to survive and blossom in spite of its vicissitudes. He belonged there. It had nurtured him. Never again would he experience the powerful sense of rootedness that it engendered in him. Each morning, he woke to a feeling of emptiness and futility. He had cast himself adrift on a vast ocean without any map or plan, spurred on by a rash hope that fortune would smile on him if he threw caution to the wind. That he was one of only a handful of Lao in a Hmong camp gnawed away at him in a way it never had in the past. He had spent his life surrounded by Hmong. Their ways were his ways. Every cultural nuance was familiar to him, every allusion. And yet these camps were here because the Hmong were fleeing from the communist regime in Laos, the regime that his blood family had in all likelihood helped bring to power. He should not be here – and yet where *should* he be? He was an orphan in more than the ordinary sense. There was no community into which he fitted, no tribe that would own him as theirs.

After six weeks, they were moved to another camp. Conditions in the first camp had been wretched enough. Here, they were far worse. Their pitiful food rations consisted of one meagre handful of rice a day, supplemented by salt or fish sauce and grain husks, a little shredded cabbage or dog meat once a fortnight if they were lucky. They lived more like animals than men and women. Disease was rife. Since only registered Thai citizens were permitted to make a living in Thailand, earning money to improve their situation was out of the question. The downtrodden refugees clung with what little energy they could muster to their faded dreams of being granted citizenship by Thailand or one of the other western nations. Submissions to the Resettlement Board took months to process and there was no guarantee that they would be successful. As a rule, the government of the country being petitioned required an undertaking from a third party that they would support the immigrant until such time as he or she became financially viable before an application would even be considered. Many of the refugees had family members somewhere in the world to whom they could appeal, or friends, however distant. Main had nobody to whom he could turn. He was stranded, unable to return to the country from which he had come, yet unable to leave the foreign land in which he had arrived. Having no better way of passing his days, he volunteered to work in the camp infirmary. Tattered wreckages of human beings hobbled from their beds for treatment, or were stretchered in, victims of circumstances that no mortal should ever have to experience. The sight of them was often too much for him to bear, but at the same time it gave him a reason to carry on with his own life. They needed his care. He could look after them.

Eighteen months went by. One by one, his friends had secured their passages into Thailand or to destinations further afield and said their goodbyes. For those left behind in the camp, death was a constant spectre. Hemmed in on every side at the infirmary by the diseased, Main wondered how much longer he could survive without contracting some fatal illness. But his dedication had not gone unnoticed. The Thai doctors to whom he answered were so impressed by his work ethic that they resolved amongst themselves to try and assist him. After some thought, they approached an ecclesiastical charity in America that had been set up to help deserving orphans, and asked whether Main might qualify for aid under the terms of its remit. He was touched by their thoughtfulness when they told him what they had done. Fanciful though it was to imagine that an organisation thousands of miles away might put up a substantial sum of money to help a complete stranger, it had been a kindly act. Not long afterwards, however, he was summoned by the Resettlement Board, and told that a lady from a Lutheran church in Minneapolis had been moved by the doctors' appeal and was volunteering to act as his sponsor. How would he like to start a new life in America? Main was stunned. He had no idea where Minneapolis was, but that hardly seemed to matter. When could he leave? He was promptly transferred to a new camp to learn basic English and gain a feel for the vagaries of western culture. Six months later, he was taken to Bangkok and despatched in an aeroplane to a point on the globe almost as far from his birthplace as it was possible to travel.

The city that had given him sanctuary could hardly have been more different to the land he had left behind. Snow, motor vehicles and concrete were all that he could see as he sat on the bus from the airport. He gazed up open-mouthed at the space-age skywalks criss-crossing between the unimaginably tall buildings as they passed through the downtown area, and later trooped uncomprehendingly through the biggest shopping precinct on the planet, when his sponsor showed him round in an attempt to make him feel at home. He was profoundly grateful for the lodgings with which she provided him, and for the generous portion of chicken supplied each day by the church. But a terrible loneliness overcame him every time he stepped out of doors. The freezing metropolis was the most forbidding of places if you spoke no more than a word or two of English and possessed no coat. The people on the streets were invariably in a furious hurry, and vehicles never stopped roaring past. He found it impossible to overcome his abhorrence for the wastefulness of the society that he had joined. So much was thrown away or expended purely for show.

It had been decided that he should earn his keep by packaging popcorn at a food processing facility. Within hours of starting work, he knew this was an arrangement that could not continue. He had not come half way round the world from a camp of starving refugees to shovel junk food into bags for distribution to the overfed. The fact that he had a vocation seemed to count for nothing in the country to which he now belonged. Who was in charge? Who made the rules? Before doing anything else, he needed to learn to speak English properly so that he could start to fathom the workings of this mystifying civilisation. He handed in his notice and enrolled to take a language course. Each morning, he would leave the house at seven, shivering with cold, to catch a bus. The college was situated many blocks from where he lived, and the journey required him to change at least once. Occasionally he would manage to catch the right combination of buses home and was back by six in the evening, but the bewildering plethora of routing choices meant that he was regularly obliged to disembark in an unfamiliar part of the city to consult a map. Because he was no longer working, he had no money. His welfare payments covered the cost of food, rent, language tuition and a bus pass but nothing more.

Little by little, his quality of life started to edge upwards. A stranger took pity on him and escorted him to a free store, where she found him a coat and a bearskin hat. Soon he knew enough English to be able to ask bus drivers which interchanges they stopped at before boarding. Friendships developed. When a fellow student at the English school discovered that he had taught Hmong dance in Vientiane, she had the idea of starting an evening class. For each three-hour session that Main supervised, he received $17 – an astonishing sum for a man from a country where it was possible to live comfortably on less than $1 a day. It meant that his days were longer still. Often he would not arrive home until ten at night. But, after several months, he had saved enough money to enrol in a tropical nursing course. Four years on from leaving Laos, he was finally able to gain a medical qualification that was recognised in the US.

'They are advertising a hospital position that looks just right for you,' the director of his dance class said as she dropped him off one evening. 'If you are interested, I could help you fill in the application form.' Main knew that cramming another set of responsibilities into his hectic schedule was out of the question. But she had been so kind to him. It would be rude not to play along. Thirty-seven other candidates had been processed by the time he took his turn and, as though to break it to him gently that they had already made a decision and were merely going through the motions, the staff member who saw him conducted the interview in Thai, a language that he found easier to understand than English. A clerk from the hospital telephoned at the weekend to ask if he could come in for orientation the following Monday. Main had been under the impression that they had finished with him, but reluctantly agreed to make the extra time and went to look up orientation in the dictionary. The definition implied that he had presented himself at the wrong building. Perhaps they had taken him to be an applicant for a different position altogether, and were now cross with him for wasting their time.

The lady who had interviewed him raised her eyebrows when he appeared. 'We usually dress a bit less casually than that,' she remarked.

He looked down at his clothes with some confusion. These were his best jeans. What else was he supposed to wear?

'You do *want* the job?'

'A job?' he said. 'Well, that is really very kind of you, I am sure, but unfortunately I don't know that I would be able to afford to volunteer for any more work at the moment. You see, I have almost no free time on my hands.'

She pursed her lips. 'The salary is really quite competitive, you know.'

'There would be a salary?' He could not work out whether she was speaking in earnest or making fun of him. 'You would pay me to work here?'

She burst out laughing. 'Did you not realise?'

'How much is the salary?'

In Lao terms, it was a sum too vast to be comprehensible. Main sat down on the floor and wept.

The director of the dance class had played a pivotal role in transforming his life. He owed her everything, and it never occurred to him to give up his teaching commitment. But in due course she took him to one side. 'You are exhausted,' she said. 'You cannot keep on with this now that you have a full-time job. It's not as though you need the money any more. It is time for you to hang up your dancing shoes. But we would very much like it if we could stay in touch. Perhaps we could ask you to adjudicate whenever we hold a competition?'

It was after one of these competitions that he found himself talking to an excited group of students. Laos had reopened its borders, and their parents had decided to make the long journey back to their homeland to celebrate Hmong New Year. 'They could take some photographs of you with them,' one of the students suggested.

'Of me? Why would they want to do that?'

'They could show them around. Somebody from your family might recognise you.'

It seemed to have escaped their notice that Laos now had a population of almost five million. But he was careful to keep a straight face. 'Which part of the country are they going to?'

'Phon Hong.'

Phon Hong was in the middle of nowhere, and miles from the Plain of Jars, where his birth family was likely to have lived. 'That is so considerate of you,' he said. 'I am very touched. I will dig out some old photos for you to give them.'

# TWELVE

Just as the finishing touches were being put to the guest house, Southeast Asian currencies collapsed. Rather than receiving 1,000 kip for every dollar they exchanged, tourists found themselves being handed 8,000, making any visit to Laos absurdly cheap. An inflation tsunami followed as the economies of the region adjusted, plunging ordinary Laotians into another period of intense hardship and strengthening the hands of those who argued that free markets were a bad idea. But Kong Keo's room rates were priced in dollars rather than kip, with the result that the guest house brought in many times more income than he and Manophet had anticipated when it opened. As though this was not enough of a bonanza in itself, westerners began flocking to Indochina in unprecedented numbers, unable to resist the bargain-price holiday deals on offer. Backpackers were banging at their door from the day they opened for business, and guest numbers picked up so rapidly that they sometimes had to put latecomers up in private accommodation. Manophet was intoxicated with his new life. At last he had at least a measure of control over his own destiny. If the *falang* who came to the guest house enjoyed themselves enough, they would recommend it to their friends and relatives back at home, and trade would boom. It was simple: all he had to do was engineer rewarding experiences for them. Quite what it was they were hoping to achieve by coming to a place like Phonsavan, he had yet to nail down, but it would surely be possible to work this out as time went by.

If there were no tourists staying, he was free to do as he pleased. What a luxury! But Manophet was not a man to let the grass grow under his feet. An hour after dusk, he would make his way to the Sangha restaurant just as he did on evenings when he had guests to escort, on the off-chance that he might run into somebody interesting. The Maly Hotel had its own restaurant, but it was to the Sangha that every other visitor to Phonsavan came to socialise in the evening. Thanks to a glowing Lonely Planet Guide recommendation, it had become a magnet for *falang*. Manophet was close to Miss Onh, the proprietor. Their two families had briefly shared a cave during the war, and he had laboriously translated her menu into English for the benefit of her foreign customers. The bond between them had grown stronger when he had brought a Japanese businessman in from the Phu Doi for a meal. He had come to Xieng Khouang to evaluate the possibility of farming mushrooms commercially, a project that would require several weeks to complete. After a few days, he had checked out of the Phu Doi and moved into a house on Highway Seven, but each morning and evening thereafter he had appeared like clockwork at the Sangha to take meals, bowing graciously to Miss Onh every time he ran into her. When the time came for him to return to Japan, he asked if he might give her a present to thank her for the enjoyment her cuisine had given him – something he had acquired during the course of his business dealings but no longer needed. Miss Onh said she would be honoured and delighted to receive such a gift, expecting to be given a consignment of mushrooms or perhaps some fertiliser. But she had misread the signals. The Japanese had presented her instead with the keys to his house.

Manophet was always happy to stand in as a waiter in exchange for a meal if he had nothing else to do. It gave him the chance to listen in on the diners' conversations and practise his English. It was not uncommon to find a gaggle of ordnance consultants holed up in one corner, sipping cold *Beer Lao* and devouring generous platefuls of food. They were seldom in a hurry, and happy to make constructive suggestions if he asked for linguistic assistance. He began to appreciate that, while certain aspects of sentence formation were governed by rigid rules, there were also plenty of grammatical loopholes – of which you needed to take full advantage if you were going to demonstrate your prowess as an English speaker. If you made the mistake of saying "he goes to the airport" rather than "he is going to the airport", for example, you were immediately written off as a hopeless amateur. But you could enhance your credibility no end by substituting an expression like "he is catching a flight", since this showed that you knew flights could be caught in English, just like colds or fish or fire. From time to time, he would run into tour company representatives on reconnaissance missions, feasting on the excellent spring rolls and weighing up whether it was safe to send tour groups to Xieng Khouang. Other evenings, he would come across dollar-a-day types, who slept on overnight buses rather than in regular accommodation and always ordered the cheapest dishes on the menu, or backpackers from the Ving Thong, a guest house similar in character to Kong Keo's that had recently opened up close by. They were invariably several years younger than him. How were they planning to spend their time in the area, he would enquire? No idea? Perhaps they might like to visit one of the jars sites the following day? He would be happy to arrange an excursion and act as their guide. Each assignment left his wallet a little fatter – though he was scrupulous about cautioning his clients if they tried to tip him too generously.

Over time, he began to acquire a reputation as a local guide. *Falang* would arrive at the Sangha and enquire where Mr Manophet was to be found. Nothing, it seemed, was more effective when it came to persuading tourists to recommend him to their friends than telling them they were paying too much for his services. And yet Manophet sensed that the jars came as a disappointment to his groups. How could he enhance the quality of the experience? He studied the writings of the French archaeologist, Madeleine Colani, the leading authority on the sites, but the tourists' expressions seemed to glaze over even faster when he gave them more information. Maybe a few good stories would help. He tried working up the local legend of how a race of giants had hewn them out of cliffs so that they could store rice wine. Then, one day, he spotted a couple of parallel holes in the ground that looked as though they might at some point have housed a pair of heavy-duty screws, and had a better idea. 'You see these holes?' he announced in an authoritative voice. 'A Russian anti-aircraft battery was positioned here during the war. Cuban forces used it to target US aircraft on their way from Thailand to Vietnam.' It was not strictly true. The gun emplacement had been at one of the other jars sites. But did that matter so much? 'The Americans didn't want to fire back in case they damaged the jars,' he added as an afterthought. The response was electrifying. Suddenly he had a different group on his hands. 'The Russians?' one of them queried. 'The *Cubans*? What were *they* doing here?'

'Laos is a communist state,' barked one of the others. 'What do you expect?'

'It wasn't back then,' the first speaker rejoined testily. 'Laos was neutral during the war.'

'If Laos was neutral, why the hell are there so many bomb craters?' a woman demanded. A moment later, they were all firing off opinions, seemingly unaware that altercations of this kind were unknown in Laos. Nobody here raised their voices or gesticulated when they spoke. It made them look absurd. But Manophet was also intrigued by the mêlée. There was something fine, something stirring about the passion with which they argued.

That evening, he sat in his chair at the guest house trying to make sense of what had happened. They were cut from strange cloth, these *falang*. Like children, they seemed to be bursting with an irresistible craving for excitement and drama. Bored by their safe comfortable existences at home, they were consumed by a hankering to plough a more dangerous furrow, even if only for a few short days. They arrived itching to be captivated, frightened, shocked, enchanted – and perhaps this was as much as he needed to know. There had been times during recent weeks when he had felt guilty that he was doing nothing more than taking advantage of their gullibility to separate them from their money. Now he could see a way of making the transaction fairer. If he could just discover how to move them, he would be able to pay them back in the sort of currency in which they longed to be rewarded. To westerners, there was apparently nothing peculiar about living for emotional pay-offs or travelling from one side of the globe to the other to seek them out. He remembered hearing one injudicious tourist describe the Lao as "perpetually underwhelmed" a few days earlier – as though lamenting their contrasting approach to life as an unfortunate collective personality defect. Apparently it had not occurred to him that the Lao might *prefer* to let the world go quietly by, having already experienced enough emotional turmoil for one lifetime.

He tested his story about the gun on other groups, with the same outcome. At the first mention of Cubans, Russians or communism, they became different creatures, bright-eyed, wary. 'I've never been to a communist country before,' he overheard a young woman admit nervously to the couple standing next to her. 'You sign up to do these things because they sound adventurous, but it isn't until you get here that you realise what big risks you're taking. I mean, there are no safeguards. If your bag got stolen, for instance, or your passport, nobody would help you. Hardly anybody even speaks English.'

She came across to talk to him as the group was breaking up. 'Is it true that people disappear over here?' she asked. 'I mean, if you say rude things about the government, for instance, and somebody reports you, can you be taken away in the middle of the night and never heard of again?'

Manophet narrowed his eyes. 'Is that what they tell you in the West?'

She took a couple of rapid breaths. 'There are supposed to be mass graves somewhere, aren't there?'

'Maybe you are thinking of The Killing Fields,' he said. 'But the Killing Fields are in Cambodia. The Khmer Rouge were never in power in Laos.'

'Sorry, I probably shouldn't be asking questions like this.'

'You can ask me questions if you like,' he said. 'But perhaps you should not speak so loudly.'

A look of panic crossed her face as she scanned the rest of the group. 'You think the secret police might be listening?'

'It is always a good idea to be careful,' he said. 'That is something we have learned in Laos over the years.'

If there was one topic that could be guaranteed to have them hanging on his every word, it was the war. At first, their obsessive interest disturbed him. Any mention of bombs, deaths or the like, and they would crowd around and badger him for more information. Describing the ugly realities to outsiders made him uncomfortable. Surely the departed had a right to be left in peace. But once the subject had been broached, it was all they wanted to hear about. It took him several weeks to realise that it was not out of insensitivity that they clamoured for shocking stories. Their curiosity was born of nothing more sinister than ignorance. As often as not, they had travelled to Laos because they had enjoyed backpacking in Thailand and assumed the experience in the country next door would be much the same. The war had never been part of their school curricula, and at no point had it been mentioned that the fighting had spilled over into Laos. As far as they were aware, the conflict had been an ideological dispute between the Americans and the Vietnamese, and had nothing to do with anybody else. And yet once the *falang* had grasped the notion that they were holidaying on a battlefield rather than in a resort, there was no satiating their desire to understand what had taken place. A collective guilt would overwhelm them as they realised how abject their ignorance must appear to Manophet, a compulsion to make amends by absorbing every fact that he could impart, and by living out any tragedy they could persuade him to share.

One group wanted to see an old Russian tank, to which he had made a passing reference in the course of trying to keep them entertained. It had been abandoned in a field several miles away by the North Vietnamese. When he told them it was too far to visit on foot, they immediately volunteered to hire a couple of jeeps. Suddenly the excursion had turned into an adventure. Tense and expectant, the party bumped along the rutted tracks, crouching low in their seats and clinging grimly to the handholds, living every bend of the road while scanning the countryside for threats, as though believing themselves to be on an espionage mission. As the rusting wreck came into view over a hill, they celebrated with volleys of triumphant clucking, and the better part of an hour elapsed before he could persuade them it was time to leave. On the way back, they made a detour to a tribal village close to one of the most heavily bombed areas of the province. A smith had a fire blazing in the forge and was beating a section of war scrap flat. Close by, women were cleaving the metal into sections and shaping it into cutlery. The group wandered between the dilapidated huts, taking pictures of the rice barns, which had been constructed on elevated platforms supported by massive rusting cluster bomb casings as a means of keeping rats and other vermin at bay. A few yards further on, a pair of split casings had been laid horizontal on the ground and filled with earth so that they could function as nursery beds for seedlings. To Manophet, the scene could hardly have been less out of the ordinary, but his guests left him in no doubt that this was a precious experience as far as they were concerned. They glanced away hurriedly when an old man missing an arm and an ear shuffled by, not wanting to be seen to be staring, trying to conceal their cameras and anything else liable to betray their unconscionable affluence.

Like it or not, war tourism was establishing itself in Xieng Khouang. The Maly Hotel had started offering war-themed half-day excursions. Even the Ving Thong had spiced up its reception area with a montage of defused ordnance salvaged from the surrounding fields. 'What happened to *your* family during the war?' a backpacker enquired one afternoon, his eyes flicking nervously between the ancient stupa that Manophet had brought them to see and a pink marker poking up from a grassy mound a few yards downhill. The marker denoted the subterranean presence of an unexploded 500-lb bomb. It was safe enough according to the experts, who had chosen not to disturb it in case they destroyed the stupa in the process. Usually, when asked to reveal details from his personal life, Manophet would pretend to have misunderstood the question and answer a more convenient one. But he liked this group. They had taken the trouble to read up on Lao history and culture, and there had been a rare warmth and sensitivity to their questions. He wrestled with his prejudice that it would be tasteless to share the miracle of Bua's return from the dead with outsiders, and an act of disrespect to the fates who had granted the reprieve. Even if he gave way and took them into his confidence, the tale was surely so improbable that nobody would believe it. By the end of the narrative, two of the *falang* were weeping openly and the mouth of one of the others had fallen open. For two or three minutes, none of them seemed able to break the silence. 'Sometimes you know straightaway that a moment will stay with you forever,' one of them confided afterwards. 'You just do what you can to prolong it.'

Bua was never far from his thoughts. His brother's experiences had obliged him to question some of his most deeply ingrained beliefs. Since early childhood, Manophet had been wary of the Hmong, his father's enemies in the war, and until recently he had never felt fully at ease when visiting one of their villages. And yet it had been the heroic actions of a Hmong soldier that had brought his brother back from the grave. Even as battle was raging around them, the Hmong had been prepared to forgive their enemies. And what about the Americans? Every Laotian from Phongsaly to Champasack regarded them as shameless imperialists and held them responsible for leaving the country in ruin. But they had taken his orphaned brother in as an immigrant, given him a new life, and made him wealthy beyond the wildest dreams of the average Lao villager. To hold America as a whole responsible for the actions of a handful of rogue politicians and megalomaniac military commanders when its citizens were such good people at heart was clearly unfair. Bua had offered to pay for Manophet to fly to America for a visit. How he wished he could say yes. His longing to travel to another country and discover how life was lived on foreign shores was as powerful as ever. Even a few hours in Thailand or Vietnam would be a thrill. But, while the authorities had made it significantly easier for foreigners to enter Laos, there was no sign of Lao nationals being given the right to cross the border in the opposite direction. Applications for passports were never successful, and submitting one would merely make the police suspicious about his motives. Ah, the freedoms these tourists took for granted! How frustrated it made him sometimes when they prattled on about the other countries that they had visited, comparing this culture with that one, or informing him that a tin of Coca Cola cost six times as much in Costa Rica as it did in Laos.

He shared a special bond with Bua. For one thing, they communicated in English rather than Lao. From the beginning, the family had been mystified by Manophet's desire to master this difficult irrelevant language, considering the initiative to be little more than a wild goose chase. Now they could begin to appreciate just what a far-sighted plan it had been. Another powerful influence was the support that he received from Bua for the career path on which he had set himself. To the rest of the family, his approach to the business of earning a livelihood had always seemed perverse. It was not the Lao way, to turn up your nose at every job opening your family managed to create for you by leveraging its small number of precious connections. As if he had not already done enough over the years to flaunt his profligate streak, he had now walked away from a steady job at the respectable Phu Doi Hotel to join a downmarket johnny-come-lately guest house that nobody had ever heard of. What did it matter if the Phu Doi was starting to crumble? It was surely only a matter of time before the government took steps to renovate it. Why was he always so impatient? But, to Bua, this was the spirit of free enterprise taking wing. It was exactly what any red-blooded American would have done, he advised Manophet. If you were too timid to challenge the status quo, you would assuredly end your life no better off than when you were born. But, if you were prepared to risk taking a promising chance, you opened up the possibility of being handsomely rewarded. Look at what had happened to him as a result of crossing the Mekong. It had been a long hard road, but how richly the gamble had ultimately paid off.

They kept in touch by writing letters to each other. It was impossible for Bua to correspond as often or as assiduously as Manophet for, where Manophet had acquired one extra sibling, Bua had acquired nine, not to mention two parents, several brothers- and sisters-in-law, and dozens of aunts, uncles, nephews, nieces and cousins. Bua was frustrated that he could not take advantage of certain advanced modes of communication that were freely available in the West, and did his best to explain a mysterious concept known as the web, around which everything in America seemed to revolve. But Manophet was unable to make any sense of what he was saying until a *falang* couple who were staying at the guest house offered to demonstrate how their laptop worked. His mind immediately started racing. There were so many possibilities. 'We should buy one,' he suggested to Kong Keo. 'We could have a website and send e-mails to *falang*. It would pay for itself in no time.' Kong Keo remained unconvinced. 'We would also have to put in a telephone line,' he pointed out. 'And it would need to be one that works occasionally. How do you suppose we could swing something like *that* with the authorities? Besides, what are the chances of being able to find an internet service provider when nobody else in Xieng Khouang owns a computer? And another thing: why are you telling guests that the jars are burial urns? We don't know that for sure. Only a few of them are thought to have contained human remains, and those might have been placed there afterwards. You should say *maybe* the jars are burial urns.' 'It is no good saying *maybe* to *falang*,' Manophet grumbled. 'It makes them think you don't know what you are talking about.'

He listened politely when tourists regaled him with accounts of holidays that they had taken in other parts of the world. There was nothing to be gained by betraying his jealousy, and their tales helped him to understand what sort of adventures left the most vivid memories. It did not take long to establish that few experiences in Southeast Asia were viewed as more rewarding than staying overnight in remote tribal villages. Westerners possessed seemingly limitless appetites for acquainting themselves with the realities of the everyday existences led by the ethnic minority peoples. Well, *that* was not such a difficult thing to arrange. Xieng Khouang was brimming over with isolated communities of tribesfolk who had never set eyes on a westerner. He picked a two-day period when Kong Keo was free to man the guest house, found three enthusiastic backpackers and set out on a trek to a Tai Dam village with a friendly head man where he had once given a bombie talk. The girl, Elizabeth would fascinate the villagers. Blue-eyed, blonde and pale-skinned, she would be unlike any other human being they had seen before. Early on, she took the lead from time to time to show that she was as intrepid as the rest of them, swaying her hips as she strode along and sending back a delicate fragrance that mingled confusingly with the familiar forest aromas. But after Manophet warned them all to be on the lookout for snakes she stayed close to him on the trail, tucking in directly behind when the path narrowed, so that he could occasionally feel her soft breath on his neck. The boys took it in turns to fall in protectively beside her.

They took breathers now and again, during which he flagged up significant wayside plants and described their medicinal uses, showed them which berries could be eaten and which must be avoided, or pointed out a creature concealed in the undergrowth or a bird in the canopy. The sun rose higher in the sky, warming the rocks, so that their clothes clung to their bodies when the trail climbed. There were two rain-swollen rivers to ford. A rope had been slung across the first as a makeshift handrail, and the party waded through the water without incident. But the second was a more awkward proposition. Manophet scanned the unsatisfactory crossing point. By the time they returned the following day, the river would have had time to subside to its usual level and should present no threat. But in this condition, with the fast-flowing water potentially waist-high at its deepest point, it represented a treacherous obstacle. Anybody not used to balancing on submerged rocks could easily lose their footing and be swept away. He took a deep breath. One *falang* accident, and his brief career as a tourist guide would be over. But there was no question of turning back. Elizabeth and Detlef had already started removing their boots and socks. Oleg was trying to unpick the tangled knot in the lace of one of his boots. He stood facing away, doubled over so that the sinews in his muscular legs stood out like bow strings. His shorts, which were pulled tight against the curve of his rump, stretched vainly back towards their accustomed position, no longer equal to the task of concealing the boundary between his tan and the pale flesh above. At last he was ready. Manophet formed the group into a chain and led them cautiously into the torrent, each braced against the impact. There was a moment of panic when Oleg slipped and lurched sideways, but he immediately recovered, and in no time Detlef, who was bringing up the rear, came yomping ashore. Flinging their arms around one another, the three of them danced and giggled like six year-olds, the water dripping from their legs.

They arrived hot and tired a little before dusk. The head man was delighted to have visitors, and Manophet had a struggle persuading him that *falang* were not in the habit of accepting free hospitality and would insist on recompensing the village financially. The sexual tensions that had simmered on the trail were suddenly a distant memory. Elated by their adventure, the backpackers washed as the villagers washed – in their undergarments beneath a communal chute, from which water brought from a nearby river along an elaborate network of split bamboo splashed down in a lazy cascade. The sky grew red, then azure. Women lit fires, and the air filled with the sweet aroma of burning pine. Cooking pots were hauled out of the wooden houses by pint-sized children grasping at the flimsiest excuse to come and gawp at the visiting *falang*. Manophet had brought a couple of balloons which he blew up and tossed over to them. What were these? The children shrieked with excitement as they chased their new playthings up and down between the huts, scampering furiously to reach the head of the queue to touch them. A whoop of dismay went up when the blue one burst with such violence that the boy in pursuit dropped the baby that he was minding, but his charge seemed to be accustomed to such indignities and let out no more than the meekest of protests.

Elizabeth came to sit beside Manophet. 'I was wondering,' she said, 'are you married?'

'No,' he said, shifting his position a fraction. 'No, I am not married.'

'So you have no children of your own?'

He shook his head.

'And yet you brought those balloons to give to the village children.' She pushed the multicoloured array of bangles that she was wearing a little further up her wrist. 'You would make a good father.'

'You think so?' He was unsure what to make of the compliment. 'I did the same thing once before, in a different village. The children here are not used to balloons.' The end of his sentence was drowned out by the sizzle of bamboo shoots landing in hot oil. 'There are many children in Laos,' he continued, as a mouth-watering vapour swirled up. 'Almost half the population is under the age of fifteen.'

'That must be some kind of knock-on effect from the war,' Elizabeth reflected. She contemplated her toes. 'It can't have been good, being a child here while that was going on.'

'No,' he said.

The transformation in her pale features was startling. Manophet had never seen a *falang* blush. 'That's awful,' she mumbled. 'I didn't realise you were – I'm sorry, I thought you were younger than that.' She took a long time over her next question. He could almost hear her thinking, weighing up how far she could go. 'The bombing was really heavy round here, wasn't it?'

He nodded. 'Our house was destroyed.'

'But your family managed to escape in time?'

'We were able to get out – although there was not really time to pack anything up.'

'How did you avoid getting hit by bombs? I mean, it must have been –?'

'We found a cave where we could shelter.'

'Like Tham Piu? My *God*.'

'Not as big as Tham Piu.'

'But you grew up with your mother and father in a cave?'

'My father was not there at that time, in fact.'

Her questions were coming faster now. 'It was just you and your mother?'

He realised he needed to go back and expand the answer that he had given to the previous question, but if he did not address her latest question there would be another misconception to correct. 'Some of my brothers and sisters were there as well,' he explained.

'*Some* of your brothers and sisters? You got separated?'

'Actually, my three younger brothers had not yet been born. I was the youngest one at that time. It was me, my two older sisters, Kone and Jun –'

'– and your mother –'

'– my mother was there, yes. But one of my elder brothers was with my father. He had been injured during the bombing, and my father had taken him to a cave. My father and my mother had run out of the house in different directions when the bomb dropped, and he had gone with my father.'

'And they were in a different cave?'

'This was a different cave, yes. A smaller cave, and not in the same place.' The narrative seemed to be twisting itself into more of a tangle every time he opened his mouth. 'But my father left my brother behind, and a Hmong soldier found him and adopted him, and he ended up in a refugee camp.' He hurried straight into Bua's story to prevent her muddying the water any further with fresh interruptions. Weeks had passed since he had persuaded himself that it was acceptable to share it with *falang*, and his scruples had now faded away. It was a tale that seemed to grow more assured with every telling. Such was his skill as a raconteur that it seldom failed to entrance an audience.

Elizabeth blinked back her tears at the end. After a while, she reached out and touched his hand. 'You Lao are so –' she gazed out into the tree canopy for inspiration. 'I think it's the way you look into the other person's eyes when you talk. A lot of people don't do that.'

'You have enjoyed today?'

'It's been one of the best days of my life.'

'I am so glad,' Manophet said. 'But at the same time I am confused. You see, I do not really understand why that should be.'

She wrapped her arms around her knees. 'It's difficult to explain. I come from a country where you never need to worry about not having enough to eat. Healthcare is free if we get ill. Education is free. The State pays us if we don't have a job. It's such a brutal contrast, coming over here. People starve if it fails to rain. They die of diseases they could easily recover from if they had the right medicine. It makes me so aware of my surroundings – even things I see every day like the stars. At home, I would hardly notice them, but when I look up at the sky here I want to cry. I don't think I've ever seen anything so beautiful.'

They ate to the backdrop of poorly smothered laughter from the watching children, who crept as close as they dared to observe Oleg's floundering attempts to gain the upper hand over the chopsticks with which he had been presented. The head man was full of stories, not all of which Manophet could follow, even though Tai Dam was easier to pick up than some of the more obscure Tai-Kadai languages. He translated as best he could, inventing details where the narrative became incomprehensible. The head man quizzed him after the *falang* had turned in for the night. How had he come to make the acquaintance of such exotic strangers? Were they unique, or were there more of them? What were they doing in Laos? Would he care to come back to the village with other parties in the future? If he wanted to make a habit of it, the villagers would be glad of the extra money. There were so many things that they needed. Manophet explained how his decision to learn English was transforming his life. Perhaps he could teach this extraordinary language to the village children, the head man suggested. Then, in a few years time, they could walk to Phonsavan and bring back visitors by themselves. Manophet smiled. It was scarcely four years since he had learned "yes" and "no" from Kong Keo. 'I could not do anything like that,' he said. 'I have no training. Most of what I know, I taught myself from a book.' 'But you have these tourists to learn from,' the head man protested. 'And you are good with children. You would make an excellent teacher.'

The experience of sleeping on the hard floor of a wooden hut, and being woken at the first glimmer of dawn by a trigger-happy rooster did nothing to dampen the spirits of the *falang*. Back at the guest house, Manophet overheard Elizabeth recounting his story to a couple of backpackers who had just arrived. She was speaking in the hushed tones to which *falang* resorted when they wished to heighten the drama of the information that they were imparting. 'His family got split up during the war,' she whispered. 'He lived in a cave with his mother and two of his sisters, but his father and the rest of his brothers and sisters wound up in a refugee camp.'

'How did they get separated?' one of the awe-struck listeners asked.

'Their house was bombed. Apparently half his family dashed out in one direction when they heard the bombers coming, and the rest fled a different way.'

'How long were they apart?'

'I didn't ask. The war didn't end until 1975, so six years, I suppose.'

'*God*! They completely lost contact? And presumably neither half of the family had any idea whether the other half was alive or dead during all that time.'

# THIRTEEN

'What *is* the Boston Review?' Manophet asked. 'Is it a newspaper?'

'It is more like a magazine.'

'How often is it published?'

Kong Keo shrugged his shoulders. 'Five times a year, I think she said.'

'We had better get our fingers out,' Manophet said, switching to English so that he could show off his latest colloquialism. 'If we make a good impression, they may mention us in the article, and then we could have American *falang* wanting to come and stay here.'

'You really think American tourists might come to Laos?'

'They are starting to visit Vietnam,' Manophet said. 'Why not Laos? I will ask Thongkham if we can borrow his jeep. Have you told the police yet? They will be jumping about like cats on hot bricks when we tell them we are going to be showing American journalists around.'

There were two of them, a man named Robert and a woman named Kieko, both about Manophet's age. They quickly showed themselves to be authorities on Lao history and politics. Not only were they able to give detailed descriptions of the early kingdoms. They could discuss aspects of the war in such depth that even Manophet was able to glean new information. Of the period since the door of the country had been slammed in America's face, their grasp was sketchier. Secretive was the adjective most commonly used by Americans to describe Laos, so they said, and it was because reliable information about the condition of the country was so hard to come by that they had decided to come and do some reconnaissance of their own. As a rule, the safest way of keeping *falang* happy was to tell them what they wanted to hear, Manophet had learned, but these two were difficult to read, and his instinct was to tread cautiously. It was not out of the question that they had CIA links. Even if they genuinely wanted to hear the worst, it could be a mistake to lay it on with a trowel. Smart people like this would not thank him for spoon-feeding them heart-rending stories.

They would want hard information – details that they could verify with their own eyes. And then there was the complication that they were Americans. Every damning piece of evidence that he presented would have the appearance of a criticism where, to other *falang*, it would simply look like an impersonal historical fact.

Their first goal was to determine the extent to which unexploded ordnance was continuing to affect daily life. Manophet took them down to the hospital, where there was a doctor who kept a register. 'One incident per week on average in this province alone so far this year,' he reported. 'That is to say, one person injured or killed. Mostly children. They see a shiny bombie, and their instinct is to pick it up or kick it. Across the country as a whole, about one death a week, and five times that number of serious accidents.' Bald statistics were probably water off a duck's back to American journalists if there was no visual evidence to support them, Manophet figured, so he took them next to MAG, the largest bomb disposal unit in the province, one of whose employees, a British soldier, kept private scrap books containing photographs of bombie victims. Bedraggled Lao with severed arms or legs gazed out from the dog-eared pages, surrounded by close-ups of missing eyes and shrapnel-peppered torsos. 'Our Administration claims it is donating eight million dollars per annum to cluster bomb clearance here,' Kieko ventured nervously. 'Is that figure wrong?' There was a snort from the irascible soldier. 'Eight million dollars is a drop in the ocean,' he retorted. 'The US was spending up to two million bucks a *day* bombing Laos during the war, and it currently spends at least fifty million a year searching for pilots who went missing in action. What's worse is the sheer bloody-mindedness of the bureaucrats that we run up against. They know where the bombs were dropped, for God's sake – it's all documented, but they won't release the information to us. And there are protocols for making most of the different types of devices safe, but they refuse to share them with us, so we have to rely on trial and error. At this rate, it will take hundreds, if not thousands, of years to clear the place up.

They drove to a small quarry, passing the orphanage that a private firm was constructing to provide a home for children who had lost their parents in ordnance explosions. 'They have grown tired of waiting for clearance teams to come,' Manophet explained, pointing to a heap of rusting metal. 'They dig up the devices themselves and leave them there to be collected. It is not a good situation. Every day children walk to school along this road.' From here, they made their way to a Hmong village. The more time Manophet spent with the Hmong, the more he warmed to them. There was an entrepreneurial flair to their character that struck a chord with him, a sense that it was not enough to spend all day watching rice plants grow, in the time-honoured Lao tradition. Mindful that villagers' perceptions of the outside world were still influenced by the stances they had adopted during the war, he calculated that it would be prudent to visit a hamlet that had sided with the US. But a feisty old crone, who stood a good twelve inches shorter than Robert, turned hostile when she discovered the visitors were Americans, then belligerent. Were they not ashamed to show their faces? The villagers had been promised protection if they would fight on the American side. They were supposed to have received new houses, a deeper well, seeds that would grow vigorously even in the harshest conditions. And yet, even though hundreds of men had sacrificed their lives, none of those pledges had been kept. No attempt had been made to stop the Pathet Lao overrunning the village. Their so-called allies had simply abandoned them to their fate and then proceeded to bomb the few houses that had been left standing. In due course, bombie accidents had claimed the lives of two of her daughters.

The mood was sombre when they sat down to talk at the guest house that evening. Manophet was rarely required to spend an entire day focussing on the damage done by the bombing, and the memories of what they had seen weighed him down. So many of his compatriots still lived in the shadow of the war. His two guests looked drained. Apparently they had always expected the press article that they were going to write to reflect badly on their own country, but now they appeared daunted by the scale of the task ahead of them.

'We're not journalists,' Robert explained. 'We're academics. It's tough for regular journalists to get pieces about Laos past their editors and into print. I don't mean to suggest the press is trying to sweep it all under the carpet. The depressing reality is that there's almost always a war being fought somewhere around the world, and current conflicts necessarily take priority over historical conflicts when it comes to reporting. News has to be new – that's the golden rule. As soon as peace is declared in a disaster zone, the media lose interest and move on to the next one. So, as far as we can see, the only way to get a piece about Laos published is to write it ourselves and place it in a journal prepared to accept articles from freelancers. If there's an exception to the general rule, it's the Vietnam War. Plenty of Americans are aware that Laos was bombed in the sixties because Vietnamese troops were using it as a thoroughfare. But the general impression is that the population here is tiny and the country is covered in jungle, so there's a lazy assumption that the bombing didn't have any lasting impact.'

'I have heard there are reports of wars every day on the news programmes in the West,' Manophet said, nodding, 'and the tourists who come here tell me they see terrible photographs all the time. But they also say these reports do not seem to be real because they see them on a nice television screen in a comfortable living room. It is only when they come and see what a war does to a country for themselves that it becomes real. That is what they tell me.'

'I don't suppose reading our article will move people to tears any more than watching the news does,' Kieko said. 'But we hope it may be seen by a few of America's decision makers. One of the things about being a historian is that you're surrounded by examples of how bad mankind is at learning the lessons of history. If we spell out some of the more catastrophic consequences of the policies implemented here by earlier generations of US policymakers, perhaps that will give the current generation food for thought and help them avoid repeating the same mistakes elsewhere in the world.'

'We're also hoping one or two of the big non-government funding bodies will pick up on the story and send some money in Laos's direction,' Robert added.

'But they do not have so much money to spend, compared to the government, I suppose,' Manophet said.

'Actually, the private sector is enormous. A tiny percentage of the funds under private control would be enough to get Laos back on its feet.'

'It would?'

'Oh yes. The gulf between the levels of wealth in our two countries is really quite obscene. The economy here is worth less than a billion dollars a year. Well, there are individuals in America with fortunes many times that size. Bill Gates, for instance, the chairman of a technology company named Microsoft –'

'I have heard of Microsoft,' Manophet broke in. 'I have seen one of their computers.'

'Well, Gates is worth a hundred billion dollars on his own. And he doesn't sit on his cash. He gives huge sums away to good causes every year.'

As though embarrassed by the whole subject, they closed their folders and diverted the conversation into shallower water. 'You don't *look* like brothers, you and Kong Keo,' Kieko observed.

'Ah, well no, we are not brothers by birth,' Manophet explained. 'But this is a practice that we have in Laos. If we are very close to another person, we may call him a brother – or a father or a son, depending on whether he is older or younger – even though we are not in fact related to each other.'

Presently Robert started quizzing him about his background. Manophet had volunteered a couple of anecdotes earlier in the day, eliciting a flutter of interest with the revelation that Vietnamese soldiers had occasionally brought in food when his family had been hiding in the Annamite mountain cave during the bombing raids, so he could hardly object to them asking personal questions. But their probing, while friendly, was a little too intrusive for his liking. He stayed deliberately vague about his time in the army. 'Oh, here and there,' he said when they asked where he had served.

'Were you at Vieng Xay?' Robert asked.

'For a while,' he admitted.

'At Camp One? At the re-education camp?'

Suddenly there was electricity in the air. They were hanging on his answer. Manophet knew exactly why re-education camps were so fascinating to *falang*. If they had been tourists, he would have told them the story about the king's unexplained disappearance as a way of stretching out the tension. But it would not do to overplay his hand. And his army training had taught him never to let his guard slip too far. He needed to be circumspect. Anything that he said to them might be reported in print, and in due course scrutinised by the Lao authorities. 'It used to be a re-education camp,' he said. 'But this is not something I can really talk about.'

'We understand,' Kieko said.

'You must forgive us,' Robert said. 'The position over here is so different to what we're used to back home. People in the West say pretty much whatever they want. If you turn on the television, you're as likely as not to find yourself listening to somebody mouthing off about some grievance or other. Nobody takes any of it particularly seriously. But in Laos you need to be more careful, I guess. Even if you wanted to make a constructive suggestion about the way the country is being run, presumably you'd be wise to keep your mouth shut.'

Manophet nodded. 'It is not a good idea to complain in our country.'

'You must feel frustrated sometimes,' Kieko said, 'particularly working with tourists. You probably had no idea how far behind Laos has fallen under communist rule until foreigners started arriving, but now you get reminders every hour you're with them.'

He could see where the discussion was leading. They were hoping he would make a few derogatory remarks about the Party. If he obliged, it would suggest to the readers of The Boston Review that he endorsed western value systems, and that might encourage them to travel to Laos and use him as a guide. He stroked his chin. He did not particularly want to spend another late-night session at the Ministry of Affairs, but the risk seemed worth taking. 'You have to understand that it is difficult to rebuild a country when there are unexploded bombs everywhere,' he said eventually. 'The government cannot build roads, for instance, and without roads it is not easy to make things better. But it is also true that we are frustrated. Everybody was full of hope when we gained independence, but the government has been promising that things will get better ever since that time, and blaming everybody except themselves when they don't. We lost faith many years ago. Most Lao have resigned themselves to being poor for the rest of their lives.'

The head man from the Tai Dam village had reluctantly concluded that he could not send his son and daughter to learn English from Manophet as it would take them too long to walk to Phonsavan. Not long after he stopped by to pass on this news, however, Manophet gave in to a couple of local Hmong boys who had been pestering him for tuition since the beginning of the year. He toyed with the idea of conducting the lessons in Hmong as a way of extending his grasp on their language, but both boys were fluent in Lao, and he decided he would be able to express himself more succinctly if he stuck to his native tongue. For the first week or two, he was conscious only of how little he knew about what he was doing. How could these unfortunate students be expected to make any headway when he was so woefully underprepared? A proper teacher would have arrived with a clear plan – where to start, how much ground to cover, what exercises to set. He should have borrowed a blackboard and chalked up the words that he was teaching them to speak so that they could see what they looked like, brought paper for them to write on, invented little ruses for keeping them engaged when their minds began to wander. Instead, he had flitted here and there, showering them with complicated vocabulary when he should have stuck to the simple building blocks, tried to explain abstruse grammatical points because they happened to crop up in sentences that he had plucked from the air. And yet, as he sat at home pondering the mistakes that he had made and lamenting his shortcomings, he felt a glow of fulfilment. In spite of everything, the boys were progressing, and so was he – as a teacher. Every blunder was a blessing in disguise, a small step on the road to improvement.

Word travelled quickly in a town like Phonsavan. Within weeks, several other children were also taking lessons – Hmong, Lao, a Khmu boy distantly related to his childhood friend, My. Manophet's doubts about his fitness to teach began to ebb away. He had become a successful tour guide without any formal training. Why should he not be able to turn himself a capable teacher? And, although teaching brought in no money, it remunerated him handsomely at a spiritual level, for there was nothing that gave him greater pleasure than seeing a student progress under his tutelage. The students, for their part, attended out of a desire to be like Mr Manophet. He was their role model. Because he had worked hard to teach himself English, he now had one of the most interesting and rewarding jobs in town. That was what *they* wanted to do when they were older. Manophet felt a more visceral connection to his pupils than to the *falang* who arrived at the guest house and then disappeared a few days later like the brilliant petals on a delicate flower. These relationships were ongoing. He knew each student's character, shared their joys and disappointments, joined in with their struggles. But there was an obstacle that grew larger with every pupil who enrolled: it was a struggle to fit more than three of them into his room at the same time. He needed a bigger teaching space. Miss Onh, the proprietor of the Sangha restaurant came unexpectedly to his aid. 'You remember the mushroom farmer?' she said. 'I am not using the house that he gave me. You could live there and turn the big front room into a classroom.' Suddenly Manophet had a house of his own and was running a school.

For perhaps the first time in his life, he had found a pursuit that reconciled him to his childhood dream of becoming a good person. At last he could begin to feel comfortable in his own skin. And yet this sense of fulfilment came at a cost. His days were frequently awkward to plan, and he needed all his resourcefulness to juggle his competing responsibilities successfully. If tourists ran into difficulties, they expected him to drop everything and give them his undivided attention for as long as it took to resolve the situation. He could be summoned from the classroom to assist with medical emergencies or sort out travel arrangements that had unravelled. On one occasion, he had to go to the police station to negotiate on behalf of an intoxicated backpacker who had managed to get himself arrested. But it was crucial that the school had a rigid timetable. To reschedule lessons at short notice was not fair on the children, some of whom were getting up at four in the morning to walk to Phonsavan for the early class. What a good thing it was to have Lao and Hmong learning side by side. As far as the students were concerned, there was nothing remarkable about such an arrangement. Their native tongues might differ, but they shared the same dreams and anxieties. What their ancestors might or might not have done to one another was not high on their list of concerns. The numerous Hmong boys who had never been to school before were often too shy to speak in front of the class. One of the best ways to bring them out of their shells, Manophet discovered, was to tease them. He would invent mischievous names for them and accuse them of preposterous misdemeanours that they could easily refute. Being able to coax a tongue-tied twelve year-old out from beneath the thrall of his own fear was surely one of the most satisfying of all the strange kicks that he received from his new vocation.

His reputation as a tour guide was now firmly established. Visitors from all corners of the globe were dropping in at the Sangha restaurant to ask where they might find Mr Manophet. He spent less and less time at the guest house – though he and Kong Keo remained close friends and referred business to one other whenever they could. Increasing numbers of *falang* were sent Manophet's way by Lane Xang Travel, a Vientiane-based tour operator that wanted to offer its clients the chance to travel to the north of the country. Originally, it had catered exclusively to affluent individuals in search of unorthodox adventures, each one requiring a tailored experience – which had meant spending many pleasant hours discussing possible itineraries with his friend, Singmakhom Daravong, Lane Xang's local agent in Xieng Khouang. But it had now taken the decision to offer its services to small groups too, encouraged by the stream of favourable feedback that it had been receiving. In due course, bookings began to flow in from western tour operators, and parties of fifteen began descending on Phonsavan in fleets of jeeps or minibuses. How could Manophet safeguard his English classes against this torrent of business? An elegant solution to the problem presented itself when a tour group arrived many hours later than scheduled after a bone-rattling journey on the country's still appalling roads. In desperation, he asked whether they would mind sitting in on his evening class. The students were thrilled to meet authentic English speakers and have the chance to try out their rudimentary language skills. The tourists, for their part, were ecstatic to be interacting so closely with the locals and making themselves genuinely useful. From that day on, a visit to Mr Manophet's English school became one of the highlights on every tourist's itinerary.

A few of the *falang* who attended were so inspired by their experiences that, on returning home, they packaged up items that they imagined might be useful as teaching aids and despatched them optimistically to Xieng Khouang. At least some of these arrived safely. A beautiful fold-out map of the world appeared from Australia, which Manophet displayed proudly on the school room wall. This was followed by several boxes of English grammar primers sent from a school in Yorkshire where they had become superfluous to requirements, biros, pencils and a hefty consignment of back-numbers of the National Geographical magazine. Other visitors sent postcards from far-off places to let him know how much they had enjoyed visiting the school, asking how many pupils were now enrolled, and chattering away as though he was one of their dearest friends. From time to time, packages of photographs would arrive, which he would hand over to his students to pick through in case any of them had been caught on film. Although he had too little time to write back to all his correspondents, he would always send letters of thanks to those who mailed gifts. As time went by, it grew increasingly apparent that he needed a more efficient means of communicating with *falang*. It had not escaped his notice that

Lane Xang had recently acquired an internet presence, at the insistence of its western customers. When an internet café appeared unexpectedly on Route Seven, he decided the time had come to get online. While the authorities would probably view the act of opening a personal e-mail account as suspicious, if not downright subversive, he had no objection to what he wrote being read by a censorious Party member if that was the price he had to pay. He had nothing to hide. Being the seventh sibling in his family, seven was his lucky number, and it took him no time at all to decide what user name to choose: lonebuffalo7@hotmail.com.

'Why do you call yourself Lone Buffalo?' an intense young tourist with an irritating British accent enquired.

Manophet described the sense of isolation that had so often engulfed him during the long days that he had spent trudging behind his parents' water buffalo.

A faint smile played on the man's lips. 'You are clever, you Lao,' he said eventually.

'What do you mean?'

'You like to keep us gullible westerners guessing, I think. You have a way of presenting the truth that makes it difficult to grasp. It is like looking at the sun through shifting clouds.'

'But that *is* the truth,' Manophet protested.

'Oh, I didn't mean to suggest the story was an invention,' the man hastened to assure him. 'But surely that can only be part of the explanation. The name might have suited you all those years ago, when you were working in the fields, but your life has moved on a long way since then. Why should you keep using it unless it is still making a relevant statement about you?'

In earlier days, his *falang* charges had been more circumspect with their inquisitions. They had recognised that he was the product of a communist state, somebody with a conflicting set of values who was liable to hold different beliefs to theirs. They were uncertain how much of their language he understood, and had been at pains to avoid offending or upsetting him by appearing too forward. Now, because he used their idioms freely and shared their sense of humour, there was no longer any reason for them to suppose that he was not tuned precisely to their wavelength. He behaved much like any other westerner when he was with them, and their wont was to embrace him as one of their own. There was no denying how precious their warmth and esteem were to him. How wonderfully affirmed he felt when he was with *falang*. His own countrymen had never held him in this kind of regard. But there were areas of his personal space onto which he wished they would not encroach quite so peremptorily. 'Once you have chosen a name, you are stuck with it, I think,' he rejoined, getting to his feet to indicate that the conversation was at an end.

'You were under no obligation to incorporate it into your e-mail address, the man called after him as he walked away. 'Presumably you would have been happy to let it drop if you were, well, in a relationship with somebody, shall we say.'

The adventure holiday companies pestered him for ideas with which to flesh out their itineraries. They had money to spend. What could he suggest? Soon he found himself accompanying groups to Luang Prabang, escorting parties through limestone cave complexes in Oudomxay province, being whisked up great rivers in motorised long-boats, trekking to hidden waterfalls with shady pools where it was safe for perspiring tourists to strip off and take a dip. How about visiting Long Chieng, one representative suggested – "the most secret place on earth" as Sousath Phetrasy, the owner of the Maly hotel, was calling it? If the Maly could run excursions to the site of the old CIA airbase for its guests, why should Manophet not be able to offer the same service? A few cursory enquiries revealed that Long Chieng remained off-limits to non-military personnel, as it had since the end of the war. Sousath had never taken anybody there. However, there were rumours that the authorities were about to grant him an exclusive licence to escort tour groups around the legendary facility – rumours that had a depressing ring of authenticity, given that his father had been the Pathet Lao's spokesman during the war and was still in a position to pull strings. Manophet responded by taking parties to see the ruined Buddha in Muang Khoun, and then inviting them to his parents' house on the way back to have tea. From her rocking chair, his mother would watch tears roll down the tourists' cheeks as he told his story, none of them grasping the significance of the fact that she could not understand a word of English.

The internet brought him closer to one of his great passions: Arsenal, a London-based soccer team. In days gone by, it had been necessary to wait until a copy of the English edition of the Vientiane Times had negotiated its tortuous way to Phonsavan to find out whether they had won their latest match. Now, supposing the phone lines were functioning, he could discover the score four or five days sooner, and read a blow-by-blow account of each game. Occasionally, English soccer matches were screened on Lao TV, and he would have the chance to watch his heroes in action on the set in the lobby at the Phu Doi. There was almost nothing that he found more exhilarating than seeing the irrepressible Dennis Bergkamp running rings around bemused defenders, or Thierry Henry firing the ball into the opponents' net from an impossible angle. A couple of years had passed since "The Gunners", as they were nicknamed, had pulled off one of the greatest feats in English soccer history by winning the two principal competitions in the same season. Although they were still playing scintillating football, their great rivals, Manchester United had been the more successful club since that golden period. No matter: The Gunners, under their charismatic manager, Arsène Wenger, would rise to the top again before long – of this he was certain. His friends could not stop laughing when he donned the oversized Arsenal shirt that had been mailed to him by a thoughtful *falang* and ran proudly out on to the dusty Phonsavan pitch to join them for a game. But he had no intention of letting a little good-natured mockery unsettle him. He would be the one having the last laugh if he could replicate some of the ball skills and body swerves of which those English Premier League players were capable.

He found the Boston Review article that Kieko and Robert had written online. The aim of the piece was unmistakeable: they were out to shock their American readers with the bleakness of their descriptions of the state to which Laos had been reduced. By the end, a depression had settled over him. It was all true, of course – the bomb craters, the accident rates, the tragic casualties, the poverty. How quickly you could forget the suffering of the folk with ruined lives that could not be put back together when your own life was on such a steep upward trajectory – when you had televised football matches to watch and promising students to nurture, not to mention a steady stream of unsolicited gifts from obliging *falang*. And yet *was* the picture as grim as the one they had painted? Westerners sometimes confided in him that the Lao were amongst the happiest people they had come across on their travels. Perhaps the important thing was not how wretched your lot was but whether it was getting more or less wretched as time went by. The article was slickly constructed. It would probably encourage another wave of *falang* to book holidays in Laos so that they could take photographs of the devastation for themselves. The more he thought about war tourism, the less he liked the idea of using the country's terrible legacy as bait. The Buddha would surely not have approved. Was war tourism so different to sex tourism, the industry that defined neighbouring Thailand? The Lao authorities had made a pre-emptive strike against that particular malaise spreading across the border by declaring it a criminal offence for *falang* and Lao to sleep together, but what steps could they possibly take to debunk the country's burgeoning image as a war destination?

He was amused to read in the article that he had served as a guard at a re-education camp, an experience that had "shaped his outlook on communism", though not altogether surprised. He had suspected at the time that they had misunderstood what he was saying. But what could you do with *falang*? They arrived with rigid ideas about re-education camps, communism and missing US airman and would clutch instinctively at the flimsiest straw of corroboration. Any factual mistakes of which they were guilty – suggesting that Dien Bien Phu was in Laos rather than Vietnam, for instance, or that it was the Americans who had been defeated there rather than the French – they wanted you to correct. But their romantic notions about the mystical East were sacred. Challenge their conviction that it possessed supernatural dimensions, and you would be on dangerous ground. Another myth that he had struggled to dispel was that he had spent time in Vietnam during his army years, an idea propagated by an eager tourist who had not been concentrating properly when he had told a group that he had trained near the Vietnamese border. But was it so wrong, allowing them to believe what they wanted to believe? They left Xieng Khouang in an uplifted state, of the opinion that they had just come through some of the most important experiences of their lives – so they would regularly claim in the letters of appreciation that they wrote him. Was that not a desirable outcome – even if it meant borrowing a story or two along the way, and employing a bit of showmanship?

Although *falang* seemed to view the practice of addressing their guide as Mr Manophet as quaint and rather endearing, it was a form of address that sent out the wrong signals to western tour operators. Times were moving on, and having no surname was coming to be seen as unsophisticated. Plenty of older Lao managed with just a single name – his father among them. In such situations, it was traditional for children to adopt their mother's surname, supposing she had one, and all his other brothers and sisters had followed that paradigm. But Manophet had refused to conform. His mother's surname was Athakhanh, and it was Uncle Athakhanh to whom he had been farmed out for adoption at the age of five, an injustice that continued to rankle. If going through life without a surname was good enough for his father, it was good enough for him – that had always been his line heretofore. But it had reached the point where the issue needed to be confronted. At length, inspiration came to him: he would fuse the Christian names of his father and mother, Moui and Douangdy, to create a surname of his own: Mouidouangdy. He recited the invented word over and over in his head. It had a good ring to it, he decided. Predictably enough, his family disagreed. What was wrong with the name Athakhanh, his father admonished? Why must he insult his mother's family by staging this public display of disrespect? The *falang* with whom it pleased him to spend his days might deem such forms of behaviour acceptable, but it was not the way decent upstanding Lao folk conducted themselves.

His father was growing frail, and Manophet did not argue back. The responsibility for bringing a large family through the war years had been unimaginably heavy, and the experience must have taken a terrible toll on him. It was not difficult to see why he found his son's way of existence so difficult to stomach – the fact that he was teaching English, the language of the barbarians who had bombed his country to pulp, to the very people who had been his bitter enemies on the battlefield, the Hmong. He did not understand how his son could accept gifts and "dirty money" in exchange for showing *falang* how much damage they had done, nor why he embraced their tawdry decadent cultural values rather than those in which he had been steeped during his upbringing. And his mother would always side with her husband when they were together. It was natural. What else would a loyal wife do? But Manophet knew that in the privacy of her own heart she was proud of what he had achieved. She understood nothing of what the *falang* who came to sit in her front room said, but she could see from their shocked expressions and tears that they were now bitterly sorry for what their ancestors had done, and that her son had played his part in bringing them to this penitent state. He had been a rebellious child and a considerable trial to them over the years. But all the time he had been searching for an obscure, out-of-the-way path that he needed to follow, and now it looked as though he might have found it.

# FOURTEEN

His father passed away towards the end of 2001. His death was not unexpected. Life expectancy in Laos was around fifty. To have survived to the age of seventy-five was no mean achievement – though this did not make it any easier to adjust to his absence. Gone was the enervating drip-drip of disapproval and disappointment, the voice invariably raised in favour of tradition, the piercing eyes, the figure of authority that Manophet desperately longed to impress and be worthy of. No longer would he feel that stab of guilty excitement whenever he chose to deviate from the course of action expected of a diligent Lao son. But being able to do as he pleased without fear of censure was not the liberating experience he had half anticipated. The lodestone from which he had taken all his bearings was gone. Each time he had a judgement to make, he found himself pausing to wonder which cause his father would have favoured. And then there was the family to think of. His father had taken so many crucial decisions over the years. Now they were on their own, and it was expected that Manophet, as the most dynamic and successful sibling, should provide some leadership. He visited his mother as often as he could during the weeks that followed. She had Kone and her husband to look after her, but Manophet had not forgotten the promise that his father had wrung from him many years back in the refugee camp. From now on, he would regard her as his special responsibility. What she would have liked best from him, he sensed, was a few extra grandchildren to add to her tally, but there was precious little he could do about that.

The English Development School, as it was now known, was making a name for itself. New students were enrolling all the time. Usually their parents were related to the parents of an existing pupil or knew them socially, but children with no obvious connection also came knocking on Manophet's door. A boy appeared one morning wanting to attend a class. He seemed reluctant or unable to explain how he came to be there. Some distant relatives had mentioned the school on a visit, he thought, but he was unable to recollect whether they were part of his father's family or his mother's, or what their names were. At the end of the lesson, he stayed behind, shifting awkwardly from one foot to the other. Would it be all right for him to sit at a table and write a note to one of the storekeepers at the other end of the town? He was supposed to be paying an account for his father while he was in Phonsavan – only, the storekeeper was not there, and he was going to have to leave the money with a neighbour. Something did not add up. Hill-tribe boys were rarely able to read or write. But Manophet was in a hurry. He had arranged to help some tourists change money and book bus tickets. And the boy had paid close attention to the lesson and seemed a conscientious sort. He would only be gone an hour or two. Giving him a friendly pat on the shoulder, he indicated his assent and headed out to his rendezvous. The house was silent when he returned. The door had been pulled to, as he had requested, and the boy was nowhere to be seen. It took Manophet several minutes to register that his bicycle, which he had left unlocked against the wall, was missing. Neither the boy nor the bicycle was ever seen again.

Success had its price. On taking up residence at Miss Onh's house, he collected all his pupils into a single class. Before long, however, he had to split the group up again – partly because, with new students appearing all the time, it had grown too big for the front room, and partly because the most recent arrivals had missed too many lessons to be able to keep up with the pupils who had been present from the beginning. He now taught an advanced class before setting off for work in the morning, and back-to-back classes for intermediate-level students and beginners in the evening, a total of three hours every weekday – on top of which, he had to allow time for preparing lessons, thinking up exercises, and marking work. Some of the students lived in far-flung villages and walked many miles to and from Phonsavan each day to attend. Others, for whom the distances involved were too great, came to stay with relatives in Phonsavan for weeks at a time. Most were boys. In many families, it was still assumed that girls would spend their lives raising children and would have no call to use English later in life. The students were so much more diligent than he had been at their age, even though there was no guarantee that their hard work would bring them any reward. Some, he knew, rose before dawn to feed their chickens, but were still slaving away at their English in the classroom at eight in the evening. For the Hmong, who made up at least a quarter of the class, the challenge was even more daunting, since they had the disadvantage of being taught in Lao rather than their native tongue.

Once or twice a month he would cook supper for a few of the students after the evening classes had ended. It was a ritual that had come into being when a Hmong boy had arrived for school carrying a chicken, a sorry-looking specimen with a broken leg, but freshly killed and sure to have at least a little meat on it. Would teacher Manophet be able to accept it in lieu of school fees, the boy wanted to know. His family was having trouble making ends meet, and it was all they could manage at the moment. In principle, each student was supposed to pay him 1,000 kip a month to help defray the cost of providing teaching materials, but most struggled to find the tiny sum, and in practice he would accept whatever they could afford, covering the shortfall out of his own pocket. Slackers he would not tolerate, but he would never turn away a poor student as long as he or she was prepared to work hard. "If you come to school every day, it's on me," was one of his maxims. He pondered the problem. The boy's family was evidently very badly off, and this scrawny bird probably represented a significant slice of its worldly wealth. It might fill his belly for the night, but it would leave theirs that much emptier. There seemed to be only one solution: to accept the gift, but on condition that the boy and some of his friends stayed to help him eat it.

Once the precedent had been set, there was no stopping the children. They took to arriving with lemon grass, chinese celery, sweet basil, assorted chillies, rice, galanga, the occasional egg, even coffee. Meat and fish were in scarcer supply, and if the meat was offered with a shrug of the shoulders you could assume you would be better off not asking what it was. Manophet suspected that dog, monkey, snake and porcupine had all passed his lips at one time or another. Other students produced jerseys knitted for him by their parents or siblings, or vests – in the hope that these would constitute acceptable payment in kind. Free time was now in alarmingly short supply, and he had significant reservations about sacrificing any more of his evenings. But it felt good to be surrounded by other people. Men were better creatures when they were not obliged to depend on their own company. In place of the silence that usually settled over the house after school lessons had ended, banter and laughter would fill the air, occasionally a song. The students' efforts to help with the cooking generally wasted more time than they saved, and their high-spirited antics often led to his possessions being moved or dropped or stained with food. After the meal, they would let him beguile them with outrageous stories, rubbing their bellies contentedly as they listened. Sometimes, a student would fall asleep where he sat, exhausted by the exertions of the day, and Manophet would move him to a quieter place until the morning rather than waking him up and making him go home.

He discovered, rather to his surprise, that two of his students were the children of local Party officials. Even in the higher echelons of Lao society, a working knowledge of English was coming to be viewed as a useful asset, it seemed. But the majority came from families who were struggling to keep their heads above water. Any opportunity to improve their chances of securing a worthwhile job later in life was worth taking. Tong was determined to buy his family a moped. As things stood at present, a serviceable pair of shoes was beyond his means, but he knew how much time a moped would save his parents and could see that if they had more time everything else would fall into place. It did not matter that it might take years to attain his goal. If you distracted yourself with arguments like that, it would just take you longer to achieve – that was his philosophy. If you made up your mind there was nothing you could do to make your life better, your reward would be the satisfaction of seeing yourself proved right. But if you concentrated on making your dream come true, you just might be successful. Manophet tried to be impartial in his dealings with them, but it was difficult not to have favourites. There was a cheeky boy named Amphone who reminded him of himself at a younger age. His hair stuck up on end like a demented rice plant, and he could mimic all manner of animals. And then there was Bountham, who was infatuated with Noy, one of the girls in the class, but was waiting for the right moment to tell her.

He kept the schoolroom well stocked with candles. Most evenings, Phonsavan's electricity came on at dusk, and the lights could be used when he was teaching evening classes, but during the rainy season thunderstorms regularly knocked out the generators for an hour or two. Even candles were considered a luxury by many of the students, who were accustomed to making do with the light from a cooking fire after dark. The flickering flames threw trembling shadows up the classroom walls, reminding him of the evenings he had spent with the opium-addicted travelling minstrel after leaving the army, and he would struggle, sometimes unsuccessfully, against the urge to take advantage of the atmosphere and spin the children fantastic yarns about him. Was it such a sin to caricature the unfortunate fellow if his anecdotes sent a subliminal message to the students not to let themselves become dependent on opium? From time to time, he would talk to them about his father, whose spirit never seemed too far away these days. In return, the pupils would volunteer regret-filled stories of their own, tales of relatives who had passed away or seen their lives blighted by misfortune. 'You should not be ashamed if you feel sad now and then,' Manophet told them. 'All of us go through difficult times in our lives. Even I cry sometimes, when there is nobody looking. You have to be patient – maybe for many years. Other people may not believe in you. They may say you are sure to turn out to be a hopeless person. But, if you keep trying your best, perhaps your luck will change one day the way mine has changed.'

They came from contrasting cultures and backgrounds, and there was no set formula for bringing the best out of them. Some were sensitive souls who reacted badly to being singled out for criticism in class, while others only made a genuine effort to shake off their lazy habits when subjected to a public shaming. Others again responded better to an occasional reproof, followed by private words of encouragement after the lesson had ended. If a pupil made the same mistake three times in a row, Manophet would rap them over the knuckles with a ruler. It was hardly a draconian sanction, and one seldom carried through, but it was sufficient to keep the class on its toes. They saw him not merely as an English teacher. He was an innovator, a man who had the power to make things happen. Any sliver of information that they could prise from his store of wisdom would be worth having. What else could he tell them about the *falang* world, that mysterious realm into which had managed to blaze a trail? Which western traits should they try to copy? This gave him a delicate balancing act to perform. It was healthy that they should look up to him and take inspiration from his example, but only as long as their expectations were kept within reasonable bounds, and they did not expect to be handed a blueprint for success. The school could not guarantee them a passport to a better existence. If they failed to work hard, their chances of advancing themselves remained negligible. After lessons, individual pupils would seek private counsel, and he would listen patiently to accounts of the troubles that they faced at home – as often as not at the hands of hostile step-parents. And yet who was he to be offering advice on moral dilemmas? More than once, he spent a sleepless night wondering whether he had judged a pupil's personal situation correctly.

A Hmong student of about seventeen began to catch his attention. The boy was not one to push himself forward, but whenever Manophet picked him out to answer a question in class he would come back with a textbook answer that showed he had been following closely. Whether because he had an ear for languages or because he concentrated harder than other students, his spoken English was outstanding. And yet his attendance record was decidedly patchy. As a rule, Manophet did not enquire too closely about the circumstances if pupils missed lessons. They were often needed by their families to help out in the fields, particularly the female students when there was rice to be planted or harvested. As long as they worked hard when they were present, he raised no objection. But this one was so promising. He could go a long way if he could be persuaded to devote a little more time to his studies. Eventually, on his return from an extended period of absence from the classroom, Manophet took him to one side. 'You are a great trial to me,' he said, speaking in English to make it seem like an exercise. 'I see you for a month, and then you disappear again, and it can be a month or even longer before you come back.'

The boy looked uncomfortable. 'I know, teacher,' he said, shuffling his feet. 'It is very bad. I am very sorry.'

'How can I teach you good English if you are never here for more than a few weeks at a time?' He was careful to pitch the question in a friendly, even mildly jocular tone. He did not want the boy to feel he was being criticised. 'You are missing so many important sections of the course.'

'I would like to come more often.' He was struggling to hold Manophet's gaze. 'But it is difficult.'

'I understand.' He gave him a conciliatory pat on the arm. 'But it is such a pity. You are one of the best students I have ever had.'

The boy looked startled. 'I practice when I am at home,' he said, as though defending himself. 'I think about the work we have done and try to make sure I can remember it.'

'You probably have a long journey.'

He nodded. 'About twenty miles. I stay here in Phonsavan with my cousin when I come. But his house is not very big.'

'And you have to eat while you are here,' Manophet said, 'and it all costs money. Yes, I know what you are saying.'

'And I don't have enough money to pay my cousin or to pay *you*, teacher.'

'You know I do not expect you to pay me if it is too difficult for you.'

'Yes, I know this. But I feel bad. My cousin is not rich. You are not rich. People give me things, but I have nothing to give them back.'

As Manophet mulled the problem over, a bold idea came to him. Why should the boy not come and live with him in Phonsavan? The Hmong had saved Bua's life and given him the chance to make a success of himself. Was this not the perfect way to repay them? Manophet would become the boy's father. There was plenty of room in the house, and cooking for two was no more trouble than cooking for one. Freed from his dependency on his cousin, the boy would never need to miss a school class. And yet this was no trivial step that he was contemplating. Was it reasonable to ask a teenager to leave his natural family behind and adapt to an alien culture? And was he, Manophet ready to assume the extra weight of responsibility? He took the boy to have lunch with his mother one Sunday afternoon as part of a larger group of students so she could look him over. Sunday lunch in Muang Khoun was another blossoming English Development School ritual, one as popular with his mother, who loved meeting his pupils, as with his less well nourished students. She was increasingly preoccupied with dark memories now that her husband had passed on, and this was a good excuse to chase away the shadows of the past. The boy, still unaware that plans were afoot to invite him to become part of the family, was at pains to avoid infringing any house taboos with which he might be unacquainted, and reluctant to say very much. But she judged his reticence to be an asset rather than a shortcoming, and Manophet could see that she was reconciling herself to the plan.

'He is a good-looking boy,' she said when they were alone together.

'At the moment he is still shy and more interested in making something of himself than chasing after pretty girls.'

'People will talk,' she warned him.

'It could be worse,' he pointed out. 'He could be a girl.'

'You should give him a Lao name,' she said. 'He will keep his Hmong name, but he should have a Lao name as well.'

'We are getting ahead of ourselves,' he said. 'It may not happen. He may not be interested. His family may not like the idea.'

The boy took little persuading. The difficult part was convincing him the suggestion was serious. He had aspirations, like any other teenager, but also a firm grasp on reality, and his instincts told him the offer was too good to be genuine. There had to be a catch. He conjured up a raft of obstacles – there was nowhere for him to sleep; it might upset the spirits of his ancestors if he lived in a Lao house; he would not be able to see his friends – as though trying to protect himself from the crushing disappointment that he would have to endure if he embraced the dream, only to see it go up in smoke. How were his parents liable to react, Manophet asked? His family gave him nothing but his food and a space in the hut in which to sleep, the boy explained. If he wanted money – for school fees, for example – it was up to him to earn it himself. In hard practical terms, his father and stepmother should be delighted to have more room in their cramped wooden home, and one less mouth to feed. But no parent, however straitened their circumstances, would take the decision to allow a stranger to remove one of their children lightly. For a single Lao

170

man to take in a Hmong boy like this was highly irregular – there was no getting away from it. The best strategy, Manophet decided, was to send the boy to broach the subject with them himself. They would need time to take it all in, and there was no virtue in harrying them into a quick decision by appearing on the scene prematurely.

A fortnight passed – one of the longest, most nerve-wracking waits Manophet could remember having to endure. But at last the boy reappeared, having persuaded his parents that they should at least talk to his teacher. Dozens of curious pairs of eyes watched their arrival in the village the following day. The air was heavy with suspicion, even hostility. Women stopped whatever they were doing and gathered in furtive huddles. Naked children stood and pointed. The boy's father and stepmother were determined not to let him go. It was unnatural. Nobody had ever heard of such an arrangement being struck between a Lao and a Hmong. The spirits would rise up against the village if they acted with such disrespect. But Manophet had several potent weapons in his armoury: he could speak Hmong; he had the story of how his brother, Bua had been raised by Hmong parents to tell; and he could point to the fact that Lao and Hmong children learned side by side in his classroom every day, along with Khmu and Phouane. As he sang the boy's praises, assuring his parents that he was one of the most promising students ever to have studied at the school, their arguments became less adversarial. Objections gave way to concerns. Would they still be able to see him? Who could he turn to if he found it all too much? Surely there must be some kind of hidden financial cost. Each reassurance brought an incremental thaw in relations. They found it impossible not to like Manophet, and more and more difficult to regard him as a charlatan. By nightfall, he had a son.

The boy was like a cat that had got at the cream. It took many weeks for the manic smile with which he greeted every agreeable quirk of his new environment to fade into a more neutral expression. Manophet, for his part, was soon able to set aside any lingering concerns that he might have been cavalier or overambitious in rearranging their lives so dramatically. Having a child brought an end to the isolation that had thrown its smothering cloak over his private life and, at the same time, a sense of fulfilment that was altogether richer than that which he derived from caring for his pupils. Like all fathers, he was conscious of his lack of stature when set against his own father, while at the same time determined not to repeat the mistakes that he had made as a parent. Every moment he was with his son he needed to set a good example, to be strong but compassionate, neither too censorious, nor too sparing with his advice. He gave the boy a Lao name, as his mother had suggested: Lue. Week by week, they became better acquainted with one another's stories. There was little that Manophet did not already know about the Hmong way of life, but he soaked up every incidental detail that Lue felt inclined to share. This was not only Lue's heritage but Bua's too, making the information doubly significant. The one drawback to the new arrangement was that Manophet's affairs were now even more of a challenge to organise. If his schedule allowed, he would accompany Lue to the secondary school in Phonsavan in the morning and collect him when his afternoon classes ended, but there were numerous days when he had too much else to fit in – in which case Lue would have to negotiate the long walk from the house on his own.

When a new edition of the Lonely Planet Guide was published later that year, Sousath Phetrasy was listed by name in the section covering Xieng Khouang. Manophet felt deflated. It was bad enough trying to keep up with his rival as it was, and now the dice were to be loaded still more heavily in his favour. He was a capable competitor. He too took the trouble to research the sites to which he escorted tourists so that he could talk fluently and intelligently about them. And he was better placed than Manophet to tell enthralling stories. His father, Soth had been made a government minister after the war, and had subsequently been appointed Lao Ambassador to the USSR providing him with a wealth of juicy material on which to draw. Amongst other things, it was rumoured that the king of Laos had stayed at Soth's house on his way to Camp Number One, though Manophet had his doubts about the veracity of this claim. Crucially, Sousath had lived through the war as a young adult, being almost twenty years older than Manophet, and had first-hand experience of being bombed. Fearing for his safety, his family had sent him to China as a child, but he had smuggled himself back into Laos through Vietnam at the age of twelve and spent the next few years sheltering in caves close to the Pathet Lao headquarters near Vieng Xay. That story alone would surely be worth hearing a few times.

One afternoon not long after Lue's arrival, Manophet discovered that his wallet was missing. He had been carrying over a million kip to cover the cost of his tour group's evening meal at the Sangha – a substantial sum of money to a Lao. His heart started thudding. This could be awkward. Miss Onh would probably be prepared to let him have the meal on credit, but he would be expected to make good the shortfall within the next day or two. Where was he going to get hold of a million kip at such short notice? It would take him weeks to earn a sum like that. If the worst came to the worst, he would have to explain the position to the tour group and hope that they would take pity on him. In their scheme of reckoning, a million kip between fifteen people amounted to little more than a rounding error, and they were always so *nice*, these westerners. But he hated this solution. It was shabby and unprofessional. He went back over the events of the day in his mind, trying to work out where he might have mislaid the wallet. And now it came to him. He had taken it out of his pocket when a glass of water had spilled onto his trousers. It should still be on the shelf where he had left it. But the shelf was empty. The bad feeling in his stomach grew more unpleasant. 'Lue?' he called.

Lue's head appeared obediently around the door to his room.

'Have you seen my wallet?'

'Oh.' He came sheepishly forward. 'Sorry. I should have said.' There was a pregnant silence.

Manophet held his breath, remembering the bicycle he had lost a few months earlier.

'I hid it.'

'You did *what*?'

'There were people coming in and out of the house – students, tourists. I thought it would be safer.' He advanced to the bookcase and fished it out from behind a stack of National Geographical magazines. 'Here it is.'

Manophet waited until Lue had returned to his room before counting the money. It had not been touched.

They talked English as a matter of course when they were at home, and Lue was soon assisting his father in the English Development School's beginners class. Manophet arranged evening work for him at the Sangha as a waiter so that he could listen to the language as it tripped off the tongues of those who spoke it fluently, and also brought him along from time to time when he was escorting tour groups, when it did not conflict with his schooling. Introducing him to tourists as "my son" was a splendid gambit, as they took the statement at face value. The "uncanny similarity of their appearances" was even remarked on once or twice. Apparently, it did not register with most *falang* that he and Lue came from different ethnic backgrounds. Manophet had never really understood why they were so inept when it came to distinguishing one kind of oriental from another. One had even admitted to him privately that he could not tell a Japanese from a Chinese. Nor did they think to question the modest age gap that existed between Manophet and his son, but perhaps they found estimating an oriental's age as baffling a task as gauging his ethnicity. An incidental benefit of having Lue at his side was that it discouraged tourists from asking Manophet whether he was married, since they tended to assume that a man who had a son must also have a wife. How refreshing it was, not having to deal with those tiresome questions about why he still single. Lue visited his birth father from time to time, but nothing from his former life held any allure. His primary ties were to Manophet now, and his single goal was to be a credit to him and make the most of the chance that he had been given. Already he was earning his own food, and in no time at all he would be able to hold down a job that paid real money, a proposition that would have been unthinkable only a few months earlier.

By the end of the year, it had become difficult to remember living on his own in the house. It was as though Lue had always been there with him. Had he really spent lonely hours beneath this roof before his son's arrival? In his mind, those belonged to the period before he had teamed up with Kong Keo – the days of trudging along in front of the buffalo in his family's rice fields, the interminable night shifts at the Phu Doi. It suited him so much better to be surrounded by other people, and to have some responsibility for them. Why had it taken such an eternity to arrive at this happy place? These days, people felt it an honour to be able to count him as an acquaintance. They would greet him respectfully on the street and congratulate him on the work that he was doing at the school. Not that he craved public recognition. Being necessary to others was what gave him satisfaction. But it did his ego no harm to be told by respectable Lao who had once regarded him as a nobody that he was a credit to his family and to the town. Only occasionally was he conscious of the weight that now rested on his shoulders. He would never be able to walk away from the little fiefdom that he had constructed. Even if Bua came up with a way of smuggling him across the sea to America to start a better life, the answer would have to be no, for his students would be lost without him, and Lue would have his life turned upside down. But they had nothing to fear. He felt happy and settled now. He would be here for them for as long as they needed him.

# FIFTEEN

B race's eyes followed the curving sweep of the Mekong to the point where it wound around a jutting beach and disappeared behind the contour. To either side, the jungle stretched away in a brocade of scolloped green, veering up along thrusting ridges to the summits of the low hills. A tattered Lao flag on a bald pole lashed to the prow of the old boat fluttered against the cloudless blue haze. The river was low. Here and there, whitecaps danced on the surface where submerged rocks disturbed the even passage of the grey water. Surveying the deserted shores, he was reminded of the remoteness of the country that he had entered. Minute by minute, they were edging further from the safety of the western world, penetrating deeper into the sort of uncharted terrain where they could disappear without anybody noticing. People assumed he must be fearless after everything he had been through, but today there was a void in his stomach. For the first time in a generation, he was conscious of his own mortality. The pale mountain ridge in the distance seemed almost to merge into the horizon at its apex, before growing distinct once more as it descended, the serrations in the limestone karst blunted by the purple shimmer. Shadowy depressions punctuated the forest where the tree cover broke, oases of open space amidst the hungry scramble of impenetrable vegetation. That treacherous jungle! It had not changed: a world starved of sunlight in which a man could lose himself in the blink of an eye if he strayed from the path, a diabolical maze of sloping root tangles and deceptive diagonals where he could walk all day only to find himself back at the place from which he had set out.

The other two Americans were briefing Manophet in the stern, shouting to make themselves heard above the din of the engine. 'He was dishonourably discharged from the Marines,' Archie explained. 'They had no alternative, frankly. He was on a routine solo training exercise over the eastern seaboard in 1961. One of his engines failed, and the plane went down close to the Choptank river. He bailed out safely but, instead of reporting the crash, he threw his parachute in the river and quit the scene. He'd been under a lot of pressure in his personal life. He figured that, if they couldn't find his body, they'd assume it had been swept out to sea. He could get himself a new identity, his wife could claim the insurance money, and they could clear their debts and get their disintegrating marriage back together. In the heat of the moment, that was how he imagined it might pan out. He took a split-second decision and made a run for it. But they found his flying gear a few miles from the crash scene, where he'd tried to hide it, and it wasn't long before he realised he'd have to hand himself over to be court-martialled. It was big news at the time. The Washington Post had a field day. On the face of it, pretty much everything had gone his way up to that point. He'd been decorated for valiant conduct during the Korean War. He was married to a spectacularly beautiful woman, and they had four fine sons. But, once the Marines had thrown him out, the only way he could earn a decent living was by becoming a mercenary, and he and his family moved out to Chiang Mai so he could fly turbo-props for the CIA, who were running arms and supplies to the anti-communist forces in Laos during the early stages of the war.'

They reached Pak Beng late in the afternoon, and at last the deafening boat engine fell silent. From the sleepy village, which consisted of little more than a few shacks, a road of sorts snaked up the Nam Beng valley. It had not been here in the sixties. Some of the paths along which he had been marched had probably been destroyed in the course of its construction. The plan was to drive up to Dien Bien Phu, where he had been imprisoned, following the route that he had taken as closely as possible, stopping off at any towns or villages in which significant episodes had occurred. It had not been his idea. At no point had he ever suggested to Archie that he wanted to retrace his steps. But his old friend had managed to talk him into it. This was not the first time Brace had been back to Laos. At one point, he had been no more than a hair's breadth away from purchasing Lao Airlines. But doing business in Vientiane was a world apart from travelling "up-country" like this. Primitive instincts began to stir as he eyed the massive trees soaring into the sky, shutting out the light. The compulsion to strike off into the jungle when nobody was looking suddenly had him in its thrall once more. Back it all came, the obsession with fashioning an escape opportunity, the endless mental cataloguing of the factors that were liable to distract his captors' attention. It had been an insane preoccupation. What sort of fool imagined he might able to make it to safety with only the sun and the crude map in his head to navigate by, when there was no friendly territory for miles in any direction? If the guards had failed to track him down and recapture him, he would surely have perished within a matter of days. But it had been his duty to give them as much grief as possible – that was how he had seen it. A Marine he might no longer have been in name, but it remained his obligation to behave like one in a time of war.

The following morning, they drove the remaining few miles to Boum Lao, where he had been captured. Leaving the Landcruiser by the side of the crumbling dusty road, they walked a short distance down a bumpy track to the village. Wide-eyed children collected in a big semicircle, the smaller ones positioning themselves warily towards the rear of the group in case the visitors turned out to be dangerous, peeking between gaps to get a view. Who were these odd-looking men, with their pale skins and expensive cameras? As Manophet engaged the villagers in conversation, Brace tried to reconcile the layout of the houses with the pictures in his mind. He seemed to remember the ground sloping the other way. Perhaps they had approached from a different direction. Was this where they had chopped the finger off the boy who had been working for the Royalists? Manophet disappeared into one of the houses, and emerged after some time with a diminutive figure, who turned out to be the head man. 'This person remembers the attack on the village,' he said. 'He was fifteen at that time. He saw you taken as a prisoner.' The man smiled, as though delighted to be reminded of the incident. 'He says he will take us to where the landing strip used to be.' They waded across a shallow river and climbed the hill on the far side. Nothing here seemed familiar. Waist high clumps of elephant grass camouflaged scrubby thorn tangles that tore at their legs and ankles. Beneath the riot of parched greenery, the broken line of a concrete irrigation ditch could just be made out. 'The Vietnamese were hidden in a cave on that hillside,' Manophet translated. 'They had been watching the airstrip for two weeks before they launched the ambush.'

They scoured the undergrowth for relics, hoping to link the area to its past, but there was nothing to suggest it had ever been of any importance. Then, as they turned to make their way back, he bent his arms instinctively behind him, as though to allow the Vietnamese to tie his elbows. This was how each stage of the march had started. A few mouthfuls of sugar-doped rice balls, ropes looped cleverly around the elbows to prevent any heroics en route, and the party would be on its way. Now that he was walking in the right direction, the sweep of the hills suddenly made sense again. The contours were where they should be. It was all coming back: the events of that still May morning in 1965 – hidden away until now in the recesses of his mind – were as clear as if they had taken place only yesterday. They had hijacked his life, brought his war to an end before it had even begun, launched him on an odyssey that would come to define him in the eyes of the world. The breeze dropped for a moment and the tall grass stood completely still. As the air shimmered, the memories came flooding back. One moment, he had been setting down the heavily laden Pilatus Porter, just as he had the previous evening and on so many occasions before, the next, bullets were smashing into the fuselage, petrol was spurting out onto the grass, the woman in the cargo hold was screaming. And her husband, a Lao soldier, was leaping rashly from the plane as it taxied to a halt, only to be shot down in his tracks. That was the point at which he had realised there was no sense in trying to turn the aircraft around and get airborne again. It was not until many years later that he found out what had happened. The Royalist forces responsible for holding the position had been overrun by the Vietnamese during the early hours of the morning. Seven people had died in the fighting. Twenty-eight had been wounded. The screaming woman in the hold had been returning to Boum Lao with her baby, who had been receiving medical treatment at Xieng Lom. She had taken a bullet in the thigh through the fuselage, and could no longer walk.

Back in the village, they had found a woman who had witnessed the drama as a girl. 'She remembers the soldiers hitting you,' Manophet said, 'and she was crying because they were ordering you to walk to Vietnam without wearing any shoes.' The woman gesticulated at his feet, her timeworn face conveying something between horror and hilarity. Brace nodded slowly. 'They took my boots away to stop me trying to make a run for it,' he said. 'But they gave them back before we left.' The woman broke in with another torrent of recollections. 'She is talking now about a white rock.' Manophet sounded confused. 'I think she is calling – slippery?' The

Americans traded glances. 'Oh, the *ice*.' Brace started laughing. 'We'd flown some beer in, and I'd picked up a block of ice in Chiang Mai to bring along so they could keep it cool. The Vietnamese soldiers couldn't work out what it was. I guess they'd never seen ice out here before. They were chipping away at it with their bayonets, refusing to handle it in case it was some kind of chemical that was going to burn them.' Another man joined the circle. He had been the Royalist unit's radio operator, a crime for which he had been sent to a re-education camp after the war. 'But the head man was working under secret cover for the Pathet Lao,' Manophet explained. 'He made a map of the camp so the Vietnamese soldiers could study before launching the ambush. He told them the details of where every person would be sleeping.' Even within individual villages, the war had divided Lao from Lao, it seemed. 'But they are friends again now?' Archie asked. 'Yes, yes,' Manophet confirmed. 'Everything is forgotten now.'

Memories of the march through northern Laos to Vietnam crowded in on him. Uncertainty had pushed every normal reflex to one side. Where were they taking him? Was he going to be tortured? Would they kill him? At no other point of his life had he had so little idea of what to expect. Hour after nerve-shredding hour, he had trudged in a state of exhausting watchfulness, each new day potentially his last. One settlement would be sympathetic to his plight. Villagers would attend to his aches and wounds, dry his clothes, give him food while conspicuously refusing to share it with the soldiers who accompanied them. The next would seethe with hostility. Angry fingers would direct his gaze towards the remains of a pagoda recently bombed to smithereens. Men would spit contemptuously onto the ground. Half way through the journey, he had been interrogated in an old French hill-fort – not by a soldier, but by a Pathet Lao monk. He had refused to cooperate. The monk had grown angry and informed him that he would be punished. The following morning, he had been taken outside and put in front of a firing squad. The soldiers had raised their rifles to their shoulders and taken aim. This was the end. His bravado had cost him his life. But the parade had fallen out without firing a shot. The scene had been staged. He would be spared the death penalty as long as he provided written responses to certain questions, the monk informed him. He must indicate whether the Peace Corps was a division of the CIA. He must explain why he and his family were living in Thailand. And he must compare President Johnson's foreign policy to that of President Kennedy. In a daze, he had penned innocuous replies in an absurd purple ink provided for the purpose, unable to tell whether the joke was on him or his captors.

It had taken three weeks to reach the outskirts of Dien Bien Phu. On arrival, he had been imprisoned in a construction of thick bamboo slats lashed together in a criss-cross arrangement. Four or five feet square at the front, this cage had become his home for the next three and a half years. The thatched roof had sloped down to a height of around two feet over a distance just long enough to allow him to lie down. While providing some shelter from the elements, it had given no protection from monsoons or from rain blown horizontal by the wind. On winter nights, he had shivered with cold. In summer, he had sweltered in the heat. Apart from supervised excursions to the nearby hole in the ground that served as a latrine, he had remained incarcerated for twenty-four hours a day. Once every six weeks, he had been allowed down to the river to wash, but for the most part he had existed in a filthy malodorous state. At first, there had been no recourse against the mosquitoes that had descended each day at dusk, thirsting for blood. With his hands bound, he had been defenceless against their attacks. In the end, a mosquito net had been found, but it had soon torn, and in due course he had contracted malaria, the after-effects of which would blight him throughout his time in captivity. Ticks and leeches had joined the feast. Scorpions had danced along his exposed limbs. Rats had set up home in the thatch, where they would rustle and squeal, their urine splashing down on his face as he tried to sleep. During the night, they would enter the cage in search of food and gnaw at his manacled feet and ankles. On one occasion, their activities had attracted the attention of a twenty-foot python that had slithered in and become entangled in the mosquito net. '*Gunzun*,' he had screamed out frantically, until a soldier had come running to chase it away.

'Was Captain Brace flying his aeroplane from Long Chieng?' Manophet asked.

'He was based at Chiang Mai, but he did fly in and out of Long Chieng a couple of times. Apparently it was tiny in those days. He says Vang Pao, Tony Poe and a Catholic priest named Father Buchard used to sit down in the evening after they'd eaten and figure out what to do the next day – where to ambush the NVA, how to guard against the likely strike back. There was no input from Washington or the CIA. It was just the three of them.'

'Did he meet Vang Pao?'

Archie gave a soft chuckle. 'Ernie's met everybody worth meeting.'

'Some people in Laos are still afraid of him, Manophet said. 'They are worried he may come back one day with American weapons and then they think the Hmong could start another war because they would like to have an independent Hmong state.'

'Is that a realistic possibility?' Archie's son Greg asked.

'Only a few Hmong want that,' Manophet said. 'Most of the Hmong people want peace as long as they can be treated fairly.'

'It sounds as though Vang Pao doesn't have much of a life in the States,' Archie reflected. 'The CIA set him up as a pig farmer in Montana, but the locals didn't appreciate his farming methods and made it clear to him that he wasn't welcome. He and his family had to move to Florida, and that didn't work out either. They wound up in California in the end.'

'People claim he could be brutal.'

'Ernie says he was a pussycat compared to Tony Poe. And he believes the stories about him running opium are exaggerated. Most of the ex-Air America pilots that he hired – and he hired and fired a whole bunch of them over the years – well, they dispute that legend. Sure, there could have been one or two bad apples doing it to make a bit of money on the side, but every flight in to Vientiane was met by customs officials – even private charters and CIA carriers. It would have been tough to get away with it. Anyway, Vang Pao is no spring chicken. I mean, he's got to be older than Ernie and me – hardly the right sort of age to be starting a revolution. On the other hand, I guess it could be pretty dull living safely in exile after the kind of life he's had.'

They drove on to Muang Xay, where he had been interrogated. The French fort had been a massive edifice, but there was no sign of it on the hill, which was thick with trees knitted together by head-high creepers. The dense ground cover almost defeated them, but eventually they stumbled on some vine-smothered ruins. Most of the stonework had been pilfered, presumably to be incorporated into newer structures, and the underground bunker on top of which he had faced the firing squad must have collapsed or been filled in. Like footprints on a beach, the past, still so vivid in his memory, had been swept away by the passing of time. He climbed back into the Landcruiser feeling cheated, and they bumped on towards their next objective, the village where he had managed to untie himself and escape from his captors for a few hours while they were sleeping. It would not be easy to find. Try as he might, he could not remember its name, and the road was starting to diverge from the trail as it climbed. To locate it, they would need to trek through terrain that was becoming rougher all the time. He was seventy, for God's sake. He knew he had to be realistic about how much he could tackle. But, now that he was here, he was in the grip of a terrible hankering to flirt more intimately with danger again. The full gamut of hardship he could do without – the leeches, the stomach cramps, the torture of having to walk all day on perforated blisters – but he needed to be closer to the land. He wanted to experience afresh the relief of arrival after a long day's tramp-tramping in a weakened physical condition, smell the damp earth underfoot after rain and feel it spatter his skin.

'It wasn't just malaria that he was fighting either,' Archie continued. 'He had ringworm, chronic diarrhoea, open sores, sunstroke, malnutrition. A couple of times, he escaped from the cage. When they recaptured him the first time, they beat him up. The second time, they dug a deep hole in the ground and buried him up to his neck for a week. When they finally dug him out, he was paralysed. He couldn't do anything for himself. He had no idea what was going on around him. It was months before he could use his legs again, and he's never fully regained his sense of feeling below the waist. The doctors say it's a miracle he survived at all, let alone lived to be this old. But he maintains to this day that he was punished rather than tortured. It was only when he tried to escape that they made his life hell.

'In 1968, they released him from the cage and transferred him to the Hanoi Hilton. Having had no contact with the outside world for three and a half years, he was suddenly back amongst other Americans. But he was immediately placed in solitary confinement and forbidden from trying to interact with them. Apparently the Vietnamese still hadn't figured out they were wasting their breath, telling Ernie what to do. Within a day or two, he'd made contact with the prisoner in the cell next to his, who started tapping on the wall in a special code that the POWs had developed. Once Ernie had picked it up, he was away. Well, the guy next door turned out to be none other than the son of the four-star General who was commanding the American fleet in Europe at the time – a pilot by the name of John McCain.'

'I have heard of this person, I think,' Manophet broke in.

Archie nodded. 'John ran for the Republican presidential nomination against George W. Bush a couple of years ago. Like Ernie, he had a bad time of it in captivity – they tortured him when he was first captured, not realising who he was. He and Ernie were both held in Hanoi for another four years, and they became pretty close. Adding the two stints together, Ernie was one of the longest-serving prisoners of the whole Vietnam War, and the longest-serving civilian prisoner by a distance. Neither the Americans nor the Vietnamese were in any hurry to acknowledge his existence – or the existence of any of the other POWs captured in Laos, for that matter – because neither side should have been in Laos in the first place. So his name never appeared on the official POW listings. In fact, when prisoners were being exchanged at the end of the war, Nixon had to suspend the process when he found out the Vietnamese weren't planning to include the men who'd been captured in Laos.'

His story could have become entangled with Manophet's years earlier. If his engine had not malfunctioned on that fateful training flight, he would have become a squadron leader and participated in the war as a military pilot rather than as a mercenary. The task of razing Manophet's home to the ground could have fallen to him. By the same token, if his Pilatus Porter had been ambushed a few miles further to the east, in Xieng Khouang, Manophet's father could have been one the Pathet Lao soldiers abetting the Vietnamese as they set the trap. But, because their destinies had avoided colliding until a full generation later, they now found themselves together in circumstances that pitted them not as enemies but as allies, and allowed them to see how much they had in common. Although each of them had suffered terrible hardships during the war, it was the war that had ultimately launched both men on the long road to success. Recognising the courage that Brace had shown as a prisoner and his dedication to the military code of conduct while in captivity, President Ford had granted him an unconditional pardon. Once that had become a matter of record, lucrative job offers had started to come his way. His book had sold tens of thousands of copies. He had ended up moving in distinguished circles. As for Manophet, he had been able to drag himself out of poverty because a tourist industry had been born in Xieng Khouang on the strength of its wretched war history. And there was one more parallel. Brace's family, like Manophet's, had gone through the unsettling experience of seeing a family member return from the dead. Brace's wife, Patricia had remarried while he had been in captivity, on the assumption that he could not still be alive – only for him to reappear years after her second husband had died in an accident.

They gave up on the village whose name he had forgotten and advanced to Muang Khua. Perched on the banks of the Nam Ou, it had been a pretty little hamlet when he had passed through it all those years ago, but time had not treated it kindly, and it was now a collection of tumbledown shacks. Rather than stopping, as they had originally planned, they pressed on towards the Vietnamese border and, late in the afternoon, reached a bald red and white striped barrier across the road. Manophet climbed down and went to talk to the soldier manning the sentry box. In 1965, the highway to Hanoi had begun at this point. On the Lao side of the frontier, there had been no asphalt, only the trail along which Brace had been escorted. This was where his march had ended. A few yards across the border, they had handed him over to a different group of soldiers, who had loaded him onto a truck and transported him the rest of the way by road. Before taking their leave, his captors had clapped him on the back and wished him well. A grudging mutual respect had developed during the long walk. Brace had impressed them with his resilience, and they him with their professional attitude to the job they were doing. Manophet's conversation with the sentry ran on for several minutes. At length, he returned. 'We cannot go forwards into Vietnam,' he said. 'There is no longer a crossing point here for civilians.' He had warned them earlier that they were unlikely to be allowed through. 'That took a long time to establish,' Archie observed. Manophet grinned. 'I did my best,' he said. 'I was asking him for permission to walk across the border and stand on the other side so we could take photographs and say we had been in to Vietnam.' He dropped his eyes and contemplated the ground. 'But the answer was no.'

'The first time he actually set eyes on John McCain was at the White House.' Archie took a swig from the bottle of cold *Beer Lao* that Manophet had somehow managed to procure. He was in full flow now. 'They knew each other pretty well by then. They'd shared their life stories through the prison wall, played chess games in their heads using tap-code. They even came into physical contact at one point, when they were being transferred from the Hanoi Hilton to a different facility in a truck. They couldn't see anything because they were blindfolded, so they tapped out their identities on the legs of the men sitting next to them during the journey, and one of the guys next to Ernie happened to be John. But it wasn't until Nixon's White House reception for ex-POWs that they had the chance to meet. Ernie swears he never shed a tear while he was in captivity, but he broke down and cried right there on the White House lawn when he and John finally came face to face.

'His wife wasn't interested in trying to put their marriage back together, but he and one of the nurses at the hospital where he was treated after his release – Nancy – took a shine to each other, and it wasn't long before they tied the knot. They've been married almost thirty years now. He had quite a life after he was freed. He was one of the first westerners to enter Kuwait when the Gulf War ended, back in 1991. They needed a helicopter specialist to coordinate the logistics of putting out the fires in the oil wells, and Ernie was the guy they turned to. A couple of years after that, he was sent to meet Gorbachev for discussions about a joint aviation venture the US had going with Russia. When Alexander Haig visited Beijing, Ernie was the guy who received him. The US Ambassador was out of town, and he was the next most important American on hand. But then the Tiananmen Square crisis flared up, and he and Nancy had to get themselves out of China on the first plane that would take them. He ran a marijuana spraying programme for the Mexican drug enforcement agency where his helicopters were sabotaged with cross-wires and shot at by the drug barons. Nothing seems to phase him. I guess situations of that kind are tame by comparison to what he went through here.'

That night he dreamed he had escaped again. By surreptitiously twisting and turning the soaked bamboo ties securing the rear of the cage over the course of many weeks, he had weakened them to the point where they could be snapped open. Using a sharpened bamboo pick, he had loosened his shackles and neck rope, and wriggled free. The Vietnamese were after him. He needed to move quickly, but he was in terrible physical shape as a result of months without exercise. Rain was crashing down from a livid night sky, making the jungle trail slippery and treacherous. On the steeper sections, it became a mudslide. It was easier to feel his way forwards on all fours. He had no idea where the track led. All he cared about was that it was heading uphill. If he could reach a mountain top, he would be able to signal to friendly aircraft using the aluminium shard that he had discovered by the river as a mirror. He had been hiding it in the thatch above the cage where the guards could not find it. But his strategy was fatally flawed. Every inch of the land was covered in trees. There was nowhere for a helicopter to land. And where was the sense in climbing a mountain in the middle of the night, when all the reconnaissance aircraft would be on the ground? He would have to delay until daybreak. But he could not go much longer without food or water. If he pilfered fruit from the trees, they would know he had passed this way. Perhaps it would be smarter to slip into a village and raid the communal kitchen. No, that plan was no good either. The village dogs would raise hell. Dogs! Suddenly he could hear barking in the distance. The guards were tracking him. All the time they were getting closer. If only it would stop raining. Losing his footing, he skidded off the path and went tumbling down a steep embankment, tearing his hands on the stubby thorn bushes as he tried to break his fall. His body thudded against a boulder and came to a jarring halt in a gully. Looking up, he saw a soldier standing over him, angry, vengeful, pointing a rifle at his head.

He was gregarious by nature – a trait that had made his long period of solitary confinement difficult to endure. But here, hemmed in by old memories, he found he needed time on his own. Once again, he could taste the madness brought on by not knowing whether he had any realistic hope of coming through his ordeal. How close he had been to losing his way. One tiny alteration to the sequence of events all those years ago, and his body would now be buried near Dien Bien Phu in an unmarked grave. By inadvertently inflicting a serious loss of face on one of the guards, he had earned himself a severe beating. It was not the first that he had suffered, but this one had resulted in a progressive paralysis spreading up from his toes during the days that followed. Little by little, his mobility had deserted him, until he had barely been able to feed himself. He had lost control of his bladder and his bowels. The guards had left him lying all day on the floor of the cage in pools of his own excrement, covering their noses with handkerchiefs when they approached. His situation had become unendurable. There had been no purpose to carrying on any longer. His mind was made up. All he had to do was let his weight sag forward onto the rope by which he was always tied. He could remember feeling it bite into his neck. Soon afterwards, he had passed out. By rights, his life should have ended there and then. But a few moments later he had recovered consciousness. Deep down, the instinct to survive was still at work. Within hours, his will to live had returned.

Steering gingerly around the shoals and eddies, they wound their way slowly home along the river Ou. The white-haired war hero sat rocking almost imperceptibly from side to side in the prow of the boat as he contemplated the boulder-studded hills. In Boum Lao, he had shown the pictures in his book to the villagers, and the artist's impression of the cage in which he had been imprisoned, to help them understand who he was. In Mouong Kheo, he had obediently played along with his friends' agenda, posing for photographs close to the mound where he had faced the firing squad, narrating excerpts from his story whenever they had asked him to do so. And yet there had been an unspoken understanding between them from the beginning that his journey and theirs were separate. His face was turned to the west now, his eyes trained on a bomb crater high on the pastures that swept along the slope of a curving ridge, the evening sun bathing the top of his head with a golden light. Children were playing on a sandbank, laughing as they splashed along the edge of the strand. The smallest boy caught sight of the boat and started waving. For a moment they thought Brace had not noticed him. Then they saw his hand rise slowly from his lap to return the greeting.

Manophet walked up from the stern and took the seat opposite him. 'You are feeling OK, Captain Brace?'

'Hey, call me Ernie,' he protested. 'Yeah, I'm fine. I used to use this river as a navigation aid when I was flying. It looks a whole lot smaller from up there.'

# SIXTEEN

B usiness had been slack for some time – a delayed reaction to the 2001 attack on the Twin Towers in New York – and Manophet had no hesitation in accepting an offer to work part-time as a paid interpreter for the Mines Advisory Group. Although MAG had always been primarily concerned with the disposal of unexploded ordnance, more commonly known as UXO, it also ran a programme of educational outreach to the hill-tribes, organising expeditions to remote villages of the kind Manophet had undertaken on his own initiative in earlier years. Four or five people would travel as a group – consultants, local guides, interpreters. If they were trekking to a Hmong village, Lue would sometimes tag along to streamline the process of building a rapport with the villagers. More often than not, they stayed overnight, obliging Manophet to reschedule his school classes. With more than sixty children now attending the English Development School, this could be a complicated exercise. A new subject had been added to the school curriculum: soccer. There were enough boys interested in playing to make up two full teams, and games took place each week in a nearby cow field. Early on, a couple of the girls had joined in, but they had since fallen by the wayside, deterred by the fiercely competitive ethic that had developed amongst the boys. Manophet refereed as best he could, haring up and down so as to be in as good a position as possible to judge whether the ball had crossed one of the imaginary lines circumscribing the pitch. There was one rule above and beyond those found in the laws governing Association Football: players were permitted to speak only in English while they were on the field of play.

Back in the days when he had been working with Kong Keo, keeping backpackers entertained had been an exercise in trial and error as he tried to get a feel for what kind of stories they could relate to. There had been nothing to stop him throwing in a mischievous exaggeration here and there to gauge its effect, or a spurious detail. But, as soon as he had started working with organised groups, his leeway for improvisation had been dramatically curtailed. Most of the bigger tour operators appointed *falang* to co-supervise their Laos adventure trips, specific individuals who worked with him month in month out, meaning that "The Manophet Show", as one of them had coined the storytelling routine with which he beguiled their clients, could no longer chop and change. Gone were the days when he could explain away an inconsistency by suggesting that his English must have let him down. And yet, now that the script was set in stone, he sometimes found himself wondering whether every word of it was true. It had developed over the course of several years, layer building upon layer, reinforcing its own sense of authenticity each time it was repeated until any deviation jarred like a blasphemy. But while each recollection, taken on its own, seemed utterly real, a few were not easy to square with the rest of the narrative. Could he have invented one or two of these awkward anomalies? Was it possible that his mind had somehow bundled some of those early flights of fancy in with the truth?

One tour group leader admitted over a beer that he felt uncomfortable taking parties of *falang* to visit ethnic minority tribes. 'We might as well be taking them to a zoo to study exotic animals,' he argued. Manophet reassured him that villagers found it just as entertaining to have a collection of peculiar-looking strangers to stare at. 'But giving them a taste for the outside world could have undesirable repercussions,' came the reply. 'Perhaps it might be better to leave them to their own devices.' Manophet appreciated the man's sensitivity. It would not have occurred to *falang* from bygone generations to question the wisdom of interfering in the lives of others. On the other hand, sympathising too freely with his point of view might give him the idea that Manophet believed the practice of visiting hill-tribe villages was unhealthy and should be stopped, something that would be disadvantageous to all concerned. The tour operators were conscientious. They made sure community taboos were not infringed and that no litter was left behind. One company had gone so far as to arrange for its clients to mail copies of their photographs to him so that he could pass them on to the villagers when he next passed that way. And yet even initiatives launched with the best of intentions were capable of backfiring in a place like Laos. While the Hmong and the Khmu were always delighted to be presented with pictures of themselves, the residents of a remote Akha village that he had once visited had been traumatised to see their likenesses captured in photographs, concluding that their spirits were now imprisoned in the flimsy squares of paper as a result of their visitors having cast evil spells on them. Manophet was uncertain how the episode had ended, but there was every prospect that it had involved the unnecessary spillage of innocent blood.

When the 2004 edition of the Lonely Planet Guide was published, Manophet and Kong Keo were both mentioned by name in the section covering Xieng Khouang and given glowing tributes. It was a triumphant moment, one made all the sweeter when a tourist drew their attention to some lines in a paperback entitled *Another Quiet American* that had been published a few months earlier and was becoming popular with discerning *falang*: "A mention in *Lonely Planet* was key to survival in Laos' quickly developing tourist industry; if you didn't make the book, you didn't stand a chance." Now they had their own entries. What a coup! But within a few months Manophet was beginning to wonder whether the incremental prestige was as much of a boon as it had initially seemed. MAG wanted more and more of his time as an interpreter, even as the number of students enrolled at the school was continuing to swell – and yet tourist assignments were suddenly pouring in again from all sides. Often he had no option but to go back in to town after teaching his evening classes to ensure that he remained on top of his day jobs. He would return home exhausted, long after dark, to find Lue already asleep. He knew he should not let himself slump down into his chair as there was a danger that he would nod off without cooking his evening meal. But his stomach had a tendency to ache when he ate late at night, and the mere thought of chopping ingredients made his eyelids heavy. So much of his spare time had disappeared that it was no longer possible to visit his mother in Muang Khoun every Sunday. He needed time at weekends to prepare teaching materials for the following week's classes, and the tour operators now seemed to expect him to be available at any hour of the day or night every day of the week.

Encouraged by Lonely Planet's assurances that Laos was now safe to visit, intrepid Americans were an increasingly common sight around the Plain of Jars. Kirk was one of the first bomber pilots to arrive. He had followed his orders with a clear conscience during the war. Communism made the lives of those forced to live under its shackles a misery, and it was in their long-term interests that it should be snuffed out before it could take root. Every possible measure to prevent the bombing raids causing collateral damage to civilians had been taken, according to those in command. Did this mean he had been unaware that innocent men and women had suffered during the onslaught? Of course not – and he had regretted that. He was not a monster. But such tragedy was endemic to conflict. It was the price a nation had to pay if it wanted to secure a stable and prosperous future. As the years had gone by, however, there had been a gradual shift in his outlook. It was not that he was any more sympathetic towards the idea that the US government had deceived its servicemen, as the conspiracy theorists would have the world believe. On the contrary, there had been excellent military reasons for being economical with the truth. Rather, it was that he now felt uncomfortable knowing so little about the people who had been on the wrong end of the bombs that he had been dropping, and the realities of life on the ground during the war. High above the battlefield, in his cockpit, he had always been one step removed from the consequences of his actions, never close enough to see the casualties inflicted by the ideological battle that was being fought. History would judge whether the US government had been right or wrong, but purging this shameful personal ignorance was his own responsibility.

In 2005, as part of this process, he took the decision to travel back to Vietnam. His wife, Carol understood without him having to explain. 'You need to smell the place again,' she said. 'I'm coming with you.' Amongst the landmarks he had a hankering to set eyes on was Mount Phou Pha Thi, from where the US had directed its bombing operations. The military personnel stationed on the karst summit had assumed it to be unassailable on account of the precariousness of the ascent, but they had been overrun in a surprise attack before helicopters could be scrambled to evacuate them, resulting in the largest single loss of US ground forces during the war. However, Mount Phou Pha Thi lay just across the border, in Laos. Would the Lao authorities be prepared to let him in for a few hours to take a look?

He had scarcely thought about Laos during the war. All his missions had been over Vietnam. Although he had occasionally jettisoned surplus bombs over deserted regions of the thinly populated country on the way home to his air base in Thailand, he had never been ordered to target it directly. And yet every book that he read in preparation for his return to Indochina made it clear that Laos had been an integral piece of the jigsaw, and digressed at length onto the Secret War. What had become of that unfortunate little buffer state? Still communist, still rumoured to be holding US airmen missing in action in remote prison camps, it lurked on the fringes of public consciousness, furtive, mysterious, a land in which few Americans had ever set foot. Kirk grew fascinated. Were they authentic, the portraits painted by Hollywood, the stories of opium lords and infernal impenetrable jungles? Trying to see Mount Phou Pha Thi would probably be too complicated, he concluded, but they could reach Xieng Khouang easily enough. And so, instead of flying home directly from Hanoi, he and Carol detoured to Phonsavan for a three-day visit.

The idea of escorting a US bomber pilot and his wife around his homeland gave Manophet pause for thought. If the man was going to march about spouting right-wing mantras in an effort to justify himself, it would be tough to strike up any kind of rapport with him, and none of them would enjoy the next few days. What were they doing here? He could understand them wanting to visit Vietnam, but why Laos? Why Xieng Khouang? He was apprehensive when he collected them from the airport but, as they traded tentative questions, his suspicions started to ebb away. They had not come to preach a gospel. They were here to listen. He could afford to draw them in, just as he would any other tourist. There was no reason not to tell his story. The subterranean chamber beneath the mound at Site One on the Plain of Jars would be the perfect place. It was too small to accommodate a full-size tour group, but it would be just right for the three of them. He let them stand for a moment in the half-darkness, soaking up the cave-like atmosphere, taking in the narrow slanting beam of sunlight filtering in at one end, the faint resinous smell wafting through from the surrounding pine trees. He could recite the tale in his sleep. He must have regaled hundreds of tourists with it over the years. But today something held him back. *The Manophet Show*. Was that what he had become – a showman who relied on stage effects and material selected on the basis of whether it gratified his audience? This role as tour guide had been thrust on him so unexpectedly. There were things that he would perhaps handle differently if he had his time again.

'Everything happened so fast when they attacked our village,' he said. 'We had no warning. They had sprayed petrol on us before that. We did not understand why the rain was oily, or why it burned our skins, but it did not hurt us if we stayed indoors. Then they came back to bomb us. A bomb landed next to the house where we were living, and it caught fire. There was a lot of smoke. People were shouting and crying. People hurt, people dead. Flames. Shrapnel and debris flying everywhere. The bomb crater is still there in one of the fields. Everything was very confused. We were afraid the bombers would come back, so my mother grabbed some things and ran out of the door with me and two of my sisters into the forest. There were a lot of enemy soldiers there. We had to be very careful and we kept moving around so they could not find us. There was no rice because the bombers had destroyed all the rice fields. We had to live off plants from the forest. We ate roots and berries. We were always hungry. It was very difficult. My father had gone out of the other door of the house with my other brothers and sisters. We wandered around the forest hoping to find them. My mother thought it would be best to head towards Vietnam because that was where the Pathet Lao were in control. But my father went south, towards the capital with most of the other refugees, so the family was split in two. After that, my parents did not see each other again for six years.

'Eventually my mother found a cave where we could shelter. Rain came through the roof in the wet season, and it was always cold and dark, but it kept us safe from the bombs. So that was where I grew up: in a cave. We were there for six years – from when I was two years old to when I was eight. Usually it was too dangerous to go outside during the day because of the bombers. My mother would go out at night time to search for food. We had to be careful about lighting fires because the smoke could give us away. An aeroplane or an enemy soldier might be able to work out where we were hiding. If we lit a fire inside the cave, it made it very smoky, and the air was not good to breathe. Sometimes we just ate our food without cooking it, but then our bellies would hurt for a long time afterwards. A few times, some Vietnamese soldiers came to the cave to give us extra food – a few handfuls of rice, maybe. They tried to teach us about politics, but we couldn't really understand what they were saying. There were three other families in the cave with us. One family went out looking for food one night and came back with some roots that they had found. They were not a good colour, but they ate them anyway because they were very hungry. After a couple of hours, foam started coming out of their mouths and they were rolling around on the floor of the cave in terrible pain. By the next morning, they were all dead. Two of the men from the other families carried the bodies away and buried them. The roots must have been poisonous because none of the other families got sick. Maybe chemicals had been dropped on them from aeroplanes.

'My mother says I was very naughty when I was little. She was always telling me not to leave the cave in case the bombers saw me, but I used to creep outside when she was not looking, and then she would have to come and find me. It was even worse when we were in the forest. There were enemy soldiers hunting for us, and it was important to keep as quiet as possible, but I would never do what I was told, and I was always making too much noise. There was nothing for my sisters and me to do in the cave. My mother used to make up stories to keep us from getting bored. She said the war would end soon, and we would go back to our farm, where there would be plenty of rice and fish to eat. We stopped believing her. We thought we would be there for ever. And all this time we had no idea what had happened to my father and my other four brothers and sisters. Maybe they were alive. Maybe they had died in the bombing. But when the war did finally end, we heard they were in a refugee camp on the border with Thailand. You cannot imagine how excited we were. We were dancing up and down and hugging each other. And, six years after the bombers destroyed our village, we finally got back together.

'We should have been the happiest family in the world. But while we were still hugging and kissing we realised my older brother Bua was not there. "We thought he went with you," my father said. "No, no," my mother said, "he did not come with us. We thought you had taken him." My brother had been wounded when the bomb exploded. My mother assumed my father had rescued him, but in fact both of them had left him behind on the battlefield. So then we all started to cry because we knew he must be dead. It was very sad. After we had finished grieving, we carried on our lives without him. We went back home and built a new house, and my parents went on to have three more children. But that was not the end of the story. Later on, we discovered that some Hmong had found my brother lying on the battlefield. They told him they would try to help him find his family, but it was impossible in all the confusion. Bombs were still falling at that time and people were running away as fast as they could. The Hmong did not know what to do, so they picked him up off the ground and took care of him. When he got better, they decided to raise him as their own child. He could not remember anything from before his accident, even his name, so they gave him a Hmong name. Many years later, they swam across the Mekong to Thailand together. They lived in a refugee camp there, and eventually he was given an opportunity to move to America. But then, in 1994, we found out that he was living in Minneapolis. Some Hmong friends of his came back to Laos and showed his photograph around in case anybody recognised him. And my mother saw the picture, and she knew it was her son. So we started writing letters, and eventually we were reunited with him twenty-five years after he disappeared from our lives.'

It had been years since Kirk had dreamt of being in combat, but he woke that night in a cold sweat, still living the nightmare that had jolted him from sleep. The port engine was on fire, and the cockpit was full of smoke. He had known this would happen sooner or later. There was a procedure to be followed. He could get through if he just stayed calm. But when he leaned on the rudder there was barely a response. Had the hydraulics failed? The instruments were giving crazy readings, and it was impossible to tell. He shouted to the crew to prepare to bail out. Silence. Where the hell were they all? Dead? He would have to put out a mayday himself. But where was his headset? And why was the goddamn river to the south when it should have been to the north? Without the navigator to help him out, he had no idea what coordinates to give. His mind started flashing up images of his life back home, the wide sweep of the golden wheat plain rolling away to the snow-capped mountains on the horizon, the promise of a hero's welcome, the dark-haired girl waiting by the phone for news. Suddenly, straight ahead, he could see Mount Phou Pha Thi. It was racing towards him. If he could not haul the plane off its bearing, he would smash straight into the control tower, wiping out America's aircraft guidance capability. At a stroke, the war would be over. Could he move the rudder manually? With one last superhuman act of will, he jammed it hard against the hurtling air, and at last, as though in slow motion, the plane heaved a fraction to the south. But all the time he was losing height. Branches were starting to separate out of the green fuzzy-felt blur below. He was going down in dense jungle.

Thousands upon thousands of trees clothed the ground, packing the deep ravines that sliced between the great limestone karsts, giving the illusion of a gentle contour, only the loftiest peaks denying them a foothold. Back and forth across this impenetrable vegetation he had flown with his heavy bomb loads over the past few months, never dwelling for too long on the question of what lay beneath the canopy. Savage uncharted terrain would soon gobble him up, fast-flowing rivers, thunderous waterfalls, sheer cliffs, unstable mountainsides littered with boulders. Fallen trees and rope-like creepers would block the way. Creatures unknown to the outside world would compete to bring about his demise, snakes that slithered across the forest floor, poisonous spiders dangling from overhanging branches, leeches at the ready on hungry outstretched twigs. And, at the heart of this wilderness, there would be hunter-gatherers, primitive men who did not play by the same rules as westerners, animists who would babble away in incomprehensible tongues and wag their fingers as they debated how to punish him for enraging the forest gods by blowing chunks of their native land into the sky. Few human beings inhabited these parts, their training instructors had been at pains to stress. That was why it made sense to offload unused bombs here rather than trying to land with them still on board. But the tribal mosaic in Laos had never been properly mapped, and they could not be categorical in their assurances that nobody would be living in the drop zone. Kirk's chest heaved. Which would be preferable: a slow lingering death in this vengeful place, or to perish swiftly in the imminent fireball? The starboard engine sputtered and failed. The last lights in the cockpit went out.

'Why the hell don't we ever *hear* about these people?' Kirk fulminated. 'They commemorate the serviceman who lost their lives here. They praise the bravery of Vang Pao and the Hmong, they acknowledge the audacity of the Vietnamese who stormed Mount Phou Pha Thi. Every American missing in action has half a dozen people up at Capitol Hill lobbying for them. But what about the ordinary Lao who lived in the villages that we bombed? Don't they count? Why do the media never give us their side of the story? It all makes me feel so goddamn *ignorant*.'

'I tell you what gets me,' Carol said. 'It's the complete lack of bitterness that he displays. He tells the story like it was a *natural* disaster – something nobody had any control over. Maybe I'm just easily duped, but I really like the guy. I have so much time for him.'

'It would be easier if he hated us,' Kirk said, 'or if he was dishonest or full of communist shit or wanted to rip us off. But he's *like* us. He speaks English like it was his mother tongue. He thinks the way we think. He has our sense of humour. You know, I asked him if he'd heard of Ernie Brace – that guy whose story I got fascinated with when I was reading up on the war. "Sure, I know Ernie," he says. "I had an e-mail from him a couple of days ago, but I've been too busy to get back to him."'

'I kept wanting to cry,' Carol said. 'When he looked up at the stars and whispered, "God, what a beautiful evening," for instance. It was so – I don't know – personal. Just us and him. Us representing the nation that almost wiped out his entire family, and him taking time out from teaching at his school to show us round the mess in his back yard that we never got round to clearing up.'

Two more days of Manophet's company did nothing to disillusion them. He introduced them to Lue, invited them into his house as though they were old friends. Other guides might have pretended not to know that Mount Phou Pha Thi was out of bounds, and taken them on a wasted journey to Houaphan province as a way of parting them from a little more of their cash, but not Manophet. It was not as though they were new to strange realms and cultures. They were seasoned travellers who had explored plenty of other unlikely corners of the world. And yet this experience was different. It had them on tenterhooks from beginning to end, left them at once elated and heartbroken at the end of each extraordinary day. From the outset, they knew this was a man and a land from which they could not simply walk away when the trip came to an end. An unbreakable connection was being forged between them.

'We want to give you a leaving present,' Kirk said to Manophet on their last night. 'What would you like?'

Manophet thought for a moment. Then his face lit up. 'Would you be able to give me a soccer ball for the school?' he asked. 'That would be –' it took him a moment to find the right superlative – '*awe*some,' he chuckled mischievously, delivering the word with a pronounced American drawl. 'The one we use at the moment is wearing out. We have to keep stopping our game to blow it up.'

'How about three soccer balls,' Carol suggested.

'How about three soccer balls and proper kit for the whole team,' Kirk countered.

Manophet stood dumbfounded.

'Boots as well, of course.' Kirk added. 'Those kids can't go on playing barefoot without shirts. They're too good for that.'

'My gawwwd,' Manophet cried, spreading his hands like a bemused orang-utan facing a penalty kick. 'Clothes! They might even let us play in the National Day Cup if we wore some clothes.'

Manophet sought to include all the ethnic minority villages in the area on his itineraries. Some were more welcoming than others. Some had more craftsmen to keep tour groups occupied, or more war artefacts to display. But he made an effort not to concentrate his business on the most popular destinations so that the income brought in by the *falang* could be shared around. Besides, villagers were prone to grow tourist-weary if westerners trooped in and out too frequently, stripping the experience of its mystique. One afternoon, he was at a Hmong village that he had not visited for many months, a sorry place where there was little to do or see. Living conditions here were amongst the worst he had seen. Few of the huts had floors, and what clothes the children had were threadbare. The group made a half-hearted effort to occupy itself by taking pictures of a diseased pig. But then a smudge-covered boy appeared. He had fashioned a mock aeroplane from banana leaves, folded and laced together with creeper, which he now hurled forth in the optimistic hope that it would fly. For a second or two, it looked capable of staying airborne, only to nosedive into the dirt. Undeterred, he dusted it down and made a few adjustments, working purposefully, as if well-versed in the art. The second launch brought the same outcome as the first, but by the third he had managed to correct the aerodynamic defects of his projectile, and it swooped magnificently across to the next hut along, where it buried itself in the yawning cleavage of a village woman who was outside sweeping her yard. Manophet could not stop himself from laughing out loud. 'He is so ingenious,' he cried. 'I want him to come and live with me.'

It was not meant as a serious suggestion, but his words hung on the air. The villagers here were piteously poor, and his house could easily accommodate a third person. 'Would you like that?' he asked the boy impetuously. The boy, who had no idea what was being offered, nodded eagerly. 'Maybe I should talk to your parents,' Manophet said. Not surprisingly, the boy's mother was outraged when she was sounded out. 'He is only young,' she pointed out indignantly. But she had seven other children to feed, and the more Manophet talked, the calmer she became. They agreed that he should return the following day with Lue so that she and her husband could quiz him about the experience of becoming Manophet's son. Manophet pondered hard that evening. On the face of it, this was an easier decision than the one involving Lue three years ago. The boy would have an older brother to show him the ropes, talk his language, help him settle – beyond which, it would be good for Lue to have a sibling to keep him company. Like Lue, he would need a Lao name, of course. Perhaps Phong would suit him. And yet raising this boy would be a more exacting challenge than raising Lue. There was entrepreneurial blood in Lue's veins. It had been his idea to come to Manophet's school to take English lessons. He had always been determined to do his best to improve his own lot. This boy, by contrast, spoke not a word of English and was not even fluent in Lao. He had rarely set foot outside his village. There was no guarantee that he would be motivated to shape his own destiny, let alone ambitious. As far as he and his family were concerned, anything was better than the poverty trap into which he had been born. That was the basis on which the transaction would be struck. But Manophet's mind was made up. Not only would he follow his instincts and take the boy in. This time he would go a stage further and formally adopt him.

The arrangements were concluded with a minimum of fuss, and a shell-shocked Phong travelled back with them to Phonsavan the following day. For the first few weeks, Manophet feared he would be unable to make the necessary adjustments. He became very shy when *falang* were present, doing his best to look invisible even as Lue seized the opportunity to practise his English. He had never been to school before, and the discipline of sitting in a classroom for hours at a time did not come easily to him. But there was one element of his new existence to which he took like a duck to water: soccer. Where Lue aspired to be the best English speaker of his generation, Phong aspired to be the best football player. Everything was solved. Everything, that is, apart from the added pressure on Manophet's time. During the rainy season, when it was difficult for the ordnance disposal teams to work, and all but a handful of eccentric or dim-witted tourists had the sense to stay away from Laos, his life fell back into balance. There was time enough to see his mother every weekend, prepare lessons, write to the kind *falang* who sent him postcards or gifts, even to dream of travelling overseas. But during the remainder of the year he was chaotically busy. Sometimes he wondered what had possessed him to assume so many complicated responsibilities. 'I cannot afford to take it easy,' he sighed when his brother Bua told him during a phone conversation that he was displaying all the symptoms of a man with a stomach ulcer, and advised him to cut himself a bit more slack. 'I have to keep my act together. Too many people depend on me. If I take time off, I will let them down. Whatever it is, it will just have to sort itself out.'

# SEVENTEEN

Manophet would have liked Lue to study at university in Vientiane or Luang Prabang, but the fees were beyond his reach, so they agreed that he should enrol instead at Phonsavan's newly opened English language teacher-training college when he finished at secondary school. He was hoping to take charge of the junior classes at the English Development School at some point in the future, and this would equip him with the skills that he would need. Once he had completed the course, Manophet decided he was ready to start working as a tour guide. At first, he needed constant supervision like any other raw recruit. But, as the months went by, he grew in confidence, until he was able to supervise groups of two or three on his own, leaving Manophet in a position where he could allocate more of his time to the ordnance clearance agencies. UXO Laos, the umbrella organisation through which most of the overseas-funded projects were channelled, had offered him a permanent position as a translator after receiving a sizeable tranche of funding from the Japanese. It would mean spending extended periods in the field with bomb disposal teams, and would require him to stay away from home from time to time. But the prospect of a higher, more predictable salary was difficult to resist, and it seemed too good an opportunity to turn down. He would be free to continue as a freelance tour guide as and when time allowed, and Lue would be able to provide some cover when he was out of town, both as a guide and at the school.

He toyed with the idea of learning Japanese, conscious that it would be easier and safer for all concerned if he could speak to the consultants in their own tongue rather than trying to understand their broken English. But he quickly realised that he had too much on his plate already to go through with it, for his household no longer consisted of just three people. A few months before, Lue's younger brother, Vanh had started taking English lessons at the school. Was this any different to the situation five years earlier, Manophet had asked himself. Why not invite Vanh to come and live with them? And, once Vanh had arrived, it had not taken long for another brother, Ped to follow suit. It was never quiet now. Somebody was always chasing around or trying to get help with their homework or inventing a new game. One night, midway through a chaotic dream in which the boys were trussing one another up in *baci* string, he became aware that his father was looking on. There was nothing surprising about his presence. It was as though he hung suspended half way between the floor and the ceiling all the time, but only occasionally chose to reveal himself. Neither of them made to talk. There was a shared understanding that everything that needed to be said had already been said. He seemed philosophical about his son's domestic arrangements – the fact that he was still unmarried, and yet fathering four boys. If it troubled him that they were Hmong, there was no hint of it in his face. Manophet went up to the temple the following day to make an offering, as was traditional when an ancestor appeared in a dream. The watching *falang* probably found his act of devotion amusing, but their scepticism did not bother him. The sacrifice did nobody any harm, and where was the virtue in disrespecting an ancestral visitation by pretending it had not taken place?

It was not as though he lacked for children. More than a hundred and forty were now coming to the school for English lessons. But perhaps it was the cornucopia of youngsters descending on his house every day like flocks of birds, only to fly off again as soon as their classes ended, that had impressed on him the importance of having children of his own. There was such fulfilment to be had from heading up a family. He was closer to his mother now that he had provided her with a clutch of grandchildren. She would, no doubt, have preferred a more orthodox train of events – a nice Lao wedding to a nice Lao girl, followed by an orderly succession of offspring – but his interests were aligned with hers in a way they had never been before, and she was touchingly fond of the boys. How happy she had been when they had all travelled to Muang Khoun to help with the harvest. He also shared a closer bond with Bua now that his life was so intricately interwoven with Hmong lives. Since first returning to Laos in 1997, his brother had paid two further visits, and he and Manophet regularly exchanged e-mails and spoke to one another by phone – though this never seemed compensation enough to Manophet for the time they had been unable to spend together as children. So many years had been lost. Bua took a special interest in his Hmong nephews. Why was Phong known as "duckling"? Surely that was not a kind thing to have nicknamed him. Manophet pointed out that there was nothing duckling-like about his fleet-footed performances on the soccer pitch. The sobriquet remained in use only because Phong had grown attached to it. None of his brothers had nicknames. As far as he was concerned, it was a mark of special affection on his father's part.

People talked behind his back, but this was nothing new to Manophet. Xieng Khouang was richly endowed with busybodies who seemed to have nothing better to do with their time than take a magnifying glass to untraditional behaviour of whatever complexion and share their findings with anybody prepared to listen. His mould-breaking life had exercised many a loose tongue over the years. But at least they conducted themselves with a modicum of decorum. *Falang* were altogether more of a liability. 'I never see you flirting with the girls at these places,' one tour leader had had the temerity to remark to him after a few beers at a popular watering hole in Luang Prabang one evening. 'But then again I never see you flirting with the boys either, I suppose.' The words had been spoken in the friendly spirit sometimes employed by westerners to show that they regarded and accepted you as one of their own. But he was not one of their own. He was Lao, and he was uncomfortable with the guide's lack of respect for his privacy. There were certain things you did not discuss with other people. Another time, a tourist had backed him into a corner after discovering from Lue that he was single. 'I thought you said you had a wife,' he protested indignantly. Manophet's heart sank. He had let the information slip to deflect an inconvenient line of questioning, forgetting that Lue would be joining the group later on. Now there was no easy way to extricate himself. Awkwardly, he adjusted the angle of his baseball cap so that more of his face was concealed. 'My wife lives in America,' he said eventually. 'Her father was in the Royal Lao Army during the war, and he took her with him when he fled the country.' The blood drained out of the man's face. 'She also took our daughter,' Manophet continued, almost inaudibly. 'I have not seen either of them since that time.'

The official adjusted the collar of his uniform slightly, so that it formed a perfectly symmetrical circle around his neck. It was customary in such situations for a functionary to appear in uniform, however lowly his position in the hierarchy. It gave his pronouncements added authority and placed the citizen sitting on the other side of the desk at an incremental disadvantage. A couple of files marked "Official" had been prominently laid out to lend weight to the impression that the State had been busy preparing its ground for weeks, if not months. Moving at a stately pace, the man opened a drawer and sifted through a sheaf of papers. At length, he located the one for which he was searching, created a space for it on the desk by shifting a carousel of rubber stamps to one side, and laboriously cleared his throat. 'Today's meeting,' he began, in a clipped, businesslike voice, 'has been arranged to apprise you of an important decision that has been taken at this Ministry.' He paused to scrutinise the document now in front of him, giving his portentous words time to sink in. 'This is a *strategic* decision that will produce significant benefits for the capital of Xieng Khouang, a province recently declared by the Government of the Lao People's Democratic Republic to be one of the most progressive and rapidly developing in the country.' Deliberately, he adjusted the position of his chair. 'Far-sighted initiatives of the type about which we are speaking can impact many lives, and it is inevitable that the interests of a small number of individuals may sometimes be damaged when they are implemented, even as the wider community benefits. As a result of the diligent efforts of this Ministry, it has been possible to limit the number of individuals who will be adversely affected on this occasion to merely three or four. Unfortunately –' he left the word hanging in the air for a moment or two, while pressing his fingertips together in an inscrutable arch – 'you are amongst those who will be required to make a sacrifice.'

Manophet glanced across at Miss Onh. They had known something unpleasant was in the offing. The Ministry of Building and Municipal Works did not summon common or garden householders without good reason. They had envisaged being informed that they were infringing an obscure piece of planning legislation, which could result in serious charges being brought against them if they could not arrange for the requisite wheels to be greased. But the wording used by the official was ominous. Normally he would have set out his stall by telling them they *might* be required to make a sacrifice.

'What is this great project, sir?' Manophet asked him.

'Our nation is growing rapidly,' the official rejoined, 'and especially Xieng Khouang province, where the volume of motorised traffic has increased by 79% during the past four years. As a result of this economic miracle, it has become necessary to modernise certain road junctions – and specifically the intersection between Interstate Highway Seven and the road to Muang Khoun, which is becoming gridlocked during busy periods. This junction needs to be widened.'

'But that is where my school is,' Manophet protested, 'my house – I mean, Miss Onh's house.'

'That is exactly the point to which I was coming,' the official said, drumming his fingers tetchily on the desk. 'The house that you own is in the way.'

'But couldn't the road be widened on the other side?'

The man contorted his face into a condescending grimace. 'It is surely self-evident that it would inconvenience a far greater number of people if the road was widened on the other side.'

'But even if we could take the house down and re-erect it, we wouldn't be able to move it backwards,' Miss Onh protested. 'There isn't enough space.'

'You are to be congratulated on taking the news in such a sensible spirit,' the official said. 'That is precisely the conclusion that our engineers have reached. I am sorry, but the house cannot remain there any longer. It must be removed. You have two months to dismantle it.'

Manophet held his head between his hands. Compensation was negligible if the public need was clear when a situation like this arose – and the junction was crying out for an upgrade. It was Miss Onh who would lose out financially. It was her house. But, as her tenant, it was he who would find himself without a roof over his head. 'Where am I going to teach?' he muttered in a desolate whisper.

'We are aware that the premises are currently in use as a school,' the official countered, evidently riled by the suggestion that his superiors might have overlooked this detail. 'Indeed, there has been extensive consultation between this department and the Ministry of Education, which has made representations to us that a way should be found for this school to remain open.'

Manophet straightened up hurriedly in his chair and did his best to look businesslike, hoping the official had not mistaken his lament for insolence. There was a boy in one of his classes whose father held a position of some importance in the Party. Perhaps he had put in a good word for him. Indeed, it was not inconceivable that his uncle, the provincial Vice-Governor had sought to find a way of sweetening the bitter pill.

'Here in Xieng Khouang province, we recognise that making education available to as wide a cross-section of the population as possible is a desirable goal,' the official continued, 'and one that is not easy for the State to achieve on its own. Our enlightened leaders do not insist that the province should retain a monopoly on the provision of education, and they have shown exceptional resourcefulness and imagination, I hope you will agree, in deciding to grant you an unusual concession.'

'A concession!' Miss Onh exclaimed, happy now to join in the official's game.

'It is my pleasant duty to inform you that the Governor of Xieng Khouang province has consented to make over to you a plot of land off the road to the northeast of the junction, on condition that you erect a building that will serve as a school, but which may also function as a dwelling house.' The official was now looking extraordinarily pleased with himself. 'The building must be completed by the end of June or the concession will lapse.'

Manophet took a long walk to clear his head. For years, the authorities had been unresponsive to his efforts to obtain financial assistance for the school, giving no indication that they even acknowledged its existence. Now, out of the blue, they had dealt him a wild card so outlandish that he was not immediately sure whether to be excited or depressed. The land that he was being offered lay directly opposite the cow field in which his students played football. It would be difficult to think of a more perfect location. For a moment or two, he allowed himself to dream. The outside of the house could be painted a sunny, cheerful colour: lemon yellow, perhaps, with orange trimmings; and the windows would be grey-blue. It could have a first-floor balcony at the front, from which he could supervise soccer practices. Downstairs, there would be a big L-shaped room in which he could teach – that would be the best way to cater for the largest classes. He could stand at the apex, and have half the students sitting along one axis and half along the other. A quiet, scholarly atmosphere would prevail. There would no longer be any need for him to raise his voice to make himself heard above the noise of the traffic. And he, Lue, Phong, Vang and Ped would have a house of their own to live in. Just imagine that! Shaking his head, he let out a resigned sigh. Why was he bothering to put flesh on the bones of this absurd fantasy? Houses cost money to build. It was all very well, the authorities making this grand gesture, but how was he supposed to conjure a hundred million kip out of thin air? It was enough of a struggle to find a hundred *thousand* kip at the moment, with five mouths to feed and his school expenses creeping inexorably higher month after month.

Then an outrageous idea came to him. Perhaps he could ask Carol and Kirk to lend him enough money to pay for a house to be built. They had been as good as their word since returning to the States, wiring funds to his account so that he could buy Arsenal strips and boots for the whole of the school's first team, not to mention several soccer balls. And they would be returning to Laos in a few weeks time for a second visit. What if they offered to buy him a present at the end of the trip instead of giving him a tip, as they had before: would it be out of the question to ask for a property loan instead? A hundred million kip might be a veritable fortune to a Laotian, but to Americans it was pocket money. Besides which, they would be investing in an asset that they would continue to own, as opposed to giving away capital. Surely that ought to be attractive from their point of view. He wrestled with the ramifications of the proposal. The dangers of living off American largesse had been drummed into him from an early age. It was because the country had allowed itself to become dependent on American capital that it had fallen into economic ruin when the *falang* imperialists had pulled out. Every schoolboy knew that. But Carol and Kirk had made their earlier gift without attaching any strings. They had no desire to interfere in the way the country was run, as far as he could tell, or make anybody conform to ideologies hatched in the West. It would never be possible for him to repay the loan, of course. The house would remain theirs, and eventually they would want to sell it – at which point he would be out on the street again. But what alternative did he have? If he took the moral high ground and went to meet them with no begging bowl in his hand, the school would have to close, and that would be the end of it.

Mount Phou Pha Thi was still out of bounds, but Kirk was determined to get a view of the fabled command post, and they drove to a vantage point near Sam Neua from which it was distantly visible. There were other sights to see in the northeast, and Manophet made sure the journey was not wasted. The government had grudgingly begun opening up some of the caves where the Pathet Lao had been headquartered during the war to the public as a way of raising revenue, and they spent the afternoon exploring. 'They used to use this one as a theatre when I was training for the army,' Manophet recalled as they toured the vast Elephant Cave. 'They brought us here once to see a propaganda film. Another time, we had to go up onto the stage and sing a song in front of all the other soldiers, each person in turn. "Rites of passage" you call it, I think. My gosh, that was something I really did not enjoy having to do.' Afterwards, he drove them on to a Yao village to watch the local craftswomen at work, pointing out Camp Number One in the distance through a gap in the hills. Towards the end of the day, as the sun was sinking low in the sky, they stopped off at a deserted airfield, to which the jungle had begun to lay claim. Banana leaves strewed the ground along the perimeter fence, and a riot of weeds had broken through the tarmac of one of the taxiways. 'This is where they brought the Royal Family in 1975,' Manophet said. 'They were taken from here to Camp Number One. Some people say the king and queen were made to do hard labour like the other prisoners. Other people say they had special living quarters where it was not so harsh. Nobody is certain what happened to them. There is a story that one day, after they had been here a few years, a soldier took them out for a walk into the forest and came back without them.'

He put off mentioning the house for as long as possible. When the subject finally came up, he glossed over it. 'Something will turn up,' he said. 'This is how things happen in Laos. Word gets round that somebody has a difficult situation and, after some talking and maybe some agreements, another person comes forward to help them out.' Carol and Kirk nodded politely, but Manophet could tell that their interest was piqued. 'Are you sure the government hasn't done this purely to show itself in a good light?' Carol asked him when Kirk was out of earshot. 'I mean, they must know perfectly well you can't afford to build a school. Let's suppose for the sake of argument that somebody else stepped in and put up the money on your behalf. Don't you think there's a danger they might say they'd changed their minds and withdraw the offer?' Later that evening, after Carol had retired, Kirk asked him casually how much it would cost to build a school. Manophet prevaricated for a while, but eventually named the figure. There was no merit in pretending he had not researched the question. 'But perhaps it would be better to build a house with a big schoolroom on the ground floor,' he suggested. 'If it was just a school, the building would be empty for most of the time.' He kept them off the subject during the drive back to Phonsavan, entertaining them with stories from his army days. 'One time, I had to walk home to Muang Khoun from Hanoi along this road,' he said. 'I was too poor to buy a bus ticket. All the way, I couldn't stop thinking about a soldier I had been training with. He was engaged to his childhood sweetheart, but the camp was too far away for him to go and visit her, so he wrote love letters and arranged for a messenger to deliver them to his village. After many months, he came to the end of his training. He was so happy as he walked along this road because now he would be able to get married at last. But when he arrived in his village his sweetheart was not there any more. She had grown tired of waiting for him and married the messenger.' A cow sauntered out into the road, and he slowed to let it cross. 'That soldier is still single,' he said. 'Maybe he will always be single now.'

They took their leave promising to see if they could think of a way to help. Manophet tried not to let his hopes rise too high, but he had overheard them talking on the last night of their visit, and he had a good feeling. 'How often do you get a chance to make a real difference to a community?' Carol had been saying. 'And we would have the satisfaction of knowing that *all* our money is being spent on the people it's intended for. I mean, I'm not saying the charities that we support back home are doing anything wrong, but part of what we give them is always siphoned off to pay their bean counters and form fillers. And Manophet would be able to continue teaching kids for years and years to come.' Kirk had sounded just as fired up. 'Well, *some* of the money is bound to end up in the pockets of local facilitators,' he had countered. 'That's just the way business is done in certain parts of the world. In the West, the taxman takes a cut; over here, it's a local government official – but the principle's no different. Anyway, assuming Manophet has his figures right, it would be no more expensive than the hot tub that we paid to have installed in my mother's house, so it's hardly going to break the bank.' When the news finally arrived, it was better than Manophet had dared to hope. Rather than lending him the money, they had decided to gift it to him outright. He threw his cap so high in the air that it caught on a tree branch, and Phong had to climb up and retrieve it. He was at a loss to know how to respond. None of his attempts to put his gratitude into words came close to conveying it adequately. He took photographs of the building as it was taking shape and e-mailed them to his benefactors, along with accounts showing where the money was going. There was a nervous moment when he discovered he would need an additional twenty million kip to cover the cost of linking the property to the local electricity grid, but he need not have worried. Kirk and Carol had no intention of letting the project fail at the final hurdle.

The older Manophet grew, the shorter the days seemed to become. He was now teaching five one-hour classes a day, one before work and four in the evening, and spending hours a month photocopying handouts at the Phonsavan Copy Centre. The photocopier rarely failed to sabotage his efforts to make a swift getaway. Its favourite gambit was to pick up several sheets of paper at once and suck them down into its inkiest recesses before spluttering to a halt. Heroic efforts were then required on the part of the store manager to extricate the trail of mangled paper. But the antediluvian contraption was no one-trick pony. It was also skilled in the more demanding art of persuading the ink cartridges on which it subsisted to explode, and could stage impressive displays of electrical mayhem, when all the lights would come on simultaneously and copies would fly out in every direction until somebody succeeded in scaling the barricade behind which the plug was located and tearing it out of the socket. On other days, jets of smoke would come belching from its innards, and a stench of smouldering plastic would fill the air. But the school had advanced too far for Manophet to contemplate reverting to a purely aural style of teaching. Some of his brightest pupils were applying to universities, and he owed it to them to do everything he could to maximise their chances of success. The soccer team was another significant drain on his time. It was now capable of putting ten goals past most of the other local sides in under an hour, and he was having to drive the first eleven to other provinces in an unreliable minibus to take on less brittle opponents. Buoyed up by their seemingly unstoppable progress, the boys had optimistically set their sights on winning the National Day Cup – to which end, they had talked him into holding extra training sessions at weekends. It all added to the number of hours he spent away from his family. He was not seeing his sons as much as he would have liked. Too often, Lue was left in charge of his younger brothers. Ignoring Bua's advice that he should be taking more care of his health, Manophet decided to cut down the number of hours that he allowed himself for sleeping.

Up to a point, staying up until midnight paid handsome dividends. Conditions were perfect for making inroads into the backlog of paperwork that was prone to accumulate if he failed to keep on top of it, since he was the only person in the house still awake. But the boys were receiving no more of his attention than before. How could he be a better parent? They should not have to queue up at breakfast to unburden themselves of their unsolved problems from the previous day. Somebody should be at home with them when they were not at school, cooking proper meals and looking out for them. He held out against the obvious solution for as long as he could. A marriage of convenience at this point in his life would surely be no more tolerable than the one his parents had attempted to arrange all those years ago. But perhaps the boys' presence would slant the household dynamics. And he was in a stronger bargaining position now. In no time, he would have a house of his own. The time had come to let his head rule his heart. If nothing else, taking a wife would put a stop to all the tittle-tattle. People might even conclude that he had planned it this way from the beginning just as Joy, one of his students, imagined. 'I want to live my life like yours, teacher Manophet,' he had confided. 'I want to work hard for many years to become a successful person, and only after that to marry and have some children. I can see that this is how a clever man organises his life.'

She was flattered by his interest. He was older than she would have liked, but his standing in the community was such that his age quickly ceased to be important. Everybody had a good word for him, and his school was gaining quite a reputation. There were even a few adults sitting in on his evening classes, hoping to pick up some English – a secondary school teacher and a couple of enterprising tuk-tuk drivers. He had ploughed his own furrow rather than following his parents' wishes, it was true, but such behaviour was coming to be regarded as acceptable in these enlightened times – particularly if it brought financial rewards. Although her parents expected her to throw in her lot with a man of their choosing, according to custom, she felt confident she would be able to talk them round. He was a handsome devil. There would be no qualms on *that* front! They strolled together, usually at weekends since he could not spare much time on weekdays. She had never thought of Phonsavan as a beautiful town, but he knew where to find pockets of unspoiled green space no more than a few yards away from the dusty clatter of Route Seven, concealed oases of tranquillity where the scent of blossom hung in the air and tiny creatures trilled ecstatically from the branches of shady trees. As though in a dream, they wandered undisturbed along red earth lanes between clusters of picturesque wooden houses. And yet he remained quite businesslike with her even as the azure of the sky and the perfumes of evening set her heart pounding at the brush of his hand. Perhaps this was what happened to a man as he grew to maturity. In one sense, she liked this strength in him, this ability to resist the sentimental tendencies to which the other boys with whom she had strolled were prone, and yet it filled her at the same time with a wistful regret.

She took a few days to make up her mind when he asked her to move in. While it seemed of no consequence to him that this was not how things were usually done in the society in which they lived, appearances mattered to her. His intentions were honourable – of that she was in no doubt. The question was whether the neighbours would be so charitable in their judgements. What if word found its way back to her friends or even her family? It was not that she was unable to appreciate the reasoning behind the invitation. Better to experience life in his unusual household and make sure the presence of his four sons was not too disruptive than to wait until they were married to discover the arrangement was unworkable. And yet, at the same time, it seemed quite wrong, putting the understanding that was flowering between them to the test while it was still so tender. At length, she acceded, not without reluctance, to his request. She found it difficult to carve out a place for herself in the busy ménage. They already had set routines, between which any innovation needed to be fitted. Everything seemed to revolve around the boys. She had imagined they would be more independent, but Manophet was forever breaking off to help this one or share a joke with that one. Not that they were over-demanding or badly behaved – on the contrary, they seemed easier to get along with than she had feared. Perhaps it was just a question of showing Manophet that he needed to adjust his priorities. At the end of the first week, she laid down a marker by spending all the money he had given her to buy groceries for the house on two luxurious desserts, one for him, one for her. Just for once, the boys would take second place. Manophet surveyed the cream-clad monstrosities with disbelief. He had seen enough. The relationship was over.

The lemon-yellow house was completed, and Manophet, now a property owner, moved in with his family. The townsfolk treated him like a local celebrity. Smiling passers-by scurried up to shake his hand and exchange greetings as he walked along the street. Old acquaintances who had written him off as a wannabe or a man of straw took great pride in bragging about their long-standing friendships with him. The transition in his fortunes was at times too great for him to comprehend. Nor did his lucky streak end there. Carol and Kirk offered to fund the purchase of a minibus, on condition that the Lao government contributed an equivalent amount in the form of a tax rebate. *Mirabile dictu*, the authorities played along. Now he was able to set off for football tournaments in Luang Prabang or Vientiane without half expecting to spend the weekend by the roadside waiting for breakdown assistance. He basked in the admiration that came his way as a consequence of the enhancement to his status, though he could have done without the attendant presumption that his pockets must be full of kip. The truth of the matter was very different: his weekly photocopying costs rarely came in below a hundred and fifty thousand kip, and his petrol bills were dismayingly large. But it seemed churlish to fret about the flies in the ointment. He could not wait for the visit that Kirk and Carol were planning for 2010. Kirk was hatching elaborate plans to charter a helicopter to take them to Mount Phou Pha Thi, and also wanted to retrace the route that Ernie Brace had taken when he was captured. Manophet's desires, though less grand, were just as powerful. He was dying to show them around the school that they had endowed.

# EIGHTEEN

'You are Fred Branfman?' Manophet exclaimed. 'The person who wrote *Voices from the Plain of Jars*? Oh my gosh.' He looked up at the tall, grey-haired American, half wondering whether his leg was being pulled. 'What a lucky meeting. That is my most favourite book!'

'Well, it was the refugees who wrote it, of course,' Branfman demurred. 'I was just a middle man. But it was my idea to visit the camps and encourage them to describe what they'd been through, and I did a lot of the translating. And then there were the drawings, of course. Those were just as important – *more* important, you might say, because it was tough to turn what was being said to us into English that captured the full horror of their ordeal. In a way, the drawings bring the reader closer to what the refugees experienced than the writing does. You know, I lost those drawings. I felt terrible. I wanted to look at them again years afterwards, and I realised I hadn't the faintest idea where I'd put them.'

'And then Channapha found them,' one of the others chipped in.

Channapha, the group's founder, a woman in her thirties with big silver-hoop ear-rings and a captivating Lao smile that arrived without warning from time to time like the sun breaking through a bank of cloud, gave a shrug of the shoulders, as though to suggest she did not deserve any credit for the discovery. 'That was how *Legacies of War* came into being,' she recalled. 'I was in Washington for a meeting with one of the grantees of the Foundation that I was working for at the time, and when I introduced myself he launched into this tirade against the bombing in Laos – because he was smart enough to know that Khamvongsa was a Lao name. The next thing I knew, he was delving into one of his filing cabinets and pulling out all these shocking drawings –'

'– because, as it turned out, this guy was somebody who used to work with me as an intern, and he'd had the sense to take them home with him when the office that we'd been sharing got closed down after I left,' Branfman explained. 'Otherwise they would almost certainly have been thrown away.'

'And the *awful* thing,' Channapha continued, 'is that I had no idea Laos had ever been bombed. I was only six when my family fled across the Mekong, and nobody told me *anything* while I was growing up. Laos wasn't on the school history curriculum. I had no inkling of what my parents or the country of my birth had been through.' She let out an embarrassed squeak, something between a laugh and a sigh. 'Anyway, now *I* have the drawings to stop Fred losing them again.'

The objectives of *Legacies of War*, the organisation that she had recently set up, were to heighten awareness of the Secret War across the USA and to raise funds to regenerate the most blighted areas of Laos. This delegation, which was visiting Laos on a fact-finding mission, was probably more highly accredited than any Manophet had yet been asked to guide around Xieng Khouang. 'What was it that had made you interested in the refugees?' he asked Branfman. 'Were you an aid worker?'

Branfman shook his head. 'To be honest, I was only here because I didn't want to be drafted to fight in Vietnam. Like a lot of people, I felt the US had no business being there, and I was damned if I was going to be a party to the felony. I spent a couple of years as an educational advisor in a village called Ban Xa Phang Meuk, which was where I learned to speak Lao. Then, in September '69, I went to Vientiane for a few days and hooked up with a guy called Tim Allman, who was freelancing for The New York Times and Time Magazine. While I was there, he got a call to say that hundreds of refugees had just arrived from the north of the country. Laos was partitioned at that point in time. There was a Royal Lao Army zone in the south and a Pathet Lao zone in the north, and these were the first people to have made it out of the area controlled by the communists. Tim wanted to get an interview with them, of course, and he asked me if I could come along and interpret, so we hopped on my motor bike, and drove over to the Pagoda at That Luang, where they'd been dropped off. They were just sitting there in a big circle, clutching a few possessions. What I heard that day changed the whole course of my life. We picked a family at random and asked if they'd ever seen any bombers over the Plain of Jars. They looked at us as though we were crazy, and told us they'd spent the past five years trying to *avoid* getting bombed. Every family we spoke to told the same story. Up to that point, the US government had always categorically denied bombing northern Laos so, to us patriotic souls, these were astounding and terrible revelations. Tim wrote up the story, and the following month the government was forced to admit that it had been lying through its teeth.'

'It was Fred and Tim who blew the whistle on the Secret War,' Elaine confirmed. Elaine had been a member of one of Manophet's tour groups a couple of years earlier, and it had been her idea to bring the *Legacies of War* team to meet him. 'The cat was finally out of the bag.'

'Unfortunately, all that happened was that the Administration switched to claiming it had never bombed any *inhabited* villages in northern Laos,' Branfman continued. 'Well, that was no more truthful than the original lie, of course, but I needed hard evidence before I could challenge it publicly, and that was when I had the idea of publishing *Voices from the Plain of Jars*. So, between '70 and '71, I went around the camps talking to as many refugees as I could.'

'My father and some of my brothers and sisters were in one of those camps,' Manophet said. 'Maybe you even spoke to them.'

'Needless to say, the security services were mad as hell when they found out. A journalist friend of mine was told by a CIA operative that they considered having me assassinated, but apparently they concluded it would be too risky because I had such close links to the press – not that you can ever be sure how much truth there is to stories like that, of course. In the end, they decided the best strategy would be to destroy my credibility by getting me denounced as a communist. One of my close Lao friends was threatened with indefinite imprisonment if he didn't cooperate, and my closest friend, Ngeun was told he would be conscripted into Vang Pao's army – which was as good as a death sentence for a former Pathet Lao soldier. But they were brave men, those two. Both of them held their nerve.'

'And after that the only option left to the CIA was to have you expelled from the country, right?'

'I was expelled at the beginning of '71. That was a surreal experience. The Lao Secret Police turned up at the Lane Xang hotel one morning to arrest me. They spent the first couple of minutes apologising. I knew one of them pretty well, and he was acutely embarrassed. He kept explaining that it wasn't their decision. The Americans had strong-armed the Lao government into giving the order, and there was nothing they could do. I gave my room key to a member of the CBS News team that I was working with and asked him to retrieve my papers before the CIA could move in and destroy them. Then I took the secret police out to breakfast on the way to National Police Headquarters to make sure he had plenty of time to complete the job. As for the politicians, they backtracked inch by inch, the way politicians do when they've been caught with their pants down. I challenged Nixon's claim that we'd never bombed any inhabited villages later that year in a Senate sub-committee hearing. I actually went so far as to call William Sullivan, who'd been American Ambassador to Laos up until 1969, a liar on national TV. A couple of years later, in '73, I was able to prove it – albeit in a roundabout way – by borrowing a radio from a CIA pilot friend and showing that US bomber crews *still* weren't checking whether there were civilians in the villages they were hitting. And so, little by little, the whole truth emerged. All in all, I was a major pain in the ass as far as the authorities were concerned.'

'Fred is what you might call America's conscience when it comes to Laos,' another member of the group volunteered. 'Our politicians did unspeakable things to this country in our name, and yet huge numbers of Americans have no idea what went on over here. They don't even know where Laos is.'

'Which is the cruellest irony of all,' Branfman said, 'because the people living on the Plain of Jars during the war had no idea where America was either – let alone, why it was bombing them. We systematically killed or maimed tens of thousands of civilians in a neutral country that half of us can't even locate on a map, and that naturally leaves the world with the impression that we don't actually *care* what we did.'

'But the Americans who come here are not like that,' Manophet objected. 'When they understand what happened, they become very emotional. They have difficulty not to cry and they say how ashamed they feel, and ask what they can do to make things better. And after they go home again they send back gifts for my school – even if they are not very rich. I am so grateful for the things they have given to me and to my students.'

'Well, thank God *some* of our fellow Americans have got the message that we need to do something to improve our standing in the world,' one of the others said.

Channapha nodded vigorously. Earlier on, the group's official photographer had persuaded her to pose for a picture with Manophet. Standing side by side, wreathed in smiles, the pair could almost have passed for a recently married couple.

'Most of our countrymen remain convinced that we're the good guys, and automatically assume that anybody who suggests otherwise is some kind of crank,' the new speaker continued. 'Do you remember the sense of disbelief when the World Trade Centre was destroyed? Everybody they interviewed was dumbstruck. And the politicians *still* don't get it. Here we are, thirty-five years on from the Secret War, bombing neutral countries as though they were put on the earth purely to provide us with a bit of target practice – only, this time we're using unmanned aircraft, like we're playing some kind of computer game. Can you *imagine* a more invidious way of behaving towards a country where you have no legal right to be? How do they suppose ordinary Americans would feel if the Chinese or the Russians started operating drones over Wisconsin or Oregon, and eliminating people they didn't approve of, along with a few incidental civilians? I mean –' he looked at Manophet – 'don't *you* ever get mad at us?'

Manophet took a mouthful of food to give himself time to think. His first instinct was to remain non-committal. It was rarely advisable in Laos to be too frank about what you thought or felt, particularly if you did not know the person to whom you were talking. But he had learned that, when *falang* asked such questions, it was usually out of curiosity rather than to lay a trap. 'I do get mad sometimes,' he said eventually. 'When I see a little boy in the hospital because he stepped on a bombie. He knows nothing. One minute he is playing in the field, and the next minute his body is full of metal arrows. They are made so the doctors cannot take them out without tearing pieces of his flesh and hurting him even more. What sort of human being invents a weapon designed to cause the greatest possible pain for another human being?'

A sombre silence settled over the group. The refusal of the US to sign up to the international ban on cluster munitions that had been ratified three months earlier weighed heavily on everybody present. The current generation of politicians could hardly have given a more dispiriting signal that they were cut from the same cloth as their predecessors.

'You went to Tham Piu yesterday?' Manophet asked. 'I used to take tourists up there when I was a full-time guide.'

'*Used* to?' a quiet man named Brett queried.

'I don't go back so much now. I think it is OK to show people a village where they have used old bomb casings to make a rice store, or to grow seeds in them, or make war scrap into spoons. But I am not so comfortable going up to Tham Piu with a bus full of tourists.'

'That was my idea,' Branfman said apologetically. 'And you're right. There were too many of us yesterday. But the place had such a powerful effect on me when I came back in '93. I wanted the others to have the opportunity to see it. I was on my own then, apart from the guide. Even the climb was eerie.' He paused to rearrange the chain around his neck. 'There was no wind. The grass was completely still. Nothing seemed to be moving – the trees, the clouds. The path isn't treacherous, but it gets steeper the further you go, and I kept losing my footing. Every rock that I dislodged seemed to be significant. It was impossible not to wonder whether it might have been flung out onto the hillside by the force of the blast. There was a chill around the entrance to the cave, where the air from inside was making its way out. Well, I guess that must have unsettled me, and when I got inside I had a lot of difficulty breathing. I kept imagining the villagers huddled together in the dark – cold, emaciated. I pictured them sitting on the rocky floor with their knees drawn up to their chins, trying to keep warm, listening to the sound of the aircraft lining them up, scared out of their wits, but at the same time assuming they were safe. And when I asked the guide where they were buried, he just looked down at the floor. I was standing on them.'

One by one the group stopped eating. The quiet American shook his head. In the background, the television blared away aimlessly.

'That was the first time you came back to Laos since they expelled you?' Manophet asked eventually.

Branfman nodded. 'It was before regular tourists were allowed in. One of my old Pathet Lao contacts got me a permit, a guy called Soubhan. And then I was here again a couple of years ago to help make a film called *The Most Secret Place on Earth* – which was previewed earlier this month in Phnom-Penh, as it happens. We went over to Long Chieng to shoot some of it. It had been closed to outsiders for years, but the son of a guy I used to know, Soth Phetrasy, was able to get us in.'

'You knew Soth Phetrasy?'

'He was the Pathet Lao's spokesman in Vientiane when I was there in the early seventies, and I used to take journalists over to interview him. I was never too sure what kind of condition I would find him in. The Royalist government made a habit of cutting off his electricity without warning to make him uncomfortable, or his water, even his food, but he never let it get to him. He was an extraordinary guy. I really admired his tenacity. And then it turned out that it was his son, Sousath who'd managed to get the film crew a permit to visit Long Chieng – taking advantage of his father's connections, presumably. Not that Sousath had any of his father's charisma. He had a tough time of it during the war, I guess, but I didn't take to him myself.'

Manophet's spirits rebounded somewhat from the plunge that they had taken at discovering his rival had a prior claim on the illustrious visitor. 'I never managed to get a permit to visit Long Chieng,' he conceded.

'It's a ghost town now,' Branfman said. 'The airstrip's still there, but we had a hard time believing it could ever have been one of the busiest airports in the world, let alone the second most heavily populated place in Laos.'

'I can't understand how they were able to keep it secret for so long,' one of the others interjected. 'The Soviets must have had satellites capable of spotting a piece of infrastructure that size. Surely it would have been in their interests to leak a few photographs to the US press.'

'I guess that might depend on where the satellites were pointing. They were probably more interested in what was going on further north. And there wouldn't have been any information flowing through conventional channels because journalists weren't allowed into the Pathet Lao zone. They say the CIA did a world-class job of covering the whole thing up. It was their biggest operation of all time, wasn't it?'

'Don't look at me, Brett,' the first man countered, putting up his hands. 'But presumably you had to research all this stuff when you were writing your book, so I dare say we can take your word for it.'

'Not that quiet Americans ever get involved with the CIA, of course,' Brett chuckled.

'You are Brett *Dakin*?' Manophet said. 'The one who wrote *Another Quiet American*?'

'You've read it?'

'I did not have time to finish it,' he admitted. 'But a lot of *falang* have talked to me about it and they think it is very good. Have *all* of you written a book about Laos?'

Laughter greeted this suggestion. 'But Elaine is also writing one, I think,' one of them ventured.

'Oh –' Elaine looked mildly flustered '– well, maybe. OK: probably. I have a title, at any rate: *Across the Mekong River*.'

'When you came to visit Laos in '93,' Manophet said, turning back to Branfman, 'you had not been to the Plain of Jars before that time?'

Branfman shook his head. 'I'd spent half my existence living and breathing the place. I'd read about it, studied maps, talked to people who'd lived there, written endlessly about the bombing. But I'd never been near it. I was desperate to spend some time here.'

'As a sort of catharsis,' one of them suggested.

'It was a long-delayed grieving process – that was how I thought of it. What happened during the war turned me into a political animal. For the next few years, I was on a PR mission, working around the clock to get the truth into the public domain, briefing journalists, addressing committees, haranguing senators. It was a role I felt I had no option but to play, but I was never comfortable with it. I might have come as close as any westerner to the victims of the war, and yet my connection to those people was second-hand at best. In my own eyes, I was a charlatan. I had no personal experience of what they'd been through. America had trashed Laos, and yet my countrymen were putting not so much as a dime towards trying to get it back on its feet. It wasn't as though we didn't have the money. All around me, Americans were frittering obscene sums away on God knows what. But we were only prepared to spend it on ourselves. I started to hate my own people. I was desperate to get out of the US and stand on the Plain of Jars for myself, witness the devastation, put the events that had taken place into proper context. But when the Lao government finally allowed me across the border, it was a terrible let-down. Vegetation grows back quickly in this part of the world. Forests had sprung up. Instead of jets screaming overhead, there were birds singing in the sky. The wildlife had returned. New villages had been built. For the first few days, I was afraid it would be impossible to establish any kind of connection with the horrifying realities of the bombing. It looked as though I'd left it too late. And then I made that visit to Tham Piu.

'After that, it became important to me to try and comprehend how this travesty had come about. What had happened to unhinge the individuals who ordered the bombing? They were the democratically elected representatives of a nation that regarded itself as the most advanced civilisation on earth, and most of them had presumably started their careers as decent, well-intentioned human beings. But these same men had cold-bloodedly perpetrated one of the most savage and indefensible acts of inhumanity in history. How had their consciences sanctioned this? What is it about power that causes a man's moral compass to stop functioning, I started asking myself?'

'I guess they convinced themselves it would be an acceptable price to pay for preventing millions of people coming under communist rule, with the years of pointless hardship that would entail,' somebody suggested.

'But intervening against regimes that impose defective ideologies on their fellow countrymen is the best way of *perpetuating* them,' a man who had not spoken before countered. 'Think of Cuba, North Korea, Laos. Communism fell apart quicker in those countries where we stayed out of the way and left the protagonists to stew in their own juice.'

'And of course I don't mean to suggest that Americans have a monopoly on the abuse of power,' Branfman said. 'The Royal Lao Government was a disgrace when it was in office. It may not have gone around murdering innocent civilians, but officials routinely helped themselves to whatever they could get their hands on – money, women. There wasn't even a pretence of governing for the common good. That was why we opposed it so vehemently when I was here in the sixties. Whereas the Pathet Lao seemed to be genuinely concerned with the wellbeing of the people at that time. I can't tell you how disillusioned I was when they finally took office.

The idea that corruption levels could *increase* had seemed inconceivable, and yet their blueprint for governing the country seemed to have been lifted straight out of *Animal Farm*.'

Branfman had told his story, and now he wanted to hear Manophet's. 'My brother came back in 1997,' Manophet said, as the narrative built to its climax. 'On behalf of the family, I was holding up the sign. It was a big day. I was, you know, suspecting a lot because I was a soldier before. I was trained in Vietnam. Russian instructors told me, sometimes you will see the CIA come to your family with someone's picture and try to get information. I thought: fifty percent it could be true, fifty percent it could be false, you know. And I keep holding the sign, and finally he walks out. When he saw his name, he dropped everything in front of the gate, and he runs to me. I couldn't say any words to him, because he was shaking me, asking, "Are you my brother, are you my brother?" I can't recognize him because it's too hard. Then he said "Where are our parents?" Behind me is my family, my father, my mother and my sister, the rest of the family. He pushed me out of his arms and he ran to my parents. All of them were crying. Twenty-nine years went by, but we came back to see each other again. It was the biggest day. And he got to visit only ten days. And the government only allowed him to visit Vientiane. Ten days went by like ten hours. My mother's stories with the three children in the caves, my father's stories with the three children in the refugee camps, my brother's stories with the Hmong family on the way to America, life in America. My parents nearly forgot him. The family nearly forgot him because it's been too long. And then one day somebody show up and it was like –'

'– rising from the dead,' Branfman suggested croakily. 'What was his age? Was he older than you?'

'He was twelve years older than me. He missed both sides of the parents because the house was burning, and he ran out by himself. So he got lost. And the next day he found a Hmong family, and the Hmong family kept telling him, "Come with us. Soon you'll find your parents." That's why in my class there are many Hmong children. Yeah, my son is Hmong,' he added, pointing at Lue.

'Do you have a wife?' Branfman asked.

'My wife has gone to America,' Manophet replied without hesitation, 'to Connecticut. Her father was a soldier in the Royal Lao Army. When the war was ended he fled the country. But he was afraid for his family could be harmed if they stayed behind, so later on he came back to take them away with him.'

'Including your wife.'

'And also our daughter.'

Elaine put a hand to her mouth.

'She was two,' Manophet said. 'I have not seen them since that time.'

'But you could surely –'

'The Lao government will not give me a passport.'

A long silence ensued.

'Sometimes I feel I would like to be free like you,' Manophet said, 'to go away to other countries, or travel round without having to let the police know where I am going, meet somebody from abroad and not have to tell a Party official what we said afterwards, and why the other person wanted to go to a certain place. Sometimes I feel I have had enough of trying to put other people's lives back together after they trod on a bomb. The man with no eyes, the one we saw outside – you remember him? He couldn't support his wife and children after that happened because he couldn't work any more, so I built a fishpond for him in a bomb crater near his land so they could have more chance to feed themselves. Lots of digging, and finding the right kind of fish to live there, and how to feed them – all that kind of thing. And the fish were swimming in the fishpond, and he was very happy again. And then one night they all died. They were just floating on the top of the water the next morning. Maybe some poison in the soil left over from the war. When things happen like this, I want to go away from the Plain of Jars with all its bombs and suffering forever and have an easy life somewhere else in another country. But when I tell this to the children at school they get very sad, and they say, "Teacher, what could we do without you? There would be nowhere for us to go." And when I hear that I stop feeling sorry for myself and remember why I need to stay here.'

Later that year, the school soccer team lifted the National Day Cup in Vientiane, beating off an array of star-studded rivals, including the Police and the Ministry of Tourism, none of whom were able to match the work-rate of their unknown opponents. For a few days, Manophet struggled to conquer his disbelief. How was it possible for a raggle-taggle collection of boys from a part-time English school, most of whom had been playing soccer for no more than a few months, to have pulled off such a coup? It was not as though they had been coached by a master tactician. Like his English teaching methods, his training techniques were of his own invention, a fusion of ideas that had come to him from watching televised European soccer games and reading online articles, or were simply the result of trial and error. As much as anything, the miracle had been achieved because the boys believed in themselves. When circumstances conspired against them, rather than growing disheartened they would roll up their sleeves and make an even more determined effort than before to turn the game in.their favour. Local teams in Xieng Khouang picked up on the news and clamoured for opportunities to pit their skills against the EDS stars. Manophet watched the eyes of boys across the province light up at the sight of his side climbing out of the minibus, and soon realised that it was not their reputation that sparked this reaction, but their matching soccer strips. Perhaps he could kindle a lasting passion for the game in some of the more promising village boys by giving them EDS football jerseys to wear. He began asking *falang* for more kit than the school needed, so that he could give sets away whenever the chance arose.

Some of Manophet's *falang* acquaintances assumed that running the school and looking after tourists took up all his time. They remained unaware that he had a day job, one that made considerable demands on him and paid the salary that kept his household afloat financially. It was the least enjoyable portion of his existence. Translating documents in the office was a painless enough way of earning money, albeit a dull one. More taxing were the trips into the countryside with ordnance disposal teams. Many of the assignments were routine: metal would be detected beneath a field. The consultants and the local bomb disposal team would discuss their options, with Manophet acting as interpreter. A remedial strategy would be formulated, and he and the consultants would then retreat to a safe distance while the explosives were laid and the charges detonated. But not all bombs were the same. The consultants sometimes found themselves faced with devices they had not encountered before. Was it possible to dig away a little more of the earth? Could they be moved safely to a position where they could be blown up without so much risk to the locals? Some of the relics were massive. Manophet knew the consultants would not stand so close if they were concerned for their own safety, and he did not flinch as he relayed their instructions. But he knew it was always possible that they could misjudge a situation. The more bombs he helped to defuse, the higher his chances of having an accident. The Japanese had dispensed with the wearing of Hazmat suits since taking over from the German consultants who had preceded them. Not that a Hazmat suit would protect him in the event of a blast, of course, but he felt naked in the field without it.

He wondered, as he stood one day translating the consultants' barely comprehensible English, whether it was all worthwhile. Thousands of bombs had been made safe, yet new ones came to light with such regularity that there was still no need to go out and search for them. Every week, villagers sent in reports of freshly discovered hazards that needed clearing away. The cylindrical device around which they were clustered had sparked an argument that had already lasted several minutes. One of the consultants could see no reason for not treating it as routine, but the other was mistrustful of certain anomalies that he claimed to have descried in its construction, and wanted to be more circumspect. Caution eventually prevailed, and it was agreed that the bomb should be rolled through a quarter turn to allow them to inspect the underside. Working with painstaking care, the clearance team scooped soil away from one edge, until the rusting hulk was free to settle gently into the required position. For a moment, the second consultant looked cook-a-hoop. A couple of sinister-looking valves had now come into view. He had been vindicated. But his smile faded as rapidly as it had appeared. There seemed to be a faint hissing sound. Was it coming from the bomb? The soil? Could anybody see anything? Manophet started to translate, but his skin had begun to itch. His eyes were stinging. The air around the bomb had become thick and hazy. It was the wrong colour. Suddenly he found it difficult to breathe. His instincts took over, and he turned and fled the scene as fast as his legs would carry him, gasping for oxygen, the rest of the team following close behind.

The two consultants were flown back to Japan for expert medical treatment the following day. Manophet, who was entitled to no such favours, spent the next three weeks languishing in the Lao-Mongolian Friendship Hospital, surrounded by doctors who had no idea what was wrong with him.

# NINETEEN

*A*t first these planes shot at the different mountains. We thought that our people had nothing to do with these matters...But then they started to shoot along the road to the village, which dismayed us because they were shooting without aim and everyone became frightened and ran out to hide in the fields. At night we returned to the village and things continued...Four planes of the jet type dropped their bombs together to destroy my village and returned to shoot twice in the same day. They dropped eight napalm bombs, the fire from which burned all my things, sixteen buildings along with all our possessions inside, as well as maiming our animals. Some people who didn't reach the jungle in time were struck and fell, dying most pitifully...We hadn't done anything, nor harmed anyone. We had raised our crops, celebrated the festivals and maintained our homes for many years. Why did the planes drop bombs on us?

*Voices from the Plain of Jars* was the talisman that allowed Manophet to travel back in time and glimpse what his parents and older brothers and sisters had been through. A revulsion for war he could summon up easily enough during the course of his everyday life, surrounded, as he was, by the victims of cluster bomb accidents, but not the attendant fear, nor the desolate sense of loss that it left behind for those who had known the peaceful ways that it had destroyed. There was an immediacy to the narratives that brought home the horror of the assault on his homeland and cauterised his soul. Whenever his life threatened to become too comfortable, he would sit down and leaf through the yellowing pages. All the accounts that Branfman had collected were harrowing, but this was the one to which he returned most regularly. How often he had read these terrible words. The writer began by describing his idyllic life before the war, a time of festivals and dancing, when the rivers were full of fish, and the trees hung heavy with pomelo fruit. Manophet's parents had grown pomelo trees before the bombing. Perhaps they had known him as a neighbour on the Plain of Jars, or even been friends with him, whoever he was. If it had been up to Manophet, every child in Xieng Khouang would have the chance to read the collection of testimonies. It captured the region's tragedy so much better than any historian. And yet this was impossible, of course, since the book was in English. The only people with the wherewithal to acquaint themselves with what had taken place on the Plain were *falang*.

*Dear Fred,*

*Thank you for the wonderful e-mail. Yes, you have got my e-mail address correctly.*

*How are you? Where are you now? Are you enjoying there? I and all of my students really miss you. We really appreciate that you visited, and we are talking about you every evening during class. Tonight I'm going to lecture about Voices from the Plain of Jars to my students, the first part. I'll let you know how they react!*

*The best wishes,*
*Manophet*

*Dear Fred,*

*It's amazing to hear from you. I really appreciate what you have shared.*

*Two nights ago I presented some parts of Voices from the Plain of Jars to my pupils. It was wonderful for those younger generations to learn more about what happened to their homeland and their ancestors, and see how it affected their lives today. All the students would really like to have a copy in Lao so they can read it through with their family, friends, lover. But I told them that it hasn't already been translated into Lao, so if they would like to read and understand it, they should improve their English skills!*

*My work carries on as usual. This morning I went to the clearance site at Ban Tone school yard. The teams found 194 bombies. That was a bad shock.*

*My English classes are still full. This week there are five boys waiting outside because there are no more seats for them. They come every day. I told them to come again at the end of the month, but they said they can't wait that long.*

*I'd love to have time to walk, play, chat to people, and join other social activities like you do. It sounds more lively and enjoyable, but I don't really have time, as you know. After work with UXO during the day and then teaching until late at night, I go to bed extremely tired.*

*I'll write more soon. I've got to go out to the site again now. Take care.*

*The best regards,*
*Manophet*

*Dear Fred,*

*I apologize for shocking you, but it's true. There are 194 BLU-26 bombs, all live, about a hundred metres from the school building. The teams have already put up a fence to surround them. The students still come to school every day. The teams cannot destroy them yet because there are signals of more bombies nearby. They will try and find them first and then destroy them all together.*

*Ban Tone is a primary school with over a hundred students. All of them are from farmer families, and most of their grandparents were living in the refugee camp in Vientiane during the war. When I talked to them, they said they had seen a foreigner in the camp sometimes, and I thought it could be you!*

*I apologize for the very late response to your question. I was very sick for a week. I have a heart problem. I could not come to work, so my English class was breaking for a while. I just started feeling better a few days ago.*

*The best regards,*
*Manophet*

*Dear Fred,*

*Thank you for your sympathy about my health. I am also very upset about it, and just keep hoping it won't be too serious now I'm waiting to get the results that are being tested in Vientiane.*

*There were 167,300 people in Xieng Khouang during the early 1960s, and in the late 1970s there were 84,965, so almost half of them disappeared. Local government believe that most of them died during the war and some migrated to foreign countries.*

*I'm always thinking that you will be back to visit soon. I'll be your private translator to talk to local people here.*

*Take care,*
*Manophet*

*Dear Fred,*

*I apologize for the late response. I was very busy for the last few days. There was a conference on cluster munitions which took place in Phonsavan, and many high delegates, excellencies and internal and external press. All those participants visited the UXO sites and saw the huge demolition at Ban Tone school yard, the 194 bombies that I mentioned before, and 136 bombies recently found at Ban Nakoh agricultural field, then another 27 mortars and two white phosphorus munitions. So all that work made me very busy as an interpreter at the UXO sites, and I'm very proud with what I've done. It was a great honour for me and my family, especially my mother, who never thought that the skinny little boy who grew up in the cave with her would have done some important work for the people in Xieng Khouang and Laos.*

*The doctors do not tell me yet about my heart problem because they have sent my blood test to Vientiane. I'm just waiting to get the result, and when I've got it I'll let you know.*

*Wishing you and your family all the best,*
*Manophet*

*Dear Fred,*

*My health is getting better now after I was medicated in Vinh Hospital in Vientiane. Today is the first day for me to return to my English class after two weeks when I could not teach.*

*How are you, and where are you now? I always want to see you again, and I believe that we will have a lot of things to talk about.*

*Wishing you all the best,*
*Manophet*

*Dear Fred,*

*I'm doing fine with my teaching. Six of my former students (all Hmong) had a farewell ceremony last Saturday. They are winning Japanese government scholarships for five years studying in Japan and they will be leaving for Japan on April 1ˢᵗ 2009. Those students and their parents invited me to join the ceremony. It was a great honour for me that I could be part of the first step of their accomplishment.*

*My work with UXO Laos makes me feel stressed. There were too many accidents this year, eleven people injured and several dead. I'm still walking on UXO fields every day. The fear comes to my mind when I've seen the victims. The biggest fear is that the Japanese will cut down some budgets because of the financial crisis in their country. Maybe I will lose my job.*

*Well I'm looking forward to hearing from you sometime. Please take good care of yourself,*
*Manophet*


*Dear Fred,*

*I apologize for not having written to you for a long time. I've been working away from town, 165 km, for almost two months. But I have good news about my work. From now on I don't have to go out that far again. I discussed with my experts and my team about working away from home, and they offered me this great policy. So I'll be working only in Phonsavan until the end of the year. All of my students are cheerful about that too!*

*My health is fine, only my work is too busy. There are now 147 students studying with me. It's really hard to teach a lot of students, and it's also hard for me to refuse new students. All those pairs of eyes are really pitiful. Since I came back and started teaching, everyday many young boys and girls have come to ask me to open a new class, so I have to open one more class with 40 students, all of them young Hmong children whose parents earn less than a dollar per day.*

*Well, I'm so happy with my good news. I'll write to you more soon.*
*The best wishes,*
*Manophet*


Manophet logged out of his e-mail account and rose slowly to his feet. He had lived through more than his fair share of unlikely twists of fate, but it had been a while since he had found a development so difficult to grasp. Even the school team's National Day Cup triumph was not so inexplicable if you allowed for the opposition's conspicuous technical weaknesses. But one thing you learned as you grew older was that, whenever you felt something could not possibly be happening, it invariably was. He padded out of the house and across the dirt road to the football pitch. A line of vanishing daylight marked the horizon to the west, from where the evening sky darkened to a near-ebony blue overhead. Now and again the makings of a breeze ruffled his hair and wafted in the mouth-watering aroma of frying yellow aubergines from one of the nearby homesteads. He made a circuit of the playing area, skirting the dung mounds and the grassless patch where the cows lay down to sleep. A deal had been in the offing for several weeks, but he had been sure it would fall through, and had not mentioned the plans that he and Gareth had made to anybody else. Nobody in Phonsavan had ever been on an adventure like this. Local Party officials counted themselves fortunate if so much as a brief trip across the nearby border with Vietnam fell their way. Not even the *national* football squad had played outside Indochina. Now a team of schoolboys, a third of them Hmong, would fly half way round the world to represent their country in a pan-continental tournament. Almost two *weeks* they would be out of the country! The players would be giddy with excitement when he broke the news to them. They would find it impossible to concentrate on their class work. Their heads would be full of dreams about aeroplanes and oceans and scoring winning goals in front of thousands of spectators.

How lucky he was to have had the opportunity to move out of Miss Onh's house. Not so long ago, Route Seven had been a mesmerising blur of bicycles whispering by, but these days the great highway swarmed with beep-beeping mopeds darting here and there in the battle to outrun one another, pedestrians scurrying to avoid them as they attempted the hazardous crossing to the other side. Every few minutes, a heavy Vietnamese truck would rumble past, swerving from side to side to avoid piles of construction rubble or a tangle of wooden scaffolding, shaking the buildings as it bumped up and down through the potholes. In tourist brochures, Phonsavan was usually still described as a wild-west frontier outpost, but it was changing fast. Visit the town centre during the day and you would find a hive of commercial activity. All the time, new side-roads were being driven across the few remaining rice paddies to allow residential housing developers to plunder the last parcels of vacant land. And yet, out here beside the school, after nightfall, it was wonderfully peaceful. He breathed in a mouthful of the heady air, held it in his lungs and listened to the trickle of the little stream that ran along the edge of the field behind the house. It was as though he was standing in a faraway Hmong village, where the noisiest event of the day would be the crowing of a rooster, a place where livestock could wander safely among the huts, and children were at liberty to play in the dirt with toys fashioned from coconut shells or lengths of bamboo.

Was it naïve of him, taking Gareth at his word? He had only met the man in December – and for no more than a few hours at that – yet here he was, little more than a month later, claiming to have raised enough money to pay for sixteen of them to travel to Sweden. Even by *falang* reckoning, this was a monumental sum of money – far more than it had taken to build his house. But his instincts told him Gareth could be trusted. Apart from anything else, he was a lifelong Arsenal fan, and surely no Gunner would betray a fellow supporter. Manophet had never heard of the Gothia Cup when Gareth had first started talking about it. A World Cup for school teams: what a splendid invention. How often did it take place? How many teams took part? Well *of course* the EDS team would be prepared to represent Laos if that could be arranged! The boys would be beside themselves with excitement to have such an opportunity. But they could hardly be expected to fend for themselves in Sweden. Might it not be sensible for their coach to accompany them? Gareth seemed to consider it odd that he could ever have imagined he would not be an integral part of the party. No team travelled without its coach. Manophet put his hand to his mouth, realising the authorities would have no option but to grant him a passport. After all these years, he would finally be allowed to cross the border. Tears rolled down his cheeks. Forcing himself to accept that his dream would never come true had been one of the hardest battles of his life. Now it turned out that none of that grief had been necessary.

A frenzy of activity ensued. Documents of the kind that Lao bureaucrats were capable of taking years to process needed to be obtained within a matter of months, and Manophet was at full stretch as he laboured to keep the paperwork flowing at the necessary speed. The parents of every boy in the team wanted to meet him to discuss the trip. Their sons had come to his school to learn English. Why were they suddenly to be removed to a country thousands of miles away where English was spoken only as a last resort to kick footballs around? How could they be sure this was not a devious *falang* scheme designed to take advantage of their ignorance about the sinister ways of the imperialist world? Manophet did what he could to reassure them that Gareth was not in the business of trafficking minors, and gave solemn promises that their sons would be returned safely at the end of the tournament. As for his own family, Phong and Vanh were part of the soccer squad, but what was to be done about Ped while they were away? The best solution seemed to be to ask Lue, who was currently working as a translator for bomb disposal teams in the south of the country, if he could take some time off to mind the house and look after Ped into the bargain. Lue agreed without hesitation, as Manophet had expected, but announced in the same breath that he would like to visit as soon as possible and bring a girlfriend. Manophet knew immediately that this could mean only one thing.

She too was Hmong, though she also spoke perfect Lao, and she had an even better-paid job than Lue: she was in charge of a bomb disposal team. *Falang* were often shocked to discover that women played such roles, but a quarter of the teams in Laos were all-female, and their safety record was better than the average. The detectors were easy enough to lift with the weight spread across four people and, for the rest, it was largely a matter of keeping your wits about you. Just as essential, the women enjoyed working together, without the complicating dynamic of the opposite sex.

'So what do you think, Father? Lue asked hesitantly as they strolled behind the house after the introductions and small talk integral to such occasions had been negotiated.

Manophet's heart beat strongly beneath his ribs. His son had found himself a beautiful girl, intelligent, kind, as perfect a bride as anybody could wish for. Had eight years really passed since his first, rather awkward appearance in the classroom? It seemed so much less – and yet, in that brief space of time, he had blossomed into the responsible and accomplished young man who now stood asking for his blessing.

'What is her cooking like?' he interrogated, pretending his approval still hung in the balance.

'It is excellent,' Lue insisted. 'She knows it all from her mother. You should try her roast chicken.'

'Is it as tasty as mine?'

Lue laughed, knowing there was no right answer to this question. 'At least as good as yours,' he said. 'And she loves soccer.'

Determined to give a good account of itself in Sweden, the soccer team adopted a punishing fitness regime. They would be playing several games a day if they progressed to the later stages of the competition, and stamina would be an important factor. By 5.30 in the morning, at which time it began to get light, every member of the squad would be kitted up and ready to start. Training had a regimented air redolent of Manophet's army days, commencing with a gruelling run. He did his best to make sure the boys could survive the rest of the day by pressing mugs of Ovaltine into their hands at the end of each session. One or two members of the team were less well nourished than he would have liked. And then there was the question of height. Their opponents could easily be six – even nine – inches taller across the board. How were they to defend against teams that thrived on pumping high crosses into the goalmouth? For once, he had enough slack in his schedule to accommodate the extra demands on his time. The Japanese had failed to secure a further tranche of government funding, as he had feared, and UXO Laos had dispensed with his services. But this was a not a good time to lose his main income stream. Lue's wedding would be expensive – Manophet would need to splash out on a cow at the very least. Traditionally, guests made contributions towards the cost of the festivities on the day, but he would still end up out of pocket. And the cost of running the school seemed to creep up every month. Linda and Paul, two kind-hearted Americans, had provided him with a computer and printer, so that he no longer had to go to the copying centre. But ink cartridges cost a small fortune, and he still had to pay for the paper.

The weeks became increasingly frantic and stressful. He had promised Gareth he would book discounted flights for the boys from Phonsavan to Bangkok, where they were due to connect with the Stockholm flight, but his contact at Lao Airlines was not returning his calls. If the booking was delayed any longer, there was a danger there would not be enough seats left on the aircraft. He decided he would have to borrow some money from the bank, using the house as security, and purchase full-price tickets. But the bank insisted on seeing the house deeds before they would give him a loan. What deeds were those? Manophet had never been given any deeds. He was now so short of cash that he was not even able to tip his old friend Bounyong, the barber when he had his hair cut. He allowed his emotions to get the better of him and let out a whoop of glee when he heard that his old rival, Sousath had died a couple of years shy of his sixtieth birthday. A look of shock passed across the usually impassive features of the adventure holiday representative who had told him the news. 'He used to try and pass himself off as me at the airport,' Manophet protested, immediately regretting the gaffe and seeking to justify himself. What a wretched state he had been reduced to. It was all getting too much. He wanted to talk to Gareth about the Lao Air flights, but Gareth had already done so much for the team. And westerners never *really* understood about money. 'In London, where I'm from,' he had confided, 'we work, we have careers, we're competitive, and if we're successful we earn money – a lot of money. Getting more and more money becomes an obsession. But when I came to Laos I looked around and I suddenly thought: shit, I have everything I could possibly want and more, but I've never lifted a finger to help anybody else. And it was then that I realised I needed to become a better person.'

The weekend before the wedding, Manophet and his sons drove to one of the lakes to the east of Phonsavan to fish. It was a time-honoured family ritual – one the five of them might not have the chance to re-enact after Lue was married. Phong had wanted their swan song to be a wild bull hunt, a Hmong tradition that Manophet enjoyed even more than fishing. Armed with crudely fashioned slingshots, they would track an animal through the forest and try to bring it down with a well-aimed missile. All four of his sons had learned how to make slingshots from their birth families, and Phong was an adept tracker. There were few sensations to rival the thrill of felling one of these fearsome beasts. But success was not assured – indeed, they were more likely to go a whole day without seeing a bull than kill one, and there was also the risk that one of them would get hurt. So it was as a fishing party that they set out after football training had finished.

'I bet I catch more than you,' Lue challenged.

'How much?'

'Five kip.'

'*Five*?' Everybody laughed. You would be lucky to get a mouthful of rice for five kip.

'I am going to catch the most,' Ped announced. 'I am going to catch seven.'

'In your dreams,' Vanh retorted. 'The most you've ever caught is two.'

'Fifty kip,' said Lue.

'My most is *four*,' Ped insisted.

'What a load of –'

'That time Phong fell in.'

'*Two* fish, you caught that day. You found a lizard that you claimed was a fish, and then you went and hooked an old snakeskin that was floating along.'

'I didn't *fall* in,' Phong objected. 'Vanh pushed me.'

'Fifty kip, eh?' Manophet reflected.

'It wasn't a snakeskin, it was –'

'I never *pushed* you in. Well, not on purpose. I tripped over Father's rod and banged into you by accident.'

Usually, there were other fishermen dug in at the best spots by the time they arrived, but today they had the place to themselves. It was a bad sign. If the regulars were boycotting the lake, it probably meant there were no fish to be had – unless, by some happy chance, they were off celebrating a local festival. Manophet had been hoping Vanh might manage to land himself a keed. He never seemed to have much luck with a rod in his hand. The first two hours passed without so much as a nibble. Ped began to grow restless. This was not how their last outing together was supposed to be. They should be pulling fish out of the water by the dozen. Manophet encouraged him to be patient. Perhaps their luck would change if they spread out a bit. For his own part, half the pleasure of the experience was being out in the open with his sons, breathing the peaceful air and listening to the water lapping against the bank. He lay back and contemplated the sweeping hills beyond the far shore. Somewhere in the forest, tribesmen had been burning off tree stumps and undergrowth to make a place for new fields, creating a high haze. The fine shimmer of gold-black smoke particles was so dense that he could look directly up at the noonday sun without needing to shade his eyes. Most of the country would be sweltering under its onslaught, but here the smog and the altitude combined to temper the fiery heat, and the land basked beneath a pleasant warming glow. Half closing his eyes, he fixed his gaze on the burnished fireball as it crawled lazily across the firmament. Every now and again he could hear the faint swish of waves running up the shingle of the little bay further along the lake shore. Life was good. Kirk and Carol had once again come to his rescue by agreeing to put up the money for the plane tickets. The preparations for Lue's wedding were almost complete. His passport had arrived. Gareth had found a film crew to follow the team in the Gothia Cup. His friend, Fred had just e-mailed to say he would be coming to visit at the end of the year.

In the end, they landed a mere three fish between them. On a successful trip, there would have been so many in their pails by the end of the day that they would have had to stop in at the market on the way home to sell off the surplus. It was enough nonetheless for a filling supper. He had taught the boys how to gut fish on three or four occasions, but it was a job they did not enjoy, and they made a habit of botching it in the hope that he would despair and do it for them. What were fathers for, after all? Building fires, on the other hand, was one of their favourite chores, and by the time he had finished with his knife and washed the slimy residue off his hands a spirited blaze was dancing in the hollow at the bottom of the garden. The boys clamoured for the rice to be cooked in banana leaves, but Manophet decided it would take too long. Dusk was falling. The last stragglers were returning from the fields, the late sun attaching long shadows to their feet. The rainy season might still be a month or two off, but there was always work to be done – furrows to be dug, fences to be mended. Having had to sit still for most of the day, Vanh and Ped were now full of energy, and they tore around the garden pretending to be wild bulls and leaping over imaginary obstacles while the fish sizzled over the flames. Manophet had enjoyed the day too much to bother reprimanding Ped when he spat his fish bones onto the grass. After the meal was over, with the fire starting to burn low, they sang together, as was their custom on these occasions. Lue was allowed to choose the songs. Crickets chirped. A pale upside-down moon came floating lazily up from the horizon.

The wedding ran like clockwork. The procession arrived at the most propitious hour, and a magnificent *baci* ceremony followed. At the reception afterwards, Manophet's garden was overflowing with guests. Lue's blood family had turned out in force, and Manophet had also extended invitations to every westerner he could think of, mindful that the more *falang* he could muster the luckier it would be for the bride and groom. The foreigners all protested vigorously when invited to dance, being unacquainted with the graceful languid style in which the Lao moved, and fearful that their clumsy attempts to mimic it would ruin the spectacle. But Phonsavan folk had long since worked out that *falang* were incapable of resisting the overtures of a smiling, determined Lao dressed to the nines in silk, and they lured them one by one to the dance area as the evening wore on. That it was beyond any westerner to pick up the subtle routines around which Lao dance revolved, earnestly though they tried, was half the fun of a wedding. In two days time, Lue's bride would be back in the field detonating unexploded bombs, but today she looked as radiant as you could wish. Lue too was looking his handsome best. He had never lacked for girlfriends. At one point, Manophet had feared he might develop a taste for the good life and neglect to settle down, or even take advantage of the Hmong practice of allowing a man to marry more than one wife. But in the end he had hunkered down and chosen wisely. What a wonderful day this was. The cow was roasting away in one corner. The speeches had been splendid. Surrounded by his family and friends, Manophet felt proud, fulfilled, as happy with his lot as it was possible for a man to be.

# TWENTY

The Nam Khan meanders indolently to the north before flowing into the Mekong. In the days when Luang Prabang was still the capital of Laos, it was to the shoal of rocks that marks the confluence of the two great rivers that the king's boatmen rowed the royal barges during the annual water festival, arranged the ceremonial flowers and candles, and prayed to the water spirits for the continued health of the kingdom. These days, the perfect vantage point from which to gaze out across the panorama is Utopia, an elegant construction of stilts and wide bamboo verandas strewn with banks of many-hued cushions on which guests may recline with glasses of iced coffee and watch the late afternoon sun sink down to the horizon. Below, expansive branches fan across the divide, swathes of semi-cultivated jungle fighting for territory against the arcs of palm fronds landscaped in by developers. Butterflies glide up from the shimmer, black with turquoise splashes, extravagantly large, attracted by the *Rhynchostylis* displays along the perimeter. The sluggish tempo of the river sets the rhythm for the whole lazy scene. It is a place from which to listen to crickets and watch coconuts ripen. If you could summon the energy to cross to the lookout point and gaze out over the city, you would find the imprint of a still gentle civilization – graceful temples enclosing wide holy spaces, broad tree-lined avenues, the occasional ferry creeping across the vast unbridgeable Mekong to the northwest. It may only be a matter of time before the city is brought low by kitsch and bustle and smog, but for the moment the past retains the upper hand, and it is still possible to imagine it as it was five centuries ago, the natural capital of the land of a million elephants, unrivalled in splendour.

Gareth preferred to remain recumbent, knowing the slightest physical exertion would send sweat trickling down his clammy-shirted torso, and took a measured sip from his cocktail. All in all, he reflected, elbowing a superfluous cushion to one side, it would be difficult to think of a more splendid location in which to stage this reunion. There was nowhere else in Laos with quite the same cultural cachet. The city had been declared a World Heritage Site in 1995, and more than a million tourists had visited during the past five years. Sometimes the National Day Cup was staged here rather than in Vientiane to make it easier for teams from the north of the country to participate, but that was the exception rather than the rule. In an ideal world, the English Development School team would have succeeded in retaining the trophy and gone to Sweden as national champions, but that feat had proved beyond the boys. Perhaps it was wrong to call them boys. At seventeen or eighteen, they were young men really – old enough to marry – but they were so much shorter than westerners that one instinctively underestimated their ages. They had been training prodigiously hard all year according to Manophet, with whom Gareth had been in contact on an almost daily basis over the past few months about the trip to Sweden. But the last of the administrative wrinkles had finally been ironed out, and now they could sit back and relax. Gareth was buzzing with anticipation at the prospect of seeing his friend again. They had not set eyes on one another since their solitary encounter a few months earlier, when Manophet had been his tour guide. How good it would be to clasp him in a monstrous bear hug, shake his hand and see the twinkle in his eye again.

What an extraordinary meeting it had been. Within a matter of moments, they had discovered a common obsession: Arsenal Football Club. What were the odds of running across a man with whom you could relive every twist and turn of the Gunners' extraordinary double-winning season *here*, in the middle of nowhere? The next thing he knew, Manophet had scrapped the pre-arranged itinerary, backed up the van and driven off in the opposite direction. In due course, they had pulled up beside a football pitch where the EDS boys, kitted out in full Arsenal strips, were knocking goals past their opponents' goalkeeper almost as fast as he could retrieve the ball from the ditch behind him. As the two of them stood admiring the rout from the touchline, Manophet had shared a succession of intimate stories about the travails suffered by his family during the war, and in those few moments Gareth had felt his world shift on its axis. Until now, he had never given a second thought to the brutal actualities of war or poverty because he had never needed to. But this conspiracy of diabolical circumstances could have been his to endure if he had been born in a different age or on the wrong continent at the wrong time. He could almost taste the stench of war in his mouth as he listened. And how had his charismatic host reacted to his wretched inheritance? By offering disenfranchised children an education and providing them with the chance to experience the beautiful game, as soccer was now coming to be known. At the end of the match, the boys had clustered round, wanting to try out their English on Gareth. Had he come to Laos in an aeroplane? What fantastic luck! They would give everything they owned to be able to fly in an aeroplane.

The idea of taking the team to the Gothia Cup had come to Gareth like a flash of brilliant light. It would be the experience of a lifetime for the boys, a story they would still be telling their grandchildren in fifty years time. Having seen for themselves the lifestyles enjoyed by ordinary westerners, they would return home brimming with visions of a brighter future, determined to change the communities in which they lived for the better. Manophet would witness the dramatic events as much through their eyes as his own, but for him too the trip would be a poignant adventure. He would be setting foot outside Laos for the first time, seeing the ocean, travelling to another continent to watch his team play football in stadia packed with thousands of noisy supporters. What Gareth had not anticipated was that he himself would derive so much satisfaction from organising the expedition. It had been a steep learning curve – he had never tackled a project of this nature before. Finding sponsors and raising the necessary funds had required him to put in hours of unpaid labour, and the initiative had severely depleted his savings. But how uplifting it was to be able to look other people in the eye when they asked what you were up to and tell them you were improving the lives of the deserving. To suggest that he had renounced materialism as a result of meeting Manophet would be an overstatement, but it would never again play the same dominant role in his decision making. The satisfaction that came from helping others fulfil their dreams was so much more enduring and profound than the kicks that making money gave. Before, it had been enough to do right by one's clients at work and be faithful to one's girlfriend. Now, through his friendship with Manophet, he had learned why he needed to demand more of himself.

Months had gone by since their earlier encounter, yet it seemed no time at all since they had stood together on the earth mound in the corner of the rice field and Manophet had handed him the detonation lead. Several villagers had come out to watch: a small dark boy with a smudged face trailing a black piglet on a string; three girls, one with most of her fingers crammed into her mouth, another wearing a traditional Hmong blouse, though nothing at all below the waist; further back, a clutch of adults, including a diminutive village elder perched on a rickety wooden chair that had been dragged out from a hut. There was something incongruous about the proceedings. He had been brought here because this was how the tourist industry operated in Xieng Khouang. Apparently, it was thought the best way to keep visitors entertained. "What did you do on your holidays this year?" "Oh, I blew up a few unexploded bombs in Laos. It was quite a lark really. Some of the locals came out to watch the fun. You should try it sometime. Makes a change from skiing or going to the beach." And yet the reason they were here was that one of the villagers had lost an eye and an arm when her hoe had struck metal while she had been working the land just a few months earlier. The clearance team had since located dozens of other devices close to the site of the accident. Gareth flicked the switch, and jumped back involuntarily as a fierce explosion burst the sleepy land apart, flinging savage clumps of torn earth into the sky. Even at this distance, the force of the blast was unnerving. His ears ringing, he watched one of the girls trying to calm the startled piglet. Evidently she had seen it all before.

He glanced at his watch. On the far side of the river, a monk attired in a traditional orange robe was walking slowly along an earth track. Presumably Manophet had spent time as a monk in his younger days. It was not something he had ever talked about. The film crew was due to fly in the following day to shoot some preliminary footage. Gareth was conscious that he might have been too bullish with Manophet about his chances of persuading the two cameramen to see the project through. To his way of thinking, the English Development School's participation in the Gothia Cup constituted perfect subject matter for a short documentary, and his passion for the idea had been enough to convince the crew to come to Laos and film the necessary contextual material at their own expense. However, it was not a foregone conclusion that they would want to follow the team to Sweden. They might take the view that the storyline was insufficiently strong, or identify potential technical difficulties that he had failed to anticipate. Nor was there much prospect of the uncertainty resolving over the course of the next few days. After all, how much could they hope to learn from filming the EDS team playing football in a cow field, or conducting interviews with UXO employees in Lao? The key to whether or not the film was a success was surely how well they could capture the reactions of the boys as they experienced western culture for the first time. And, even if the crew did take the bait, it would only be possible to engage them if he could succeed in raising yet another tranche of funding to cover their fees.

It was considered polite in Laos to arrive late, Gareth recalled, consulting his watch once more – though his expectation had been that Manophet would arrive punctually, being used to the English and their ways. Perhaps something had come up at the last minute that needed his urgent attention. When you had as many responsibilities as Manophet, there was always the chance that you might be phoned out of the blue to help resolve a crisis. He chuckled to himself, remembering a post by a member of the soccer team that he had noticed on Facebook just before setting out: "My teacher says the funny sentence like this: Good day, hello world, blah blah blah, the quick brown fox jumps over the lazy dog." That was Manophet all over – so familiar with the ways of the West that you would never realise how alien they were to the culture in which he had been brought up unless you knew his story. Half past four came and went. Gareth started to feel uneasy. He was as close to Manophet as to some of his oldest friends. He had spent an eternity on the phone to him during the past few months, and they had exchanged e-mails by the dozen. He knew him through and through, so he imagined. But the fact of the matter was, they had only ever met once. A few hours – that was all it had taken. Gareth had come away from the meeting convinced that this was a man he could trust. Buoyed up by a sense of euphoria, he had hatched the scheme to take the team to Sweden, gone out and raised fifty thousand dollars, and then wired the funds to Manophet's account so that he could pay for the flight tickets, insurance, visas and passports. And yet Gareth had never set eyes on any of these documents. A terrible thought was beginning to gnaw away at him. Did he actually *know* Manophet at all? Now that he finally had a passport, was it conceivable that he might have double-crossed him and absconded with the funds?

They smiled and made you feel welcome, the Lao, took delight in the same passions – football, partying. They shared your sense of humour, gave every indication of thinking as you thought. And yet how far did you *really* understand what was going on in their heads? It was not so unusual in a foreign land to have the feeling that the natives viewed you as being there purely to be parted, by whatever legitimate means, from your money. But in Laos there were so many other undercurrents to negotiate, partial understandings that undermined your equilibrium and left you in a state of perpetual uncertainty. The communists still ruled the country with an iron fist. People occasionally disappeared. Curfews could be imposed at a moment's notice – ostensibly in response to local Hmong unrest, but quite possibly to allow shady enterprises allied with the State to engage in dubious activities without fear of being observed. The press was heavily regulated. *Falang* men were prohibited from having sex with Lao women unless and until they married them. How strictly was *that* law enforced? Over here, the rules of engagement were blurred. People did not tell you the whole truth. They did not always answer the question that you asked. They had lived through an era during which it had been dangerous to speak too freely even to close acquaintances, let alone strangers. And, before that, they had seen their country subjugated by wave upon wave of imperialist invaders and then bombed into the ground by forces of overwhelming superiority. Was it any wonder that they mistrusted foreigners? Gareth suddenly felt very alone. Manophet was the cornerstone upon which his whole involvement with this strange bewildering country was built. And suddenly Manophet was not where he was supposed to be.

They had arranged the meeting only four days ago. There was no possibility that there had been a mix-up over the date or the place or the time. And, although Manophet knew Gareth's mobile phone worked in Laos, he had not called to say he was running late. His failure to appear was ominous – there was no getting away from it. But Gareth could not believe the worst of his friend. Was it beyond the bounds of possibility that the authorities had pulled him in for questioning? There were Hmong boys in the football team. Could a Party official have got it into his head that they might try seeking asylum when they arrived in Sweden? Or perhaps they were worried about the possible Public Relations implications if western journalists attempted to interview the Hmong players. But they would need an interpreter for that, and Manophet would be the only person capable of playing such a role. Maybe the authorities were trying to strong-arm him into agreeing not to speak to the press while he was out of the country. Who could tell how paranoid they might become when faced with a situation of a kind that Laos had never had to deal with before? More likely, they were having second thoughts about letting Manophet himself have a passport. They must have had reasons for holding out on him so long. One could be sure the Party would keep a dossier on him, but it was impossible to know what sort of information it might contain. On the face of it, he was an asset to Laos. His success as a tour guide had raised the country's profile across the globe, attracting new visitors and much-needed overseas currency. Beyond which, his achievements as an educator were sure to pay dividends over the coming years as his protégés reaped the benefits of their schooling – albeit of a less quantifiable kind. Perhaps that was the problem. Perhaps it was *Manophet* they were scared of losing.

He tried to put himself in his friend's shoes. What would *he* do if he had been granted a passport after a lifetime of being desperate to have one? Steal the money that had been raised on behalf of the underprivileged students for whom he had spent the past ten years caring, and make a run for it? It made no sense. It was not as though the authorities were liable to demand his passport back after the Gothia Cup had ended. Why should he not wait until that longed-for experience was behind him before disappearing if he was secretly desperate to get out of Laos? Surely Bua would be prepared to keep him in funds while he carved out a fresh existence for himself in a new country. Besides, it would mean abandoning his house, his school, depriving the soccer team of its chance to play in

Sweden. He would cut himself off forever from the rest of his family, his students and – most importantly – his sons. The longer Gareth considered the position, the more convinced he grew that the money that he had raised had been used for its intended purpose. The boys' passports, tickets and visas were under lock and key at Manophet's house, exactly as they ought to be. It was just Manophet himself who was unaccounted for. He felt embarrassed at having ever imagined it could have been otherwise. How could he have entertained such unworthy thoughts about his friend?

More than an hour had elapsed since they had been due to meet. The moment of reckoning had arrived. Gareth slid out his mobile and dialled Manophet's number. Every instinct told him the phone would be switched off.

But after a moment the call connected.

Three rings. Four rings.

'*Sabaidee*.' It was a halting voice, not Manophet's, the voice of somebody out of place, in the wrong world.

They warn you to expect the unexpected in Laos, but it does not leave you any the better prepared. Gareth plugged his other ear to shut out the noise of crockery being stacked a couple of floors below. His first idea was that the phone had been stolen and that he was speaking to the thief. Young, male and scared – that was how the other party sounded. *Sabaidee* – hello – was one of the three Lao words that he knew. What was he supposed to do now? It was not the same as speaking in person to a stranger whose language you did not understand. You could not gesticulate to get your point across, or make faces.

The line whispered and crackled like a distant forest fire as the silence between them lengthened. Gareth knew he ought to say something, but he felt badly disorientated. It was as though he had stumbled into a cartoon landscape criss-crossed by garishly coloured roads that sped nonchalantly over precipices towards destinations of which he had never heard. Not so many hours ago, he had been six thousand miles away, heavily muffled against the cold as he trudged along pavements sprinkled with a dusting of snow to the tube station. Now he was perspiring freely under a brutal equatorial sun, peeling his tee-shirt away from the soaking mat of hair on his chest every few seconds. According to his body clock, it was the middle of the night.

'Hello?' said the voice.

The relief at hearing an English word was only momentary. The position was now even more tangled up than before. How had the speaker known to switch languages? It was as if he had been expecting the call – and yet, at the same time, was underprepared, unequipped to deal with it. The greeting sounded bewildered, resigned, exhausted, betraying a confusion of inadequacy of the kind only the voices of the young can express.

'Hello,' Gareth tried to speak calmly, 'this is –'

Then it seemed senseless to give his name. The word Gareth would only confuse a Lao speaker. He started again. 'I'm trying to get hold of –'

But this was another mistake. "Get hold of" was too colloquial. He hurried on, consumed by a sudden fear that the other person was about to put the phone down on him. 'I'm sorry, could I please speak to – is it possible – is Manophet there?'

'Manophet?' repeated the voice, even less certain than before – but placing the stress on the final syllable, so that Gareth could immediately apprehend the difficulty. Westerners instinctively stressed the first syllable of Manophet's name and clipped the central vowel. But the Lao pronunciation was different. The speaker was trying to establish whether they were talking about the same person.

'Mano*phet*,' Gareth repeated, speaking the word very slowly, to make sure it would be understood. 'Mano*phet*, that is correct.' Suddenly he knew who he was talking to. 'Lue?' he queried.

'Lue, yes, it is Lue.'

'Lue, this is Gareth, your father's friend. Is he –'

'Gareth?' the voice repeated. The same desolate monotone.

'Yes, Gareth. Is Manophet at home? Is he there?'

'He is –' A long pause, presumably a search for the right English words. Gareth had not spoken to Lue before, but his English, according to Manophet was reasonable. 'I am sorry,' the voice said. 'He is not here.'

'Good, excellent, right – I mean, no, that's what I expected. I'm supposed to be meeting him up here in Luang Prabang. But he hasn't shown up. I was wondering if you might –'

'In Luang Prabang?'

'Yes, in Luang Prabang, but he isn't here, only I'm not sure *why* not.'

'He is not in Luang Prabang any more.'

'*Not* in Luang Prabang? Oh, right, I see.' Gareth did not see. Nothing at all was clear to him except that it was important to choose his words carefully. 'But do you,' he started, 'I mean, can you tell me –'

'He is in Vientiane.'

'In *Vientiane*?' This was about the last piece of information he had been expecting to hear. 'But what on earth's he doing in Vientiane?' he queried. 'We agreed to meet in Luang Prabang.'

Another long hiatus. 'His body is in Vientiane.'

Gareth went completely still. The noises in the background had subsided, to the point where it was difficult to believe he could have misheard. Did Lue understand what he had just said? Obviously something must have gone wrong with his English, but what the hell could he have meant?

'He passed away,' Lue said. 'Yesterday morning. He is dead.'

It could not possibly be true. Manophet was forty. He had chatted at length to Gareth on the phone four days ago. Everything had been fine. He had said nothing about feeling unwell. It was all a dreadful misunderstanding, something to do with the cultural divide that separated their two countries. You did not just die without warning. Even in an impoverished country like Laos the laws of science applied.

'Lue, I'll ring you back,' Gareth said, and rang off.

Without any sense of what to do or where to go, he wandered out of Utopia and into the street. A ferocious stabbing heat greeted him, the late afternoon sun glaring pitilessly down through the haze. There was no breeze now. Gaunt saplings stood in lifeless squares of dust along the pavement, not stirring. A dog lay listlessly beside a heap of broken paving stones. Dazed, he turned across the road towards the market, forgetting there might be cyclists. There was no means of corroborating Lue's story, no other information source through which to find out what had really happened. *Surely* there must be a mistake. The timing was too brutal. What sort of God could pluck him away *now*, so young, just as he was about to realise his lifelong dream? And yet why did Lue have Manophet's phone? Gareth was dangling over an abyss, clinging grimly to a fragile thread, his childish faith that good must necessarily triumph over evil. Marooned in a country whose language he could not speak, surrounded by folk with no comprehension of the world that he inhabited, he felt more helpless than at any time in his life. To whom could he turn? And what was he to do about the film crew? There would be nothing for them to film when they arrived. It was too late to put them off. By now, they would already be somewhere over the Middle East en route to Bangkok. He slumped down against a tree. What did any of that matter? A terrible aching void had opened up inside him. His friend, Manophet, who he had been on the verge of getting to know so much better, and on whom everything hinged, was dead.

After a few minutes, he dragged himself up off the ground and started walking again. As Wat Wisunalat came into view, he remembered the monk with whom he had struck up a conversation earlier in the day at one of the smaller temples, a gentle fellow with a good grasp of English. Perhaps, if he could find him again, he might be prepared to act as an interpreter. It was after six by the time Gareth tracked him down, but he grasped the situation quickly and offered to speak to Lue. The phone conversation between them, conducted in Lao, lasted half an hour. Manophet had been violently sick. To begin with, they assumed he had eaten something that had disagreed with him and was suffering from food poisoning. But then paralysis had started to set in. His speech had grown increasingly difficult to understand. They had driven him to the Lao-Mongolian Friendship Hospital, where the doctors could see that he had suffered a catastrophic cardiovascular failure. But there were no facilities for dealing with such patients in Xieng Khouang. Treatment for this kind of medical emergency was available only in Vientiane. It would be necessary to airlift him. Bua had managed to raise enough funds to pay for a helicopter. The hospital had made the requisite arrangements. But too many hours had passed by the time Manophet finally arrived in the capital for them to save him. Lue and Kone, who had accompanied him in the helicopter, had just got back to Phonsavan after being on the road all day. His body would be arriving the following morning for the cremation rites that initiated the four-day funeral ceremony.

That night, when Gareth should have been sleeping, he lay awake dripping sweat. Images of helicopters and hospitals and funeral pyres crowded his mind, visions of Manophet in a state of paralysis, Manophet covered in black vomit. The following day, he dozed off in public spaces, coming to with no sense of where he was or what he was supposed to be doing. He bought cigarettes for the first time in years, but then gave them away. He forgot to wear sun protection, did not bother to shave, lost his passport but rediscovered it on a stone seat in a park he had visited earlier. He was in the thrall of the wrong emotions – by turns disgusted with himself for having imagined that his friend could have betrayed him, appalled that his grand plans for the boys had been wrecked, disconcerted by the news that Manophet had placed an incomprehensibly large donation in the alms box at the temple the day before he had been taken ill. Why could he not shake off these stupid distractions and just *grieve* for his lost friend like any normal person? If only he had not insisted on obsessing over administrative details every time they had talked on the phone and lightened up a bit. He had assumed there would be time to get to know him properly once they were together again, but it had been a disastrous miscalculation. Now he would never be able to get to the bottom of the unanswered paradoxes and mysteries that defined the man whose body was already being consumed by flames. And this was why he could not grieve. Even in death, the friend that he had lost was a stranger to him, a wonderful stranger that he had almost had the chance to know.

He thought of Lue getting back to the lemon yellow house after bumping along all day in a van on the dusty road from Vientiane, pictured him sitting in the empty classroom, drained, hearing Manophet's phone ring. 'I'm so sorry,' he mumbled, immediately calling him up again. 'I've been completely selfish. I had no idea what you'd just been through.'

And now, at last, the knots inside him started to work themselves loose. The two men sobbed openly down the line.

'You could come here to the funeral,' Lue suggested. 'They will bring the ashes to the house tomorrow after they have cooled down. After that, we will start the ceremony.'

Gareth had never heard a more comforting proposal. 'But I will have this film crew with me,' he remembered.

'You can bring them,' Lue said. 'Nobody will mind. There will be hundreds of people.'

Mourners passed beside the wooden box containing Manophet's ashes, which had been placed on a stand in the porch, as they arrived. A marquee had been set up in the garden. Inside, tables covered in white tablecloths strewn with flowers were packed closely together. Half of Phonsavan seemed to have turned out, men in suits, men in uniform, Hmong in traditional costume, children from the school. A slight figure peeled away from the multitude as Gareth approached and came to greet him. Without asking, he knew that it was Lue. Each of them reached out a hand, but after a moment they found they were hugging one another, two grown men, strangers, weeping silently, not bothering to conceal their tears. Gareth introduced the film crew. 'We have our cameras with us,' they volunteered. 'We could film if you like. Then you would have a record. We could do it very unobtrusively.'

As the only westerners present, they cut awkward figures among the crowd, but somehow it did not matter. The occasion united the guests, old and young, Lao, Hmong or *falang*. Gareth had been assigned to the table on which the footballers were sitting. Each player had shaved his head and eyebrows as a mark of respect, and together they created a startling spectacle. Most seemed too shell-shocked even to move. Only Nouad, the captain, who was seated directly opposite, looked in control of himself. He was unusually tall for a Lao, dark, charismatic. 'We are happy that you could come,' he said softly. A silence developed, but it seemed deliberate on Nouad's part. He held Gareth's gaze calmly, as though this was the most natural and effective means of getting to know him. And Gareth found that, rather than being embarrassed, he was at ease with this approach. Slowly, the other boys came back to life. Over the course of several minutes, they rearranged themselves so that they were grouped behind their captain in a sort of phalanx, as though to demonstrate that he was their spokesman. A single burning question occupied the minds of everybody at the table. Would it be too disrespectful to voice it? What would Manophet have wanted?

'Nouad,' Gareth said eventually, 'how do you guys feel about going to Sweden after what has happened?'

'We want to go,' Nouad said, nodding slowly. 'We still want to play.'

Two months later, fourteen Lao boys, none of whom had previously seen the sea, tasted a burger or a pizza, or travelled in a train, let alone an aeroplane, flew to Gothenburg to contest the schools' world cup along with teams from seventy other nations. They were the first football team to represent their country in Europe, a distinction that earned lavish praise from the sport's governing body, FIFA, and brought coverage on national and international TV channels. Almost sixteen hundred teams entered the Gothia Cup, female as well as male, the players' ages ranging from eleven to nineteen. The English Development School team reached the semi-finals of its section of the competition, losing on penalties after leading 1-0 with ten minutes to play, and went on to pick up the Fair Play Trophy, which is awarded to the team that shows the greatest sportsmanship on the field across all participants and most honourably represents its country. Every twist and turn of the saga was captured on film by the production team that had shot footage of the funeral, and the material was worked up into a gripping documentary. Back home in London, Gareth regularly plays the DVD. Part of him swells with pride as he relives the closing ceremony, at which the boys are presented with their medals. But he cannot watch the familiar scenes without a lump forming in his throat. And, just behind him, there is always a long silent shadow.

# AFTERWORD

*O*n *Safer Ground*, a documentary in which the story of the English Development School team's exploits in the 2010 Gothia Cup is told against the background of Laos's troubled past, was released in June 2014.

Fred Branfman, the man generally credited with blowing the whistle on the Secret War, died in September 2014. A new edition of his seminal book, *Voices from the Plain of Jars* had been published the previous year. Prior to his multi-year crusade to expose the truth, the line taken by the US Administration was that it had never bombed Laos. By the time he was done, officials were prepared to concede that it was the most heavily bombed country in the history of aerial warfare, according to a Washington Post investigation. Branfman may be heard reflecting in his own words on the events that took place during the Secret War in *The Most Secret Place on Earth*, a short film released in 2008.

Captain Ernie Brace died in December 2014, having finally been awarded the Purple Heart the previous year at the behest of former US Presidential candidate, John McCain, after four previous nominations had been unsuccessful. A few months before the presentation ceremony, *Locked up Abroad: Vietnam POWs McCain and Brace*, a retrospective recorded by the two ex-POWs, was released by the National Geographic TV Channel.

Manophet was not a smoker or a heavy drinker, and it is not clear why he should have passed away at the age of just forty. Five years on from his death, eight of his nine siblings are still alive and well, as is his mother. Only Sing, who was the victim of a motor cycle accident in 2008, predeceased him. Ernie Brace ended his book, *Monkey Paw Soup* – in which he described the trip that he took with Manophet in his own words – with the suggestion that he "died from the residual effects of a phosgene bomb he was helping to dispose of some years earlier." While it is as speculative to blame Manophet's death on the gas leak as it is to claim that phosgene was the gas involved, Brace was well versed in the technicalities of war, and he would not have asserted in writing that phosgene bombs were present on the Plain of Jars without good reason.

Another possibility is that the circumstances of Manophet's birth were to blame for his premature demise. Epidemiological studies have shown a strong correlation between under-nutrition during the later stages of a mother's pregnancy and the susceptibility of the child that she is carrying to early-onset cardiovascular disease. It is hypothesised that the foetus channels the limited resources at its disposal into developing critical organs such as the lungs and the brain, while scaling back on tasks of lesser physiological importance such as lining artery walls, leaving them more liable to rupture and bring about a stroke. Manophet's family was living from hand to mouth in the forest at the time he was born. His mother was so malnourished that she was unable to produce milk, with the result that he was the only child in the family that she was unable to breast-feed.

Following Manophet's death, a charitable foundation was set up to fund and take charge of the English Development School. Thanks to the hard work of those involved, two hundred pupils are now enrolled, and there are a further one hundred and fifty names on the waiting list. The school has six new teachers, including two of Manophet's former pupils, new premises, and an array of new teaching aids. It also has a new name: The Lone Buffalo School.

# APPENDIX: A BRIEF INTODUCTION TO LAOS

Laos is a country similar in shape to the UK when rotated end over end. It shares a frontier over a thousand miles long with Vietnam to the east, and a frontier of similar proportions with Thailand to the west. To the south, it borders Cambodia; to the north Burma and China. The border with Burma follows the course of the Mekong river, which also delineates long stretches of the Lao/Thai border as it flows south towards Cambodia. The Lao/Vietnamese border runs along the top of the Annamite mountain range, a geographical barrier that has left Vietnam less exposed to Indian culture than Laos, Thailand and Cambodia, whose languages and scripts have Sanskrit influences. In terms of land mass, Laos is roughly half the size of Thailand and three quarters as large as Vietnam. However, it has a population just a tenth the size of Thailand's, partly because it is landlocked, and partly because much of the terrain is mountainous and densely forested, less than 5% being categorised as arable land. According to the 2005 census, 55% of the population is ethnically Lao, 11% Khmu and 8% Hmong, with the remaining 26% comprising almost fifty other distinct ethnic groups (some scholars put the figure closer to a hundred), each with its own language. Three distinct language families can be identified: Austro-Thai (to which Lao, Phouane, Tai Dam, Hmong and Yao belong), Austro-Asiatic (to which Khmu and other Mon-Khmer languages belong) and Sino-Tibetan (to which Akha belongs).

Most, if not all, these minority groups originated in China but were expelled across that country's southern border, some because their tradition of growing opium was regarded as unacceptable. Once in exile, they paid scant attention to national boundaries, finding their way not only into Laos but also Burma and Vietnam. Because there is little competition for the marginal lands on which they eke out their harsh existences, sovereign authorities have historically shown limited interest in interfering in their affairs. The ethnic Lao arrived in Laos several centuries before most of the other minority groups. Driven out of China by the Mongols in the thirteenth century, shortly after the Siamese had populated south Thailand, they proceeded to occupy the fertile Mekong valley, displacing earlier settlers, a Mon-Khmer speaking group, into the surrounding hills. Over the next few hundred years, Indochina carried on much like Europe, with conflicts breaking out sporadically between the various kingdoms as they vied for ascendancy, and strategic alliances forming and dissolving. Partly because Vietnam comprised three separate provinces at this time, the balance of power in the region shifted frequently, and during the seventeenth century Laos was the dominant player, controlling large areas of Thailand. But in the decades that followed Thailand and Vietnam flourished, thanks to their extensive coastlines, while Laos fragmented into kingdoms. These, together with Cambodia, came to serve as buffer states between the two increasingly formidable coastal powers.

In the mid-nineteenth century, the French arrived to colonise the region, successively subjugating the three kingdoms of Vietnam, starting in the south, before occupying Cambodia and Laos. Thailand (or Siam) was allowed to remain independent so that it could serve as a buffer state between French Indochina to the east and Burma, now under British control, to the west – though on condition that it handed back swathes of territory that it had earlier seized from Laos. The French ruled Laos with a relatively light hand and faced little hostility prior to the Second World War, but over time their practice of allocating minor official and commercial positions to the Vietnamese in preference to the Lao became an increasing bone of contention. By 1940, when France was overrun by Germany, over half the population of Vientiane was Vietnamese. An important legacy of this period was Route Seven, the highway constructed through the Annamite mountains to connect Laos and North Vietnam. After its surrender to Germany, France answered to Japan in Indochina, but it was permitted to continue administering the region until 1944, when Vichy France collapsed and Japan took direct control and declared an end to the colonial era. Vietnam, under Ho Chi Minh's Viet Minh nationalists, accepted the offer of independence, as did Cambodia. But Laos, nervous about Vietnam's intentions and sensing it was only a matter of time before the French resumed control, indicated that it intended to remain loyal to France. The Japanese occupied Laos without delay, prompting an immediate *volte face*, but the damage had been done. Heeding the authorities' call for resistance, French, Lao and ethnic minority group guerrillas took to the jungle, and a self-fuelling period of civil unrest that would continue for fifty years had begun.

When the Japanese withdrew from Indochina a few months later, America, motivated by a desire to stymie any French initiative to reclaim its former colonies, sided with the Viet Minh, deepening the rift over how Laos should move forward. Traditionally, the Lao had been easy-going and accommodating, but now sections of the population became polarised, and attitudes started to harden. Some favoured a return to French rule, but others believed the time had come for the country to become independent. The French were supported by sizeable numbers of Hmong, who had coexisted amicably with them under colonial rule and fought willingly against the Japanese, by whom they had been harshly treated. Smaller numbers of Hmong from a clan that had been less favourably regarded by the French took the other side, however, as did many belonging to the largest ethnic sub-group of the aboriginal Mon-Khmer-speaking people in the southern highlands, the Khmu, whom the French had spent years trying unsuccessfully to subjugate. In due course, the French recovered control of Laos, at which point the roles reversed and the Viet Minh became the resisting force, allied to the Pathet Lao, a left-leaning nationalist movement formed in 1950.

The emergence of communism as a mainstream political ideology across the world caused the US to reformulate its position towards Indochina. When, in 1950, Ho Chi Minh's communist regime in Vietnam was recognised by China and Russia, America switched horses, dissolved its alliance with the Viet Minh, and started to provide France with economic and military support, primarily for use in Vietnam. In Laos, both sides were soon engaged in stealthy manoeuvring. Practical measures aimed at winning the hearts and minds of impoverished Lao villagers were painstakingly implemented by the anti-colonial Pathet Lao/Viet Minh alliance, particularly in the educational field. Meanwhile, long-standing misgivings on the part of the Hmong about their treatment by the ethnic Lao were cleverly exploited by the anti-Vietnamese faction. Not least among their grievances was the fact that they were known by the ethnic Lao as "Meo" (savages) rather than "Hmong", a word that means "a person" in the Hmong language. Other minorities such as the Mon-Khmer-speaking tribes, who had historically been referred to as "Kha" (slaves), were similarly disenchanted. Little by little, the infiltration of two provinces in the northeast of the country by the communists gathered momentum until, in 1952, the Viet Minh marched boldly on the king's palace in Luang Prabang. Road blocks set up by Hmong tribesmen under the legendary guerrilla leader, Vang Pao persuaded them to turn back without either side having to resort to arms, and Dien Bien Phu, the border town that they had occupied en route, was recaptured the following year. Two years later, however, the French were defeated at Dien Bien Phu in a bitter two-month battle, and their rule of Indochina was at an end.

The transfer of power was formalised under a treaty signed in Geneva in 1954. It was agreed that free elections should be held in Vietnam in 1956, and that Laos and Cambodia should become a neutral buffer zone into which no foreign military personnel could be deployed. Neither party to the agreement negotiated in good faith. America had no intention of sanctioning an election that would lead to the creation of a united communist Vietnam. And the Viet Minh, aware that America was in no position to disprove its claim that it had no troops on Lao soil, made no effort to withdraw them. While Laos might have been suited to act as a buffer state in a geographical sense, its population was just two and a half million, up to one and a half million of whom were hill-tribesmen, and its primitive economy was tiny. To those of a political disposition on either side, it therefore appeared to be not so much a sovereign nation as a yawning power vacuum. In northeastern Laos, the Pathet Lao ignored the Royalist Lao government and ran the provinces that it controlled along increasingly communist lines, despatching recalcitrant villagers to North Vietnam for "re-education" – assignments from which they might or might not return. The Americans responded by pumping capital into the Lao economy in the form of the largest per-capita aid programme anywhere in the world. Most of this money found its way into the pockets of local government officials and merchants, and never reached the ethnic minorities.

But the neutralist instincts of the leading Lao politicians of the time were powerful and, confounding the predictions of the cynics, they were able to set up a government of national unity in 1957, the Pathet Lao surrendering its territory and swearing allegiance to the crown on condition that supplementary elections would be held the following year to allow it to procure an appropriate level of parliamentary representation. When these elections took place, the Pathet Lao won more seats than US observers had anticipated – to the extent that ministerial positions were offered to two of the incoming Pathet Lao politicians. Panic struck Washington, and America announced that it would suspend aid to Laos until such time as they and the prime minister were removed from office. By now, the economy was so dependent on US aid that the government had little option but to accede to these demands. America duly restored its aid programmes and, when false rumours that the Viet Minh had invaded Laos began to circulate, expanded them dramatically, but this did nothing to erode the communists' growing popularity. The final nail was hammered into the coffin in 1960, when a fresh round of elections was rigged to such an extent that the Pathet Lao won no seats at all.

Laos – and particularly Xieng Khouang province, which bordered North Vietnam – had now entered a dark period of history. A military coup by US-funded forces against the new US-backed puppet government marked the onset of chaos. The Russians began supplying aid to the communist forces. In both camps, arms flowed freely to those willing to deploy them, though there was no such generosity when it came to sharing information. Neither side wanted it known that they were in breach of the 1954 Geneva settlement or the subsequent 1962 agreement, in which all parties had explicitly pledged to respect the neutrality of Laos and not to interfere in its internal affairs. Their single common interest was to keep their activities covert, with the result that the so-called Secret War took place largely unnoticed by the rest of the world. Much of the fighting focussed on the Ho Chi Minh trail in the southeast of Laos, a network of jungle paths along which the North Vietnamese ran supplies to communist guerrilla forces in South Vietnam, bypassing the narrow central part of Vietnam which had been demilitarised with the intention of cutting supply lines. However, there was also intense activity in Xieng Khouang province, where the CIA had constructed a vast secret airbase at Long Chieng. High concentrations of Hmong lived in this part of the country. Their reputation for being prepared to stand up for themselves and defend their homelands with their lives if necessary made them natural partners for the Americans, who were keen to keep US casualties and breaches of the Geneva agreements to a minimum by stationing as few military personnel of their own on the ground as possible.

The brunt of the fighting in Xieng Khouang took place on the high plateau known as the Plain of Jars – so-named because thousands of massive stone urns had been discovered at sites across the region. Scholars remain undecided about the provenance of the megalithic jars, which appear to date from the Iron Age, and their intended function is also the subject of debate. Lying at an altitude of 3500 feet, the Plain enjoys a temperate climate. Level terrain conducive to farming livestock, fruit and vegetables is watered by rivers that flow down through broad mountain valleys. The region's abundant reserves of natural resources make it economically valuable, and its rolling grassy expanses are also of strategic importance since many of Indochina's most vital trade routes pass through them, notably those leading into North Vietnam via Route Seven. Some fifty thousand villagers are estimated to have lived in the area during the fifties, about three quarters of them Phouane, a minority group loosely related to the ethnic Lao. The Pathet Lao first took control of the Plain in 1964, at which time the North Vietnamese still had relatively few combat troops in the region, though they did provide their allies with significant numbers of military advisers.

America responded by mounting covert bombing raids on northern Laos, flying two to five sorties a day at the outset. Over the next few years, Vietnam built up its presence in Laos to at least sixty-five thousand troops, deploying a total of seven army divisions equipped with Russian tanks and other military hardware, including anti-aircraft batteries. America manoeuvred CIA agents into foreign aid positions and decommissioned air force pilots so that they could enrol as employees of commercial airlines such as Air America and fly war missions legitimately. A fighting force with a substantial numerical advantage in terms of ground troops was thus pitted against a force with overwhelming aerial superiority. In 1968, there was a rapid escalation in bombing activity over the Plain after President Johnson suspended operations in North Vietnam. As Monteagle Stearns, US Deputy Chief of Mission in Laos from 1969 to 1972 explained to Congress the following year, "We had all those planes sitting around. We couldn't just let them stay there with nothing to do." The Pathet Lao moved at night in small groups, taking refuge in villages during the daytime on account of the risks of venturing into the open, so it was the villages that took the brunt of the assault, around 350 being destroyed. While the Pathet Lao were adept at removing themselves to safety when under attack, the villagers – particularly the elderly or infirm and young children – lacked survival skills, and the overriding majority of the casualties inflicted by the raids were civilian. By 1969, hundreds of missions a day were being launched against Laos, at which point the American authorities admitted to the offensive. With the Vietnamese continuing to insist that they had no counter-presence in the area, the public response was not favourable.

The villagers dug bolt-holes in the ground in an attempt to preserve their lives, or resorted to taking refuge in caves, but even here they were not safe, as the Americans developed laser-guided missiles capable of seeking out and destroying anti-aircraft batteries concealed by the Pathet Lao in caves. In one particularly shocking incident in 1968, over three hundred and fifty villagers were killed by a single missile strike on a cave at Tham Piu in which they had taken shelter. Anything that moved by day was targeted, meaning that villagers could only tend such crops and livestock as had escaped annihilation at night. By the end of 1969, the Plain of Jars had become uninhabitable, and the remaining villagers were airlifted to refugee camps to the south of the country for their own safety. B-52 bombers were brought into the attack and, with their support, the guerrilla army led by Vang Pao finally regained control of the Plain in 1969. Thai volunteers were flown in to help defend it against the fifteen thousand North Vietnamese troops stationed elsewhere in Xieng Khouang province, but America then began scaling back air support as it was negotiating for peace behind the scenes, and by 1972 the Plain was largely back in Vietnamese hands.

US bombing records show that at least two million metric tonnes of bombs were dropped on Laos at a cost of ten billion dollars – more than the combined total dropped on Germany and Japan during World War II – at a rate of one planeload every eight minutes. This figure includes ordnance jettisoned by US pilots returning to airbases in Thailand from aborted missions to Vietnam to avoid having to land with bombs still aboard, a practice considered to be dangerous. Despite remaining neutral throughout the war, Laos therefore has the unenviable distinction of being the most heavily bombed country on earth. White phosphorus, napalm, defoliants and herbicides were freely deployed, rendering the water on the Plain of Jars undrinkable, and over 250 million cluster bombs were dropped. Some thirty percent of these were released at altitudes too low to leave them time to self-arm prior to impact, with the result that they failed to explode and became an enduring hazard. Forty-five years on, fatalities continue to run at a rate of around one per week, with serious injuries occurring roughly every other day. Almost half the accidents involve children, who are frequently victims of a natural curiosity to investigate when shiny spheres the size of tennis balls mysteriously appear after heavy rain washes away the topsoil concealing them. In Xieng Khouang province, over a tonne of ordnance was dropped per head. The provincial capital Muang Khoun, a beautiful city rich in culture, was so extensively damaged that it was not considered worth rebuilding and remains a ghostly legacy, the home of a vast dilapidated sitting Buddha distantly encircled by ancient stupas.

A final ceasefire took effect in 1973, and for several months Pathet Lao politicians exuded an air of reconciliation. However, as soon as the remaining American and Thai personnel had withdrawn from the country, they took a stranglehold on power. At the time of its formation in the fifties, the movement had attracted a mixture of patriotic nationalists, who felt that an end to colonial rule was overdue, and previously marginalised hill-tribesmen. Now it was able to tap into a broader anti-imperialist swathe of public opinion. Having seen areas of their country bombed into near-oblivion, the people were united in their idea of who their enemy was, and they embraced the "Lao People's Revolutionary Party", the full-blown communist/Marxist outfit into which the Pathet Lao evolved, with open arms. The monarchy was abolished, and the king, queen and crown prince were despatched to a seminar camp in the north of the country for "re-education", a euphemism for years of hard labour from which they, like many others, failed to return. Before long, the majority of middle-ranking Royalist army officers and civil servants had followed them. Thereafter it was the turn of the skilled and educated to be taken away. The press ceased to be free. Men were prohibited from growing their hair long, and women from wearing jeans. American aid, formerly the country's life blood, dried up, and Soviet aid took up only part of the slack. The authorities' decision to ignore the advice of Marx that there should be a capitalist interregnum before attempting to transform a peasant-based agricultural economy to a communist model proved profoundly damaging. Too few officials with useful experience remained to allow government departments to operate competently. Food shortages ensued, and the economy all but collapsed.

Correctly anticipating what was coming, hundreds of senior-ranking Hmong and Royalist Lao fled to Thailand in 1975, but only a limited number of airlifts were laid on, and thousands of others who had hoped to accompany them were left behind. Many followed on foot and by boat across the Mekong. Twenty-five thousand Hmong (along with sixteen thousand Lao, Khmu, Mien and others) succeeded in escaping, but the new regime, concerned that they might regroup in exile and one day return to wage civil war, put an end to the exodus by closing the border with Thailand. A statement in the Party newspaper made its agenda chillingly clear: "We must eradicate the Hmong minority completely" (this being the faction loyal to Vang Pao, who had by this time been given sanctuary in America). Soviet-manufactured chemical weapons were almost certainly used against those considered enemies of the State. The harsh regime, coupled with grinding economic hardship, ensured that disillusioned Lao nationals, mostly Hmong, continued to attempt the dangerous Mekong crossing over the course of the next fifteen years. Eventually the Thais began forcibly repatriating those deemed to have entered the country illegally. New refugees were refused admission and sent back to Laos where, in some cases, they were summarily executed. The number of formal executions ordered by the Lao People's Revolutionary Party pales into insignificance when compared to Pol Pot's murderous regime in neighbouring Cambodia, but untold numbers perished in seminar camps from undernourishment and exhaustion.

Not all Hmong sided with Vang Pao during the war. Some fought against him, and Khmu may have made up as much as 40% of his guerrilla forces. But the majority of the diehards were Hmong, as he was, and the Hmong were brutally treated during the years that followed. Women were publicly raped. Children were maimed or poisoned to pay parents back for siding with the Americans. Babies were pounded to death in rice mortars. Youths were offered incentives to kill their own parents, even being issued with guns for the purpose. The Hmong looked to America to honour its unwritten promises to assist them in their hour of need, but the CIA was fully occupied with the task of extinguishing the furious blazes of adverse publicity that had broken out back at home. The last thing it needed was journalists taking a harder look at its long-standing involvement with the Hmong, which at this point was still largely undisclosed. The wider American public, meanwhile, had little on its mind beyond securing the safe release of US prisoners of war and establishing the fates of those missing in action. To this day, unverified reports that Americans captured in the Vietnam War are still held in Laos continue to circulate. America has granted citizenship to almost two hundred thousand Hmong, but there its largesse ends, and it is clear that the Hmong will be on their own if they now try to mount an armed struggle to engineer a transition to multi-party government in Laos.

When asked to account for their policies towards the Hmong, the Lao authorities argue that they have been trying to wean them from their slash-and-burn mountainside existences, encouraging them to live at lower altitudes where agriculture does not necessitate so much deforestation and where opium fields are less easy to conceal. It is true that the production of opium – which has always been integral to the Hmong way of life, serving as a cash crop for a people who have few other reliable income streams – dropped dramatically after 1989, at which point Laos was the third largest producer in the world. Whether this was a direct result of government policy is open to debate, however. The Hmong dispute the official version of events, contending that it was the authorities (rather than them) who controlled the opium market after the communists came to power and enjoyed the financial benefits, that it is the authorities, in conjunction with Vietnamese logging companies, who are guilty of illegal large-scale deforestation in Laos, that the rubber trees that they have been encouraged to plant in place of poppy fields are themselves an environmental hazard, and that forcibly moving them to barren lowland areas is a politically motivated strategy designed to weaken and demoralise them.

Muang Khoun was not the first great cultural centre in Laos to be annihilated. Vientiane – said to have been the most beautiful city in Southeast Asia – was ransacked by the Siamese in 1827-28. Luang Prabang, which ranked not far behind, suffered grievously at the hands of the Chinese between 1887 and 1893. For years at a time, the country once dubbed Shangri-La (a mythical, permanently happy Buddhist land isolated from the outside world) has seemed to stagger from one crisis to the next. But, not before time, the fortunes of the average Laotian have begun to improve since the turn of the century. Poverty rates have fallen sharply since free-market principles were belatedly embraced. Ordnance accidents are less and less common, and life expectancy has increased dramatically. The tourism, mining and construction sectors of the economy are all reporting healthy growth. Tribal skirmishes continue to erupt from time to time but, ethnic tensions have abated. And yet the country remains one of the poorest in the world. Four fifths of the workforce is still engaged in subsistence agriculture, and much of the infrastructure is rudimentary. Constructing roads through mountainous countryside littered with unexploded ordnance (UXO) is not a straightforward proposition, and the same goes for growing crops. While there is plenty of fertile land that could in principle be harnessed to agricultural production, seeking to farm plots that have not first been made safe by a UXO clearance team is risky.

Towards the beginning of 2010, Legacies of War, in the person of Channapha Khamvongsa, testified before the House of Representatives in an attempt to persuade the US government not to cut spending on UXO clearance in Laos. Swayed by her submission, Congress agreed to commit a hundred million dollars to the project over the following ten years, a sum almost equal to one percent of the annual gross national product of the entire Lao economy, though at the same time rather less than the sum expended every week by America on the bombing of Laos during the Secret War.

# FURTHER READING

Brace, Ernest C, *A Code to Keep*, Hellgate Press, 2010. Originally published by St Martin's Press, Suffolk, 1988

Branfman, Fred (ed), *Voices from the Plain of Jars – Life under an Air War*, second/expanded ed., University of Wisconsin Press, 2013. Originally published by Harper & Row, New York, 1972

Brown, Mervyn, *War in Shangri-La – A Memoir of Civil War in Laos*, Radcliffe Press, London, 2001

Coates, Karen J, *Eternal Harvest – The Legacy of American Bombs in Laos*, ThingsAsian Press 2013

Dakin, Brett, *Another Quiet American*, Asia Books, Bangkok, 2003

Hamilton-Merritt, Jane, *Tragic Mountains – The Hmong, the Americans and the Secret Wars for Laos, 1942-1992*, Indiana University Press, 1993

Meiring, Desmond, *The Brinkman*, Hodder & Stoughton, London 1965

Proschan, Frank, *Rumour, Innuendo, Propaganda, and Disinformation*, Review essay of *Tragic Mountains (vide supra)* in Bulletin of Concerned Asian Scholars, 28.1:52-63

Russell, Elaine, *Across the Mekong River*, Independent, 2011

Lightning Source UK Ltd.
Milton Keynes UK
UKOW06f2015280116

267354UK00007B/264/P